SPORTS MARKETING

Competitive Business Strategies for Sports

....

Christine M. Brooks

University of Michigan

PRENTICE HALL
Englewood Cliffs, New Jersey 07632

Library of Congress Cataloging-in-Publication Data

Brooks, Christine
   Sports marketing: competitive business strategies for sports /
   Christine M. Brooks.
      p. cm.
   Includes bibliographical references and index.
   ISBN 0-13-835893-1
   1. Sports—United States—Marketing. 2. Sports—Economic aspects—
United States. I. Title.
GV716.B76 1994
338.4'7796—dc20

93-39462
CIP

Acquisitions editor: Ted Bolen/Nicole Gray
Editorial/production supervision and
  interior design: Marianne Peters
Cover design: Violet Lake Studio
Production coordinator: Peter Havens
Copy editor: Krystyna Budd

©1994 by Prentice-Hall, Inc.
A Paramount Communications Company
Englewood Cliffs, New Jersey 07632

Printed in the United States of America
10 9 8 7 6 5 4 3 2 1

ISBN 0-13-835893-1

Prentice-Hall International (UK) Limited, *London*
Prentice-Hall of Australia Pty. Limited, *Sydney*
Prentice-Hall Canada Inc., *Toronto*
Prentice-Hall Hispanoamericana, S.A., *Mexico*
Prentice-Hall of India Private Limited, *New Delhi*
Prentice-Hall of Japan, Inc., *Tokyo*
Simon & Schuster Asia Pte. Ltd., *Singapore*
Editora Prentice-Hall do Brasil, Ltda., *Rio de Janeiro*

Contents

· · · · · · · · · · · · · · ·

Setting up for a Successful Venture ....

Heading for Success ....

Chapter 13   Analyzing Competitive Forces   281

Appendix A   Writing Your Strategic Plan   313

Glossary   323

Index   329

Preface

• • • • • • • • • • • • •

It is easy to get caught up in all sorts of definition problems with the word sports. To avoid such complications I use the word *sports* to encompass the entire active lifestyle industry. I include all forms of purposeful physical activity, done in both structured and unstructured settings. I recognize that this use of the term sports may be problematic for some of you since I am not following traditional definition guidelines. Strictly speaking, I should use the phrase *sports and physical activity industry*, or perhaps, even more accurately, the phrase *active lifestyle industry* instead of the term sports. While teaching I found that repeating the words *sports and physical activity industry* became rather cumbersome. Since the name of our field is Sports Management, *active lifestyle industry* seemed too radical a deviation in terminology. I solved the problem with my students by simply beginning the course by explaining what I meant by the term *sports* and then used this word to represent both components of the *active lifestyle industry—sports* and *physical activity*. In the same vein, I ask for your understanding as I use the word *sports* to represent all components of the *active lifestyle industry*.

Whatever we call it, the sports industry is a multibillion dollar segment of our society that is growing larger every day. Its monetary growth has spawned a demand for college programs that prepare students for sports business careers. The University of Michigan is one of the many schools that responded to this demand. As the faculty designed the curriculum, however, we quickly discovered that there was a severe shortage of teaching materials in the way of textbooks, computer simulations, videos, case studies, and other aids. The faculty did the best they could in gathering teaching material related to their assigned content areas. My specific assignment was to design a course that would teach students about competitive market strategies as they applied to sports. I could not find any material that discussed products, market opportunity, industry structure, sponsorship, competitive force analysis, and other business notions that were specific to sports. I was looking specifically for material that would help students learn how to think, interpret, analyze, and apply what they learned so that they would be adaptive to any sports environment. My solution to meeting these needs was to write my own material. This book is the formal presentation of my efforts.

As you work your way through this book you will find that it is a very action-oriented approach to learning. I will ask you to research markets, analyze and interpret the data for market opportunities, and then design a plan to pursue those opportunities in an organized and effective way. I also ask you to present your findings in strategic plan format.

When they first enter the classroom, my students expect I will give them a clean, neat, orderly "cookbook" outline of what I want them to do. The conversation typically goes something like this:

Student:	"I can't think of a project. Can you give me some suggestions? What are other students doing?"
Me:	"This is your chance to try anything you want."
Student:	"Well, how about a midnight fun run for overweight students? Do you think this is a good idea?"
Me:	"Do **you** think it's a good idea?"
Student:	"Yes, but what if people don't like it? I'll feel stupid."
Me:	"That certainly is a risk, but so what? You can find out if your idea is workable."
Student:	"Well, how many pages should I write for my strategic plan?"
Me:	"As many as it takes to do the job properly."
Student:	"But. . . . . . ?"

Just as I try to awaken the creative spirit in the students who are in my classroom, I will try to awaken it within you by asking you to think things through for yourself. Education experts agree that our survival in an increasingly competitive global economy requires that you learn how to take ideas and explore ways to apply them to diverse situations. You may prefer a cookbook outline but you will discover soon enough that the world does not operate on common recipes. The notion of exploring the unknown, where failure is frequently the teacher and is therefore considered *good*, is quite foreign to many students I teach. They think of failure as bad. This prevents them from following through on bizarre ideas that could be the breakthrough that sports needs. I urge you to define failure as *good*. I have had many student groups discover, after doing their market research, that their idea was not going to work. Without exception, the failure of their first idea led them to a better and more profitable idea. The discovery of failure helped them bond together more closely, and they simply explored another version of their idea. Do not be afraid to explore the unknown, fail, try again, and perhaps fail again and again. The axiom "nothing ventured, nothing gained" is true in sports business just as it is in all other facets of your life. It is persistence, effort, and creativity that ultimately lead to success. So long as you challenge yourself, and try over and over again, you will be successful.

For those of you who may find the lack of a cookbook structure frustrating I urge you to think for a minute about the consequences of staying in this mode. It's the difference between a secure but limiting existence of an oyster, and a slightly more risky but exciting existence of an eagle. The ocean provides the oyster with food and gives it protection. All the oyster must do is give up its freedom and remain attached to the same rock throughout its entire life. The eagle, on the other hand, certainly faces more danger and has no guarantee of food. Life is exciting and challenging for the eagle. It can leave its nest and fly high above the mountains to breathe the beauty of its surroundings.

Do you want to be an eagle or an oyster? Do you want security by accepting the crumbs others discard? This is what a cookbook student gets—the crumbs of other people's ideas. These throwaway ideas are almost always uninteresting and mundane. Or, do you want to create your own destiny? In this book I assume you want to fly with the eagles and face challenges. I challenge you in two ways. First, I ask you to pretend you are going to produce a sports event or take some other sports-related product idea to the marketplace. You select the event or product that interests you. Each chapter introduces you to some aspect of the venture you must consider. There are chapters dealing with markets, industry structure, sports publics, sponsorship, market research, publicity, and strategy. There are several case studies to help you experience the eagle's view from the mountain top—that is, to let you see the application of the material you are reading to the real world. Worksheets will guide you as you plan your idea, but will not provide you with the exact solution. Since the book covers many details involved in bringing an idea to market, the information in each chapter may, or may not, be relevant to your specific situation. It is up to you to decide what information applies. Second, I ask you to write a strategic plan for your idea. This step ensures that you put on your thinking cap. Talking about an idea, or reading about the endeavors of others, will not give you the personal experience you need to fly high above the mountains and come back alive. Writing it down, developing a plan, thinking through the strategy—that's how learning occurs. That's how you survive in the marketplace.

I give as much guidance as possible for those of you stuck in the cookbook mode. I do, however, attempt to break you of this habit by making you responsible for searching through the information available, analyzing it from many directions, picking out what is relevant, discarding what is not, and then making the decision to venture forth. Once you make the decision you must move forward with giant confident strides even if people surrounding you claim you will fail. If *you* want to do it, then *do it*! Mountain climbing is the analogy I like to use. You will never have perfect information, and your friends may say you are crazy to even make the effort. Those who have already made the climb can give you advice, but you are the one who is facing the challenge. You must analyze the side of the mountain as best you can, gather your resources and courage, commit to a path, get started, and be flexible enough to change direction if unforeseen obstacles block your way. Take note, though, that you cannot climb to the top of the mountain by leaving one foot on the ground. In other words, don't procrastinate—get started! Whenever you hesitate about taking the first step, picture yourself lying on your deathbed. What are you wishing you had done? Whatever it is, make sure you do it now because you can never recapture today tomorrow.

Much of the information I include in this book is from actual sports business situations. I gathered the material over a six-year period from interviews with about 100 different sports organizations, individuals, and corporations. I would like to express my appreciation to these individuals and organizations for their help and support. From their experience and advice you will:

- see that sports is a dynamic and challenging enterprise.
- be given guidelines on how to understand your consumers, markets, products, and sponsorship opportunities.
- learn strategies that will help you explore new ideas.
- learn how to move from the idea stage to the action stage.
- see that you have many career choices available to you.
- learn how to take advantage of the competitive forces that buffet almost all sports organizations.

I have one final comment. People who want a career in sports often make a common mistake. They assume all they must do is take a relevant college course, read a book such as this one, or obtain a Sports Management degree. Improving your knowledge about the industry, its products, and its markets is just one of the steps you must take. You must also prove that you can apply your knowledge to the financial advantage of some sports entity. This will almost always require some hands-on experiences through internships, volunteer projects, and other field experiences. If you complete both these steps—that is, improve your knowledge *and* practice your skills in the marketplace—you will no longer be competing for jobs with the multitude of others who did not prepare in this way. So, with this in mind, I dedicate this book to those students from my 1991 class who had the courage to test their ideas in the marketplace. Their event is now a yearly endeavor of the Sports Management Student Government here at Michigan. The first effort didn't make much of a profit, but it didn't lose money—certainly an accomplishment in itself. These students harbor in them the true spirit of entrepreneurship and the sports industry needs them. I wish them, and all of you with similar gumption, the best of luck.

ACKNOWLEDGMENTS ....

Every book represents a collaborative effort, and this one is no exception. I wish to express my appreciaion to all the people who contributed time to speak with me and provide me with material. Specifically, I wish to thank the following:

William Mergler, VP of Corporate Promotions at Volvo, North America, who gave considerable input for the sponsorship chapters.

John Barr, Director of Regional Site Communications at Eastman Kodak Company, for sharing his views on sponsorship within the corporate marketing framework.

All the USOC National Governing Body Executive Directors who so willingly discussed their marketing problems, ideas, and strategies.

All the sports consumers who were the participants of the survey research I have conducted over the past eight years.

My students who have tolerated my trial and error approach to designing the course content upon which this book is based. Their feedback (both good and bad) was an important component to the final content of this book.

Eleanor Jones, Director of Marketing/Visa U.S.A., for providing me with materials regarding the Visa International Olympic sponsorship program.

Christine Bork a masters degree student who helped code the triathlete data that was used in Chapter 6.

Mike Pyle a Sports Management undergraduate who helped gather the data on sports spectatorship used in Chapter 5.

United States Synchronized Swimming for a delightful association with their sport, athletes, staff, and officials during two research projects. The information from these projects provides readers of this book wonderful insights as to how a small sport can go about solving many marketing problems. My special thanks to Betty Watanabe, Executive Director of USSS, and Joyce Lindeman, a Board member for their support and assistance.

The many companies including Seiko, Sarah Lee, Cort Furniture, Domino's Pizza, The Kentucky Derby Festival, Miller Brewing, Coors Brewing, the National Football League, and the Pistons Basketball Team, The America's Cup among others for providing documentation about their sponsorship programs and for providing me and my students with interview time.

My husband Dennis, for not complaining when I monopolized the computer and for giving me moral support and encouragement throughout the writing of the book.

The following reviewers who provided me with excellent feedback and suggestions on how to improve the quality of the book: Ruth H. Alexander, University of Florida; Jacquelyn Cuneen, Bowling Green State University; and Terry R. Haggerty, University of New Brunswick.

Christine M. Brooks

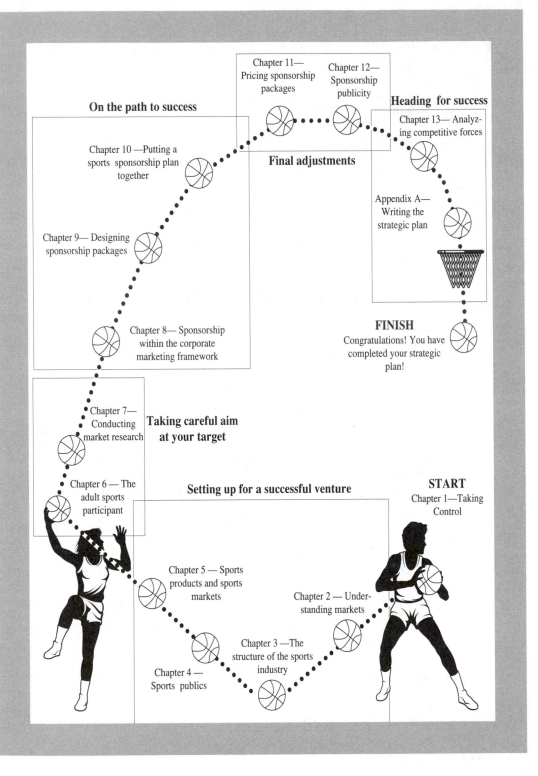

CHAPTER ONE

Taking Control

• •

Thinking is the hardest work there is, which is the probable
reason why so few engage in it.

—*Henry Ford*

If you put a frog in cold water and heat the water slowly, the frog will calmly sit there and let itself be boiled. It becomes so accustomed to the slow, continuous change in heat it does not realize that its environment will eventually become intolerable. Like the frog, many of us are in such a rut that we become used to a certain way of doing things even when we are heading toward disaster. It usually takes a major jolt to shake many business organizations, and people, for that matter, out of the same old routine. Think about it. Thousands died in the *Titanic* disaster before legislators mandated sufficient lifeboats for all passengers on ships. The *Challenger* shuttle exploded before NASA took a hard look at its priorities. Only after people die will automobile manufacturers consider building safer cars. Our lakes and rivers become polluted before we, the citizens of this world, insist that our politicians enforce environmental laws. The same is true for sports organizations. A sports organization must reach the crisis stage before its managers will consider new approaches.

The cause of inaction is, of course, people. It is so easy to become lulled into doing the same thing day after day until we absolutely have to make a change. Think for a moment about how you live your own life. Do you tend to accept the way things are until disaster looms? How much prodding do you need to move out of your comfort zone of daily living to experience the unknown or the unexplored? To be a ground-breaking sports marketing strategist you must be willing to move out of a familiar environment, open your eyes to changes that are occurring around you, and seek innovative methods of solving problems. If you do not do this, you will miss some great opportunities. In other words—you must be cognizant of when the temperature is rising, move out of the water before it is too late, and *take control!*

How do I expect you to learn to take control from reading this book? To answer this question let us begin with a thinking assignment. Find a few classmates and take some time to discuss the following questions. At first glance the questions might seem quite basic to you. It may surprise you, though, to discover how little you have really thought about them.

Here are the questions:

- What is a sports product?
- What benefits do sports products offer people?
- What are the market segments for sports products?
- How do you develop a plan or strategy for entering a market segment?
- Who are the competitors in the sports industry?
- What is meant by "market share"?

How did you do? Did you find these questions difficult? Did the terminology confuse you? Did the questions overwhelm you? If so, you are not alone. By the time you reach the final chapter of this book, though, you will be able to tackle each question with confidence. So, that is goal number one—to give you a sense of familiarity with the basic jargon and the nature and logic of competitive market strategies by introducing you to such notions as sports products, market segments, and market share. We call this the "what is" of competitive market strategy. In other words, you learn how to gather the information that is presently available. To be a successful strategist, though, you must also learn to explore "what could be." Therefore, a second thrust of this book will be to teach you how to analyze the data you have gathered so that you can design ideas and develop action strategies. So in addition to becoming familiar with the "what is," you need to become (a) intentionally creative with your ideas and (b) liberated from the fear of being wrong, a fear that serves only to prevent you from taking action. One way of accomplishing these latter two goals is to make *yourself* the boss.

YOU ARE THE BOSS

As you will soon discover, the analyzing phase is fairly simple. Once you understand what you should look for, analyzing is not much more than examining the facts as they exist. The idea and action phases, on the other hand, are often messy and confusing. The outcome of a specific market strategy idea, and the action you ultimately take, is certainly visible—sometimes it is successful, other times not so successful. To really feel what it is like to design and implement a market strategy idea, we need to put you in the driver's seat. We will do this by placing you in an imaginary job. Close your eyes for a minute and imagine yourself as the manager of a sports organization of some type. You will probably choose your favorite sport. If you are already working for a sports organization, you will probably select that sport. The sport you select really doesn't matter—just the fact that *you are the boss*. Now, go on—close your eyes and picture yourself as a sports manager.

OK. Good. To complete the imagery I'm going to ask you to do one more thing. I want you to think of yourself as more than just *any old* manager—you are an *entrepreneurial* manager. This intrigues you, right? Why are you an entrepreneurial manager? Good question! As you will discover during your journey through the contents of this book, there are vast opportunities in the sports industry available to those with an entrepreneurial bent. Entrepreneurs are the true heroes of the sports industry, for they develop new products from sports, expand the markets for sports, encourage innovation, and make a major contribution to the overall size and scope of the industry.

Be warned, though. Implementing a new venture or introducing a new idea in the sports industry, or indeed any other industry, is risky. Entrepreneurs fight tough odds, since the natural tendency of people is to resist even the best ideas. The most useful ideas that are now commonplace in our culture, such as the Xerox machine, were rejected many times over by key decision makers before they finally gained acceptance. A new idea usually means change, and change is often uncomfortable. The entrepreneurial road is challenging, time demands can be staggering, and success is often elusive. An entrepreneur must have a strong belief in his or her abilities, an overdose of determination, and a thick skin to overcome roadblocks that will cause detours and deter progress.[1]

There is only one way to prepare for any venture—*a plan*. Preparing a *strategic plan* will set you firmly on the right track. A strategic plan is a detailed outline of your analyses, evaluation, and selection of market opportunities so that you can reach your market objectives. No matter what part of the sports industry you might ultimately decide to venture into, or the type of product you hope to offer consumers, you stand a much better chance of succeeding if you have a plan to follow.

LEARN BY DOING

The best way to learn how to put a plan together is by *doing it*. This is the reason we are structuring your learning experience around your imagined managerial position. It will give you the opportunity to experience the actual process of developing a strategic plan for a venture we will discuss shortly. This will teach you how to jump through the hoops you will face in the real world. You cannot play the competitive sports market strategy game unless you can prove you are a capable player. People want to see your plans on paper so that they can be sure you have thought out your ideas carefully. You must show why you are capable and how you will compensate in the areas in which you have no expertise.

If you have done the necessary background research, writing a strategic plan will not be that difficult. You do not have to be a literary genius, but you must think creatively, have a vision that extends traditional boundaries, and communicate your ideas clearly and concisely. A strategic plan tells people what you want to do, the support your venture will need, the markets for your product, and how you will ensure profitability. If you cannot produce a convincing strategic plan you may never be truly successful as a sports market strategist. The simulation approach used here will provide you with procedures that can improve the quality of your strategic plan. Furthermore, by placing you in a realistic situation the chapter material will come to life. The goal is for you to gain enough knowledge about competitive sports marketing strategies to allow you to tackle any venture within the sports industry with confidence and zeal.

YOUR VENTURE

Your venture is to produce a sporting event or design a product that is in some manner associated with sports. Each chapter contains worksheets that will help you generate the kind of information you need to develop a strategic plan for your idea. I provide you only with general information; you will have to apply that information to your specific situation.

The following eight steps will help make the simulation a little easier to do.

1. Approach this simulation as if you were actually going to bring your event to market.
2. Go over the chapter outline to familiarize yourself with the topics you will cover.
3. Briefly scan through the strategic plan guide outlined in Appendix A.
4. Work with two or three other students.
5. After you read each chapter, make sure you understand the relevance of the material to your event. The strategic planning worksheets provide the type of information you will need to apply to your idea.
6. Read through each chapter a second time, noting areas that provide you with the information for your strategic plan worksheet. Also note on the worksheet the areas where you will have to do some additional research before you are able to answer the questions. Assign team members the task of gathering the necessary information.
7. Do not expect to complete each worksheet on the first attempt. Complete as much as possible the first time through; then do the research that you need to finish it.
8. Work on the simulation two to three hours per week throughout the entire semester.

Some of the terminology used throughout this book comes directly from the corporate world. However, where existing terminology did not exist, or did not fit a specific aspect of the sports industry, I invented new words. The future will determine if these new words are acceptable to the sports industry. In any case, you will face a whole list of terms that may be new to you. You will need to familiarize yourself with these terms, since they can help you establish an image of competence and knowledgeability.

HOW TO USE THIS BOOK ....

Figure 1.1 gives you a suggested structure for using this book. First, divide your semester into six equal time periods and then follow the plan outlined in Figure 1.1. If your semester is twelve weeks long, for example, you should cover the material in Chapters 1–3 during the first two weeks. Attempt to complete worksheets 1 and 2 and begin working on the market research project outlined in Chapter 7. During weeks 3 and 4 you should cover Chapters 4–6, complete worksheets 3–6, and continue with your research project. Give yourself a quiz toward the end of the sixth week (use the glossary for a list of terms you ought to know); after that complete your research project. Complete the second half of the semester by following the guidelines on the remaining portion of the chart in Figure 1.1.

Finally, when you cast this book aside, or sell it to future sports business students, I hope that you will carry the strategic planning process with you and that it will be the foundation upon which you will build your sports business career. *Live and study with passion!*

SUMMARY ....

This chapter suggested a strategy to help you maximize your educational experience while reading this book. I pointed out how important it is for you to free yourself from your cage of familiar experiences and be willing to step into the unknown. Then I asked you to explore what you now know about such issues as sports products and their benefits, market segments for sports and how you might attract those market segments, the competition you face, and the concept of market share. These are the kinds of issues with which you must be familiar in order to become a good market strategist. Building on what you already know, this book will perhaps help you be one of those valuable individuals who make a difference. To get you prepared for what you will face in the real world, I put you in charge of your own organization. I asked you to think of yourself as an *entrepreneurial* manager, not just any old manager. The word *entrepreneurship* conjures up images of a risk taker, a person with novel ideas, persistence, and a thick skin, someone totally unafraid of failing. That's exactly the type of person I want you to be as you develop a strategic plan for your fabricated organization. Now that you have taken control, your first task is to understand the markets for your idea.

Divide your semester into six equal time periods

Work Schedule	Beginning		Middle		End	
	Chapters 1–3	Chapters 4–6	Chapters 8–9	Chapters 10–11	Chapters 12–13	Appendix A
Chapters to cover						
Worksheets	Complete worksheets— Chapters 2–3	Complete worksheets— Chapters 4–6	Complete worksheets— Chapters 8–9	Complete worksheets— Chapters 10–11	Complete worksheets— Chapters 12–13	
Projects	Begin working on the market research project —Chapter 7 →→		Hand in your market research project	Begin writing your strategic plan from completed worksheets 1–8 (see Appendix A) →→		Finish writing your strategic plan from worksheets— Chapters 10–13 (see Appendix A)
Tests			Key concepts covered in Chapters 2–9			Key concepts covered in Chapters 10–13
Class Time	Use class time to stimulate thought and debate rather than expecting your professor to simply regurgitate what you have read in the chapters.					

REFERENCES   ••

1. For a useful introduction to the process of selling your idea to a boss, manager, or key decision maker, I suggest you read Jesse S. Nirenberg, *How to Sell Your Ideas* (New York: McGraw-Hill, 1984).

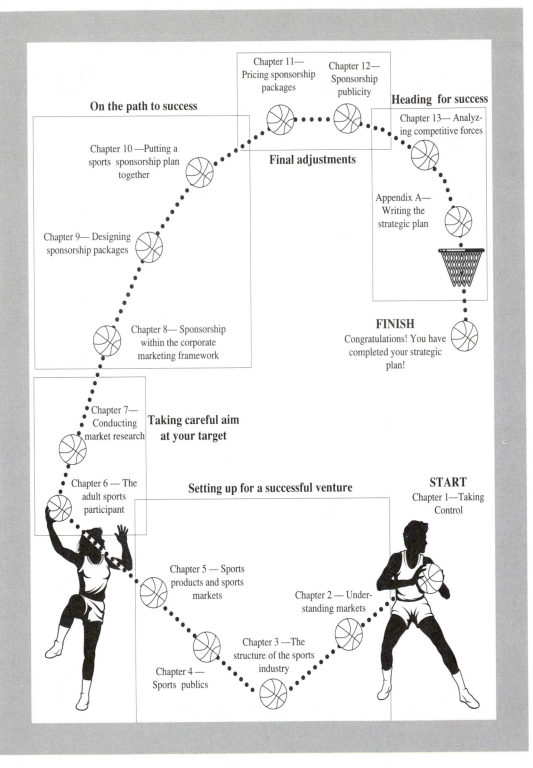

Chapter 11—
Pricing sponsorship
packages

Chapter 12—
Sponsorship
publicity

Heading for success

Chapter 13— Analyz-
ing competitive forces

On the path to success

Chapter 10 —Putting a
sports sponsorship plan
together

Final adjustments

Appendix A—
Writing the
strategic plan

Chapter 9— Designing
sponsorship packages

Chapter 8— Sponsorship
within the corporate
marketing framework

FINISH
Congratulations! You have
completed your strategic
plan!

Chapter 7—
Conducting
market research

**Taking careful aim
at your target**

Chapter 6 — The
adult sports
participant

Setting up for a successful venture

START
Chapter 1—Taking
Control

Chapter 5 — Sports
products and sports
markets

Chapter 2 — Under-
standing markets

Chapter 3 —The
structure of the sports
industry

Chapter 4 —
Sports publics

CHAPTER TWO

Understanding Markets

· ·

Men occasionally stumble over the truth, but most of them
pick themselves up and hurry on as if nothing happened.
— *Winston Churchill*
(1874–1965)

There is one very common mistake in marketing: failure to fully understand the markets for a product. If you do not know much about your consumers or why the product you have interests them, you cannot hope to fully comprehend the various markets available to you. Just because you are providing products you like yourself does not automatically mean that consumers will also want them. This is especially true when your products involve spectatorship or sports participation. You are about to read two case studies that demonstrate the pitfalls of failing to fully research the needs and wants of your consumers. The first case provides you with an inside view of the ups and downs of the World Football League (WFL) as its founders attempted to challenge the deeply entrenched, highly successful National Football League (NFL). With sufficient research, the founders of this league would have discovered there was insufficient market support for a second league. The second case takes a look at how developers tried to take advantage of the surge in golf participation. As you read this case study, the danger in satisfying your own needs by seeking higher profits without first consulting your consumer should become apparent. The fact that consumers had a love affair with the game of golf cannot be disputed. However, golf course developers saturated the market with high-priced courses that appealed only to a small segment of the market.

CASE STUDY | The World Football League

In October 1973 a meeting was held in a plush lawyer's office to discuss the formation of a World Football League, WFL—a rival league to the established NFL. Present at the meeting was the originator of the idea, Gary Davidson, a young Southern California attorney. He was short and a bit on the stout side despite his addiction to exercise. In the room were several other individuals—all men, all wealthy, and all enraptured by the idea of owning a professional sports team.

Davidson had already founded the American Basketball Association (ABA), in1967 and the World Hockey Association (WHA), in 1972. At the time, most teams in both leagues still wallowed in red ink. Some of Davidson's acquaintances describe him as a slick rip-off artist, but Davidson protested that label. He maintained that he contributed to American culture by providing an important service to the wealthy: He gave them a means of nourishing their vanity. "There is nothing better for the ego than owning a professional sports team," he proclaimed to others. Davidson appointed himself commissioner of the WFL.

Imagine you are there as Davidson begins to speak. Silence falls over the cigar-smoke filled room:

"We have an excellent opportunity available to us. The NFL has no strong rival. It has grown arrogant and complacent. There are a ton of quality players available. A number of NFL players are unhappy about their salaries. It's amazing how little the players get, considering the enormous popularity of football. You know how much a rock group like Led Zeppelin makes? It would stagger you. I don't think the mania for professional football is any different from the hunger for good rock music. It's all entertainment, and people are willing to pay big money to be entertained. We are going to war with the NFL!"

"Who would invest in a professional sports franchise?" asked Bill, a prominent commercial developer.* "Unless you're the Knicks or the Celts or the Dolphins, you don't make any money off the gate, or from television for that matter."

"That's why you go into it," replied Davidson, a little miffed at such a naive question. "Sports franchises are tax shelters. They generate nice tax losses because you can depreciate 80 percent of the cost of the team by amortizing the cost of player contracts. And, you can pass through the losses to your main business. Capital appreciation is another big factor. You buy a franchise in anticipation of the team's future market value. For example, the first eight World Hockey Association teams cost the owners $25,800 each when the league formed two years ago. The expansion teams this summer sold for $2 million per franchise.

---

*Although this case is based on fact, Bill is a fictitious character. He was invented simply to illustrate how we can use data to make market decisions.

"If you get in on the ground floor, a WFL franchise will cost you $650,00," continued Davidson. "Now compare that to the $16 million it would cost you to get an expansion team in the NFL. And with the WFL you will all be starting from scratch. This means you each have an even chance to win a championship. The $16 million you would pay for an NFL expansion team will simply ensure you of last place for many years to come."

A More Entertaining Game

Davidson holds up an inch-thick loose-leaf document and waves it in front of his enthralled audience. The basic plan is right there. The title on the document is *The WFL Playbook* (in private Davidson calls it "Mein Kampf"). The league would begin competition in 1974, consist of twelve teams, and have a twenty-game season. The starting date of July is several weeks before the start of the NFL season. In addition, several differences distinguish the WFL from the NFL. First, there is no reserve clause binding a player to the team for an extra year if he does not sign a new contract. Second, under WFL rules a touchdown would be worth seven points and an optional "action point" must be a pass or a run; there is no automatic extra point. Finally, other rule changes are designed to add more action and scoring to the game. These changes include the following:

- Goal posts are positioned at the rear of the end zone.
- A thirty-yard line kickoff is set to allow more runbacks.
- Except when a field goal is attempted inside the twenty-yard line, when a kicker misses a field goal the ball is returned to the line of scrimmage.
- A pass completion will require just one foot in bounds.
- In the case of a tie the teams will play a fifth quarter, split into two seven-and-a-half minute segments.
- There are no fair catches allowed on punts.
- An offensive back can go into motion toward the line of scrimmage before the ball is snapped.
- The hash marks are placed further toward the center of the field.
- An incomplete pass on fourth down returns the ball to the line of scrimmage.

Davidson added other attractions such as a black-and-gold football to highlight ball spin, colorful team names, stylish uniforms, and helmet insignias drawn by a famous commercial artist. He claimed that all these would add excitement to the league. At the end of the season the two top teams would play in the World Bowl to determine the champion. WFL teams would locate in cities without NFL teams, or in cities where

NFL teams were not doing well. For example, Davidson thought Houston was a viable city for the WFL because of fan disgust with the Houston Oilers. They had won only two games in the previous two seasons. He also believed the Chicago Bears and the Philadelphia Eagles were vulnerable. At the meeting Davidson also revealed expansion plans within five years to such cities as Tokyo, London, Munich, Paris, Dusseldorf, Rome, Mexico City, and Stockholm.

Television

As you listen to Davidson discuss the television package, it occurs to you that it is a bit on the skimpy side. The three networks have contracts with the NFL until 1977, so there is little chance of network TV coverage for the WFL until then. Davidson has arranged for cable stations to broadcast five of the six weekly WFL games on Wednesday nights. These games are scheduled for airing in the hometowns of the away teams. The sixth, the "game of the week," will air nationally on Thursday night. TVS Television Network— a privately owned company belonging to Dun & Bradstreet— would televise the game. Television revenue will earn each team about $100,000 during the first year. But, as Davidson explained, "this year is not for the money; it's for the exposure. TV revenue is not as critical for the WFL as it is for the NFL. The gate is the big thing in this league. The break-even point for a typical WFL team appears to be around $35,000 in average paid attendance and that should be no problem" (see Figure 2.1).

Figure 2.1   How Davidson Calculated the Break-Even Point

Davidson's league consisted of a twenty-game season. Since he did not plan to profit from television revenues, he had to rely solely on ticket sales. Using sales and cost information, you can estimate how many seats must be sold for each team to break-even. Assume total costs such as salaries, uniforms, and supplies, stadium rent, promotional expenses, transportation and meals, league assessments, interest expenses, and miscellaneous operating expenses equals $4.5 million. These are called **fixed costs**, since they occur regardless of attendance.

Assume the average ticket price is $7. The cost of printing the tickets combined with costs related to attendance (variable cost) is sixty cents. This leaves $6.40 to cover fixed costs. The attendance needed to break even, then, is:

$$\frac{\text{Fixed costs}}{\text{Price per seat–Variable cost per seat.}}$$

With fixed costs of $4.5 million, this results in the following break-even calculation:

$$\text{Number of seats} = \frac{\$4,500,000}{\$7.00 - \$.60} = 703,125 \text{ for a twenty-game season, or } 35,156 \text{ per game.}$$

Players

A professional football league requires skilled players. There were three possible sources: dissatisfied NFL players; graduating college players; and NFL castoffs. This final group was the least desirable source of players, since Davidson felt credibility with the public required top-notch NFL players—especially those popular with fans. To attract quality players the WFL would have to offer salaries higher than those offered by the NFL. According to Davidson three Miami Dolphins players—Warfield, Kiick, and Csonka— will consider moving to the WFL. He expected others to move to the WFL when their NFL contracts expired.

Playing Facilities

The WFL had one major problem, namely, finding suitable stadiums. Davidson planned to use existing stadiums until the league could build its own. In two years time the Giants planned to move to the new Hackensack sports complex. A WFL team could take over the stadium vacated by the Giants.

"There is absolutely no way this league can fail," Davidson confidently proclaimed. "We are in much better shape than the American Football League was when it first started."

"I wonder about that," commented Bill. "I understand the tax incentives. But I guess my concern is whether this country can support another professional football league."

"Of course it can," retorted Davidson. "Americans are football crazy. The NFL has a 93 percent capacity in its twenty-six stadiums. Over half the population—between 90 and 100 million—watch the Super Bowl every year. And the NFL has just started to tap into novelty items and now operates its own publishing house. With an annual gross of more than $150 million, there's no question in my mind that professional football is a growth industry. During a 10-year period ending in 1973 professional football's gross revenues rose 210 percent." What Davidson failed to mention, however, was that much of this revenue growth came from television—the exact area where the WFL had limited opportunity.

"But here's the situation you have described to us," responded Bill. "You are asking us to invest in an abundant product—even overabundant if you look at the amount of television programming there is. But the raw materials [the players] for this product are rare and subject to incredible bidding wars. And if we open our doors for business by starting this new league, we will increase the capacity to produce this abundant product. In the process we will have to bid even more ferociously for scarce materials. Now I ask you, why should I buy into this business deal? It doesn't make much sense."

A brief moment of silence follows.

"But professional sports is a different kind of business," commented a voice from the back of the room. "I have faith in Gary," the voice continued. "He's done this before, and he can make it work. I'm in." Would-be professional football team owners in the room quickly added their support. Bill decided to hold out for now until he could research the viability of such a venture.

Market Analysis

The next day Bill discussed Davidson's offer with his wife, Sally, who was a market researcher for a major company. As Sally listened, she shared Bill's concern as to whether there was enough fan support for a new football league. Had professional football reached its saturation point? Was there still room for market expansion? Sally offered to help Bill research these issues further. First she located paid attendance figures for the NFL (Figure 2.2).

Prior to 1969 the NFL consisted of two competing leagues, the American Football League (AFL), established in 1960, and the older NFL that played its first games in 1924. Other football leagues had challenged the NFL's monopoly on the game, but none was able to survive— until the AFL. Influential and wealthy backers such as Lamar Hunt and Barron Hilton helped ensure AFL success. In fact, a story circulated about a news reporter who remarked to Hunt's father that Lamar could lose a million dollars a year on his Dallas Texans (now the Kansas City Chiefs). The senior Hunt reportedly replied, "That means he has a hundred and twenty years to make it profitable."

As Sally probed the data, she discovered that it took the AFL seven years to reach an average attendance of 35,000. During the 1960s the two leagues battled for markets and players, driving up team expenses. In 1970, the two leagues agreed to end their suicidal battle by merging. The popularity of professional football mushroomed through the 1960s. At the end of the 1970 season the combined NFL-AFL had a total attendance of 9.5 million, almost double what it had been ten years earlier. By 1973 total attendance hit 10.7 million. Average attendance had increased to 59,000 per game.

Obviously, there was little question that attendance had been increasing over the years. The data showed this quite clearly (Figure 2.2). However, Sally also noticed that the attendance was increasing at a decreasing rate (Figure 2.3). Her graph indicated that there was a 5 percent increase in attendance at professional football games between 1969 and 1970. Between 1970 and 1971 attendance increased 6.6 percent. But after the 1970 season there had been a steady decline in this increase: Thus between 1970 and 1971 there was a 5.7 percent increase; between 1971 and 1972, a 3.7 percent increase; and between 1972 and 1973, a 3.7 percent increase. Sally felt that if this trend continued there might be no increase in attendance in 1974 and perhaps would decrease after that.

Figure 2.2 Attendance at Professional Football Games between 1960 and 1973

YEAR	American Football League Average Game Attendance	National Football League Average Game Attendance	Combined AFL-NFL Total Attendance
1960	16538 (56)	40106 (78)	4,054,452
1961	17904 (56)	40675 (98)	4,988,816
1962	20487 (56)	40851 (98)	5,150,723
1963	21583 (56)	42486 (98)	5,372,340
1964	25854 (56)	46561 (98)	6,010,924
1965	31828 (56)	47285 (98)	6,416,405
1966	34291 (63)	50829 (105)	7,497,413
1967	36439 (63)	53026 (112)	8,234,621
1968	37642 (70)	52520 (112)	8,517,317
1969	40620 (70)	54430 (112)	8,939,500
1970	52381 (182)		9,533,333
1971	55362 (182)		10,076,035
1972	57394 (182)		10,445,827
1973	58961 (182)		10,730,933

Source: Robert L. Trent, *The Encyclopedia of Football* (New York: A. S. Barnes 1977), p.685.

The figures Sally and Bill had available to them showed the average game attendance for the AFL (column 2), the NFL (column 3), and total professional football attendance (column 4). The number of games played during the season is in parentheses.

Sally calculated total attendance for the AFL and the NFL by multiplying average attendance by the number of games played. For example: In 1960 AFL attendance was 16,538. Total games played were 56. Therefore, total attendance was $16,538 \times 56 = 926,128$. To compare total attendance for the two leagues, she plotted them on this chart.

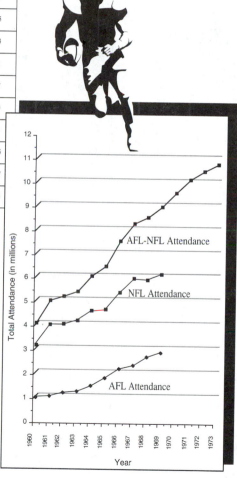

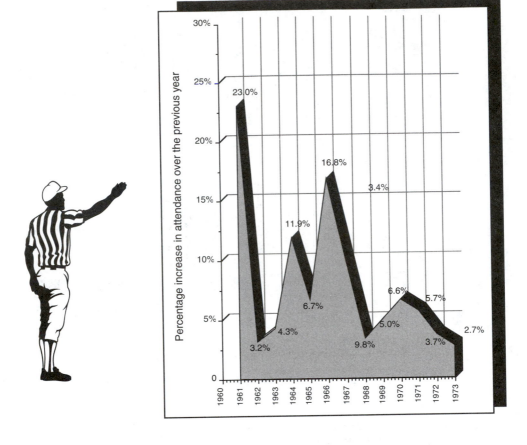

Figure 2.3 The Gradual Plateauing of Attendance at Professional Football Games

Sally noticed other facts:

- The number of professional football games had increased from 154 in 1960 to 182 eight years later.
- Virtually every major city had one or more teams.
- The season now overlapped baseball at one end, and basketball at the other.
- Television appeared to have reached its saturation point.
- The country was in a recession.
- There was very little similarity between the old AFL and the WFL in its first year. There were only twelve NFL teams in 1960, and only one of the networks was televising professional football.

- With the exception of New York, the AFL stayed clear of NFL markets.
- The AFL caught the mania of professional football just as it started in earnest.

Bill looked at Sally's analysis. "I don't know about this," he said. "It's just possible that professional football hysteria has peaked." He wondered if there was something they were overlooking? Should they pass up their only chance of owning a professional football team? How much trust could they put in Davidson and his associates?

One Year Later

The scene now shifts to the New York's St. Regis-Sheraton Hotel. The year is 1975 and the atmosphere gloomy. This time Bill was absent. He and Sally had decided not to buy into the league. Davidson had sold his twelve franchises, but many fetched far less than the $650,000 asking price. Only one of the original owners could be considered super rich. The remaining owners were newly rich promoters and business owners like Davidson. There was also a group of thirty-four nameless and faceless individuals who put up $50,000 each to purchase the Detroit Wheels.

The season started well, and for a time Sally wondered if she had misread the data. The WFL played its first nationally televised game in Jacksonville, Florida, on a hot and steamy July evening. Over 60,000 spectators packed into the stadium. Nielsen reported a 16 percent national rating, and the Southern California *Sun* had a healthy Nielsen rating of 11 for its opening game. Philadelphia announced a 55,534 paid attendance. From that point on, though, the situation quickly deteriorated. Both the Philadelphia Bells and the Jacksonville Sharks admitted to padding attendance figures. Out of a reported sale of 121,000 tickets Philadelphia had received money for only 20,000. "What can I say? I lied" said the team's executive vice-president. "I never thought those figures would come out." On November 13, the final playing date of the WFL regular season, there were 14,245 at Honolulu, 14,794 at Birmingham, 13,339 at Memphis, and 28,213 at the *Sun*'s game. These figures were well below the needed attendance of 35,000 but on par with first-year attendance figures for the AFL.

At the assembly in the St. Regis-Sheraton, six of the twelve franchises were without owners. Unpaid salaries amounted to $4 million, the Internal Revenue Service (IRS) had started proceedings against some of the teams to collect back taxes, players had cars and homes repossessed and Gary Davidson had been ousted from the role of commissioner. As it turned out, Sally had correctly predicted the 1974 NFL fall in attendance—it was off 4 percent from 1973. The Birmingham Americans won the first World Bowl, but owner of the Americans Bill Putnam ran out of money because of the huge bonuses he was paying to NFL players who promised to jump to his team. Meanwhile the IRS tried to take over his player contracts and sell them to the highest bidder, and the TV contract for the 1975 season looked glum. Chris Hemmeter, a thirty-five-year-old millionaire from Hawaii, devised a new plan for the revitalization of the WFL. Hemmeter traveled about 15,000 miles a week as he gallantly attempted to breathe life back into the WFL. Hemmeter's plan to make the team's gate receipts and TV-radio income relate to the team's revenues generated much enthusiasm.

The 1975 Season

After the disastrous 1974 season most people were surprised to see the WFL survive into 1975. However, the entire season collapsed when the WFL failed to obtain a national television contract. The league died a quiet death halfway through the 1975 season. At the end, Hemmeter had this to say: "We failed in marketing . . . most of us are bankers and we lacked charisma." Had this observation been made before Davidson put the WFL plan into action, he might have commissioned some research that would have led him to develop a more viable market entry strategy, or he might have decided to abandon his WFL plan altogether.

....

....

CASE STUDY | Golf Course Expansion

In 1988 Kit Bradshaw, director of publicity for the National Golf Foundation (NGF), declared golf to be the fastest growing sport in America. Its popularity and growth cut across different classes, races, and sexes. The number of golfers, defined as those who played at least one round in the past year, grew by 34 percent between 1985 and 1988. The NFG estimated that 23.4 million people played at least one round of golf in 1988. At this growth rate 30 million would be playing the game by the year 2000. The industry had grossed over $20 billion a year, and conservative forecasters were predicting a golden future for the sport. Terry Williams, director of McKinsey & Co., a business planning and consulting firm used by the NGF to study the market for golf, predicted that the industry would gross $31 million by the turn of the century. With the introduction of the right programs McKinsey & Co. believed golf could reach $40.7 billion. There had been a sharp increase in the sale of golf equipment since 1985; the aging group of baby-boomers (people born between 1946 and 1966) were dropping out of their more strenuous activities, and many were opting for the slower pace of golf; and the game had expanded beyond its traditional white, professional male constituency to a broader spectrum of consumers that included women, Hispanics, and blacks. There was a rapidly expanding senior golf market for those of at least sixty years of age (Figure 2.4). Seniors played around 30 percent of all rounds of golf and were becoming an increasingly significant economic force in the financial growth of the industry. By the year 2000, the data suggested, 35 percent of golfers playing more than ten days would be over fifty-five years of age, and 53 percent would be over forty-five years old (see Table 2.1 for a description of how the NGF made these estimations).

By all appearances, golf was on the verge of becoming a national

Figure 2.4   Age Profile of Adults Who Play Golf at Least Ten Days a Year

In 1986, the 65-plus age group was the smallest category of fairly frequent golfers. They represented 12 percent of all golfers. By the year 2000 this age group will have grown 98 percent and will represent 17 percent of all golfers.

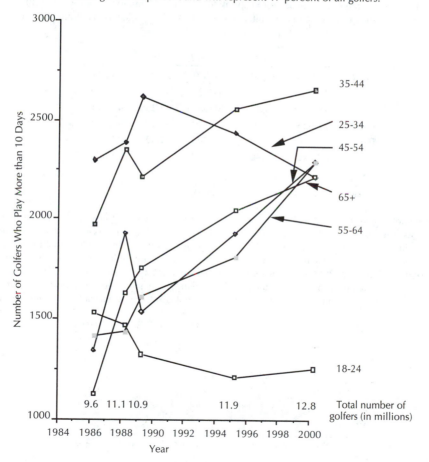

mania—a sport that was reshaping lifestyles, spending habits, real estate development, and investment patterns.

Two Years Later

At the 1990 National Golf Foundation Summit cynics dubbed the projection "the great golf boom that wasn't." Financial failure threatened hundreds of golf equipment and apparel manufacturers that had geared up

Table 2.1 How the National Golf Foundation Estimated the Number of Golfers in the United States.

Predicting how many golfers there will be in the year 2000 is based partly on fact and partly on estimation. The following gives you a step-by-step guideline of how you can estimate the number of golfers in the United States.

Step 1: Obtain reliable estimates of how many people there are within the population. The Census provides you with past and future population figures. In the chart below you will find there were almost 28 million people 18-24 years of age in 1986. This age group is expected to shrink to just over 25 million by the year 2000. There were 178.3 million people 18 and older living in the United States in 1986. The projection is 202.6 million for the year 2000.

	1986	1988	1989	1995	2000
18-24	27,973	26,904	26,591	24,281	25,231
25-34	42,984	43,961	44,024	40,962	37,149
35-44	33,142	35,321	36,548	42,336	43,911
45-54	22,823	24,151	24,872	31,297	37,223
55-64	22,230	21,799	21,544	21,325	24,158
65+	29,172	30,400	30,992	33,764	34,882
TOTAL	178,324	182,436	184,571	193,965	202,554

Source: U.S. Bureau of the Census, *Current Population Reports.*

Step 2: Obtain reliable survey data that will provide you with the percentage who golfed for each age category. The 1986–1989 figures listed below are from the Simmons Market Research Bureau Survey of Leisure in the United States. After examining trends for each age group for these three years, you can then judge what trends you might expect to see in the future. It pays to stay on the conservative side. For example, in the calculation below the percentage increase through the year 2000 is kept the same for all except one age group. The percentage for the 45-54 age category has been increased 2 percent because of the evidence indicating more individuals within this age group are playing golf each year. In the other age groups the percentages were similar between 1986 and 1989.

18-24	13.6%	13.0%	14.4%	14.4%	14.4%
25-34	12.4%	14.9%	14.7%	14.7%	14.7%
35-44	14.0%	13.5%	14.5%	14.5%	14.5%
45-54	10.7%	11.7%	14.3%	15.3%	16.3%
55-64	10.4%	12.1%	10.9%	10.9%	10.9%
65+	6.7%	7.9%	7.8%	7.8%	7.8%
TOTAL	11.5%	12.5%	13.0%	13.0%	13.0%

Source: Simmons Market Research Bureau, Inc. Study of Media and Markets.

Table 2.1 *Continued*

Step 3: Calculate the number of golfers in each age category by multiplying the percentage in step 2 by the population size in step 1. For example, there were

0.136 X 27,973,000 = 3,804,000 18–24-year-old golfers in 1986.

There are expected to be

0.144 X 25,231,000 = 3,633,000 in the year 2000, or 171,000 less than in 1986.

18-24	3,804	3,498	3,829	3,496	3,633
25-34	5,330	6,535	6,472	6,021	5,461
35-44	4,640	4,768	5,299	6,139	6,367
45-54	2,442	2,826	3,557	4,788	6,067
55-64	2,312	2,638	2,348	2,324	2,633
65+	1,955	2,402	2,417	2,634	2,721
TOTAL	20,483	22,666	23,922	25,403	26,883
Increase		2,183	1,256	1,481	1,480
% Increase		10.7%	5.5%	6.2%	5.8%

Other Statistics: There were almost 20.5 million golfers in 1986, 22.7 million in 1988, and an expected 26.9 million in the year 2000. (This figure does not match the 30 million predicted by the National Golf Foundation because the NGF figures included children.) There were just over 2 million more golfers in 1988 than there were in 1986, which represents a 10.7 percent increase. There were 5.5 percent more golfer in 1989 than in 1988, and so on. Based on the trend information, you might expect the number of adult golfers to increase about 1 percent a year through to the year 2000.

for the boom. Experts believed that half the golf clubs in Florida were in financial trouble. Many would have to restructure if they wanted to survive. Nor was Florida the only state with problems. The apparent cause of the problem? Developers had built the wrong type of golf courses in the wrong places. Private clubs designed to cater to the needs of high-priced housing developments especially felt the economic pinch. In New England, for example, at least six of the residential golf course developments had filed for Chapter 11 bankruptcy. A sober Golf Summit panel member concluded, "It's similar to the so-called tennis boom—suddenly the industry lost 10 million players who never existed."

What was the explanation for the financial failure of so many businesses associated with golf in light of the NGF's rosy forecast that the country needed one new golf course a day for the next ten years in order to serve the growing millions of golfers?

Some Background

To many nongolfers the sport still conjures up images of aging, upper-class paunchy businessmen. In reality, however, the game has expanded its appeal to a broad spectrum of society. Over 50 percent of the players hold clerical, sales, or blue-collar jobs. From Sugarloaf Mountain in Maine to the ninety courses in San Diego County, legions of Americans, including an increasing number of women, are demonstrating that golf is a game for all ages and social classes. The pursuit of par, whether at $50,000 or $5 a round, is an enduring avocation for the millions who tee it up each year.

To meet the growing popularity of golf over the past thirty years, the number of golf courses in the United States has more than doubled. Most of the facilities were built during two time periods. The first boom occurred during the 1920s, when developers constructed 4,500 golf courses. Between the mid-1950s and the mid 1970s developers added a further 6,000 courses, most of them public. As an alternative to country clubs, public courses opened up a game previously considered the preserve of wealthy retirees and business executives. It was during this time period that more blue-collar and factory workers started to play. By the mid-1980s golf had entered a third boom period, so that by 1988 13,626 golf courses dotted the American landscape.

Once a developer buys the land, the cost of building a golf course can range between $150,000 a hole to $350,000 a hole. The architectural work alone can cost $1 million to $1.5 million, with a basic layout that includes a clubhouse, maintenance area, and cart storage shed costing around $3.5 million. Signature courses can run in excess of $30 million. After construction, maintenance runs about $25,000 per hole a year.

From an investment point of view the market value of a golf course should depend on cash flow. As is true for all sports, though, emotions and ego always manage to play a role. A golf course is very visible, and it is often difficult to convince the seller that cash flow should be the basis of its price. From a logistical financial point of view, if there is no cash flow after considering debt, the course is overpriced.

Golf as an Investment

As 1988 drew to a close, the NGF members expressed their pleasure with the growth of the sport. The statistics were indeed impressive (Table 2.2 indicates some of the more important statistics). Given these statistics, golf looked like a winner, a true growth sport. The statistics were enticing enough to attract the attention of Wall Street. Investors formed limited partnerships, advised big institutional money to commit funds to golf courses, and tried to forge alliances with large golf development companies. Caldwell Banker thought the golf course business was big enough to justify forming Golf Properties Marketing Group of Phoenix, Arizona. This division of Caldwell attempted to match buyers with sellers of existing courses.

Almost 90 percent of the new courses built between 1987 and 1989 were tied to real estate development. Residential real estate devel-

Table 2.2   An Analysis of the Growth of Golf Between 1970 and 1988

	1970	1975	1978	1980	1982	1984	1986	1988
Golfers (millions)	11.2	13.0	14.0	15.1	16.0	17.0	20.2	23.4
Rounds Played (millions)	266	309	337	358	379	403	421	487
Golf Facilities	10,188	11,370	11,885	12,005	12,140	12,278	12,384	12,582
Private	4,619	4,770	4,872	4,839	4,798	4,831	4,887	4,897
Daily Fee	4,248	5,014	5,271	5,372	5,494	5,566	5,585	5,748
Municipal	1,321	1,586	1,742	1,794	1,848	1,881	1,912	1,937

opers had watched private golf clubs raise entry fees and dues twofold over a ten-year period. They figured they could add golf courses and fancy clubhouses to their developments, and this would enable them to charge 40 percent to 50 percent more for a housing lot overlooking a course.

At one time two companies dominated the golf course business: American Golf and Club Corporation of America. American Golf owns or operates approximately 120 private resort and daily fee courses in sixteen states, whereas Club Corporation owns or manages around 200 courses worldwide and has in excess of $500 million in revenues. The increased interest in golf as a real estate investment has made it tougher for these two golf course development companies to buy new courses at their real market value. The investment popularity of golf courses almost tripled the number of bids a seller received, so that by 1988 it was not uncommon for one golf course seller to have six to eight bids.

Golf courses also garnered the attention of foreign investors. The British, Koreans, and Japanese began to bid prices up way beyond the actual market value of the business. The $115 million acquisition of the Riviera Country Club in the Los Angeles area by Japanese investor Maurki Schogi, for example, really shocked the industry. Riviera was certainly one of the most prestigious golf courses in the world, but insiders estimated its true value at $50 million. Until the Riviera deal, golf properties were assessed on income, and since traditional golf courses generally produced minimal income, they had nominal value. However, by using assets rather than income as the value strategy, courses were sold at two or three times their actual market value.

Pending Problems in the Industry

In 1991 the golf industry reported that only prestige resorts and daily fee courses, which don't charge membership fees, were faring reasonably well. Investors quickly discovered that only resort locations could demand high fees, for golfers expected to spend more money at these places. They also expected to pay higher fees inside major markets. Apart from these situations, though, there were limits to what people would spend on a recreational activity like golf. There were other problems with data interpretation. Demographics are a valuable source of information about the market potential of a sport, but they are often misunderstood.

The golf industry misinterpreted the data in many ways, including the following:

- The sharp increase in sales of equipment was an indication of an equipment replacement boom, not a golf boom.
- Golfers who played frequently—that is, at least twenty-five days per year—accounted for about half of all golf spending. The number of frequent players had not changed over the years.
- New golfers are not golf fanatics. They have a variety of interests. They want to sail, go white-water rafting and scuba diving, and play golf as well. In other words, they are fanatics of exercise or activity, not golf. Many are also "experience" fanatics. In other words, they are searching for new and exciting things to do in their lives.
- Real estate developers built two-thirds of all private courses. They built most of the golf courses too far from large population centers and were unable to draw sufficient players to overcome fixed costs.
- Based on the demographics of the golfers most of the new courses needed to be cheaper public (daily fee or municipal) operations.
- Developers overestimated the allure of golf-front property. Nearly 70 percent of home buyers in communities with golf courses don't even play golf. In addition, excessive use of pesticides and other chemicals aggravated many communities, especially in parts of the country with scarce water supply.
- Developers faced high operating costs, often running about $1.2 million per year. With the economy slumping, companies were firing white-collar executives and cutting perks such as golf club memberships. It became less chic to pay the higher fees to play a round of golf on the pretense of exclusivity and status.

ANALYSIS OF THE TWO CASE STUDIES

The individuals involved in these two case scenarios made a common mistake—they forgot to consult with their consumer. They assumed that the consumer would want their product simply because it was available. This assumption is usually wrong, particularly when it comes to spectatorship or sports participation. In the golf case, it was clear that more people were playing the game, but developers built the wrong type of golf courses. The benefits offered by the real estate magnates did not compensate most golfers for the cost of playing golf on those particular courses. Real estate developers simply sought to satisfy their own needs—higher prices for their homes and lots—and thought they could do this by taking advantage of the desire people had to play golf. They did not care about, nor did they understand, physical activity behavior. Consequently, they saturated the market with golf courses that were attractive only to a small segment of the market.

Similarly, Davidson introduced what he believed to be a new and improved version of professional football. What Davidson did not even consider—or perhaps what he simply chose to ignore—was that he faced a deeply entrenched, highly successful competitor in the NFL. You need a better strategy than reckless optimism when you have a new product on the market. If Davidson had analyzed the situation in the same detail as Sally, he could have planned his strategy differently. Davidson needed to assess the size of the market for professional football, the untapped consumer needs, and how he could carve out his own niche by meeting those needs with another professional football league. The individuals to whom Davidson sold franchises were equally guilty of ignoring market needs. All they saw was a tax shelter and glamorous notions of owning a professional sports team. Davidson presented them with limited data and only a scanty assessment of the potential market, but the owners chose to overlook these shortfalls. Further, the NFL easily adopted the rule changes that made professional football more exciting; this quickly diminished any novelty the WFL may have had over the NFL. Unfortunately, the WFL also suffered serious image problems. Sports organizations and their products are highly visible. The press is quick to pick up on issues that will adversely affect the public's perception. Padding attendance figures and not paying players became insurmountable public image problems for the WFL to counter.

The Purpose of Consumer and Market Knowledge

To develop a competitive strategy you need to know three things:

- a thorough understanding of the components of your product
- a thorough knowledge of the needs of your consumer
- a thorough knowledge of how product components and consumer needs fit together

The two cases you just read provide examples of some sports managers' tendency to think of the consumer as a market pawn. The cases also indicate the danger of not fully understanding the product you are packaging for consumption. In each case the product took precedence over market needs. In the end the consumer decides whether to accept or reject a sport on the basis of whether or not it meets perceived needs and desires.

If you want to keep abreast of changing conditions in the marketplace, you must collect some form of data. There is more to it than simply collecting information. If a sports organization is to be responsive to its markets, it must not only keep abreast of competitive and environmental changes by collecting information, but also be in a position to cope with them. As you read through this book, you will notice many situations where sports organizations know what they must do but do not have the resources for implementing the necessary programs. Without resources, what you know can often be irrelevant, since you cannot act on your information. As the golf course developers discovered, it is also important to cope with environmental concerns from a societal standpoint. They were not aware of the growing consumer resentment toward careless use of resources. Had they been, they might have developed and marketed their courses differently.

The purpose of market research is to help you make better decisions. The more sophisticated the management, the more data they will generally want. The WFL almost completely overlooked the importance of research. The enthusiasm of owning a professional football team, and a good sales pitch, blinded the owners to the need to determine market potential for their new venture. Even the simple research Sally did was enough to show that there was a poor likelihood of success.

Even when you have data available to you, there is no guarantee you will make a correct decision, especially if you interpret the information incorrectly. The problem with the research done for NGF, for instance, lay not so much in its accuracy as in its incorrect application to the marketplace, in addition to their rush to capitalize on an overestimated trend. It is not uncommon to find managers who accept research without questioning its meaning and implication. If the researchers and real estate developers had been more familiar with actual golf consumption behavior, the golf industry might have interpreted its data differently and applied the findings in a more productive and profitable way.

Subjective Analysis

The statement "There's nothing like experience" contains an element of truth. You will find that some market problems just do not lend themselves to formal research. The measurement tools may not be accurate enough, or they may be completely lacking; the statistical techniques may be underdeveloped, or there may simply be too many variables. If you had done market trends for either the WFL or the golf industry, you would have based many of your projections on subjective decisions. You would have gathered the data available from the past and present and tried to predict where the trends were going. Although this is a useful and often used strategy for predicting the future, such predictions do not always work out as expected. Affecting the trends may be other variables that either you overlooked or were not evident to you at the time.

There is one more point about research you should know. Although a formal research project is usually important, it is expensive to do—costs can be over $50,000. If you lack research funds as many sports organizations do, you will have to be very creative in gathering your data. Observations and comments from consumers, as well as other sources, will often give you a good feel for what competitors are doing, changes in consumer preferences, and shifts in the marketplace you should watch out for.

SUMMARY

This chapter addressed how important it is for you to collect and analyze relevant data when you try to assess the marketability of an idea. You saw how easy it is to become so excited about a product that you assume everyone will be equally excited about it. Your idea is simply the first phase; you must then find out if there is a market for your idea. If there is, you must decide what form your idea should take to meet the needs of the consumers within that market. Factors such as trends, economic conditions, other competitors, environmental issues, and consumer needs are all essential parts of the data puzzle you must piece together so you can see as much of the picture as possible. As you saw in the golf situation, though, you seldom have all the information you need, and the partially assembled puzzle will often present you with a rather abstract picture that is difficult to interpret. This makes it easy to misread the picture you have put together. Certainly if you are missing the consumer need pieces, you will find it almost impossible to correctly interpret the picture before you. Your success in the planning and implementation of your idea will depend directly on the quality and quantity of information at your disposal. It will also depend on your ability to interpret and use this information prudently. It is sometimes quite difficult to find data relevant to your specific idea. You will usually need to collect information that will help you understand the entire spectrum of the market in which your idea will exist. If your idea is to conduct a three-on-three basketball tournament on your campus, for example, you need to know market trends throughout the country, as well as market trends in your city and on your campus. A good place to begin is in your library. Make an appointment with your librarian and ask this individual to show you where you can find market data. Sources you can look for include

- Simmons Market Research Bureau, Inc., survey reports.
- National Sporting Goods Association Reports.
- U.S. Bureau of the Census current population reports.
- Various sports associations such as the NGF and NFL.
- Knowledgeable experts. There may be a listing of companies or other organizations where data relevant to your idea is frequently collected.
- Magazines that are in some way related to your idea. Good publishers will often collect data on their reader demographics, trends, and other basic titbits about readers. Some publishers will share this information with you.

Once you have obtained your data, you must keep in mind one important dimension in your ability to correctly interpret what you have gathered, namely, that you must have a reasonable understanding of the sports industry and how its structure can affect the success or failure of your idea. In the next chapter we pursue this topic in considerable depth.

STRATEGIC PLAN WORKSHEET–CHAPTER 2

What you should know about your markets

Your Goal   ....

To understand how important data are in assessing the potential of your venture.

Background   ....

Check when completed

- What is your event?
- What is your sport?

Market Analysis   ....

Check when completed

- What are the market trends for your sport? (Do an analysis similar to that done by Sally.)
- Where is the sport headed — declining, improving, stable?
- What markets are served?
- What are the opportunities for your organization now? Five years from now? Ten years from now?
- What is the future of your sport in terms of market need, acceptance, and profit potential?
- What significant factors within the environment will affect your specific sport business or product now? Five years from now? Ten years from now?

REFERENCES   ....

The case study "The World Football League" was developed from the following sources:

BURCK, CHARLES G.   "Why those W.F.L Owners Expect to Score Profits." *Fortune*, September 1974, p. 142.

GLUCK, HERB.   *While the Gettin's Good—Inside the World Football League*. New York: Bobbs-Merrill Company, 1975.

JOHNSON, W. O. "The Day the Money Ran Out." *Sports Illustrated*, December 1, 1975, p. 85.

MARSHALL, J. "Once and Future League." *Sports Illustrated*, April 21, 1975, p. 29.

TWOMBLY, WELLS. "Super Flop 1." *New York Times Magazine*, January 12, 1975, p. 10.

"The Numbers Game—Don't Knock Losing." Forbes.

December 15, 1973, p. 47.

HARTLEY, ROBERT F. "Marketing Mistakes," Chapter 10. *The World Football League—The Tainted Promise.* John Wiley & Sons: New York. 1986.

The case study "Golf Course Expansion" was developed from the following sources:

BERGSMAN, S "Fore! Investors Eye Golf Courses." *Barron's*, November 13, 1989, p. 104.

ELDRIDGE, L. "Golfing Surge Burdens Courses." *Christian Science Monitor*, April 21, 1989, p. 14.

GLENN, R and McCORD, R. *The Whole Golf Catalog* (New York: Perrigee, 1990).

LENER, J. *A Boom, as Younger Players Flock to the Links, New York Times, June 25, 1989, p. F13.*

RUDNITSKY, H., and KOSELKA, R. Extrapolation Madness, Forbes, December 24, 1990, p. 56.

SCHOLL, J. "Why Investors Should Beware the Boom in Golf." Barron's, November 12, 1990, p. 20.

TANNENBAUM, J. "Golf Entrepreneurs Feel Fairway Is Sure Way to Green." *Wall Street Journal*, January 23, 1989, p. B2.

WILLIAMS, L. "What's a Fast-growing Sport with a Designer Label? Golf." *New York Times*, September 4, 1989, p. 1.

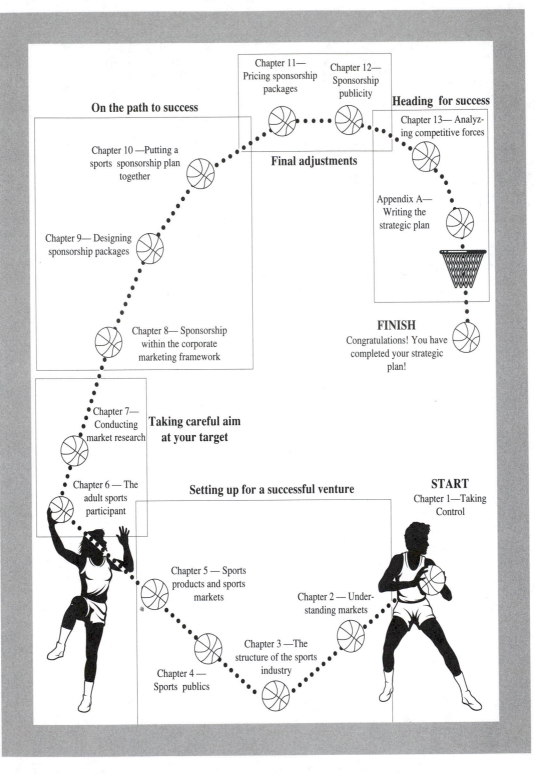

CHAPTER THREE

The Structure of the Sports Industry

• •

All for one, one for all.
—*Alexandre Dumas, The Three Musketeers*

If we include the professional, amateur, and recreational aspects, sports compose a sizable industry so tightly intertwined that it is often difficult to differentiate the contribution of each component. By *industry* we mean a group of organizations producing products that are close substitutes for each other.[1] Under this definition the sports industry is just one component of a larger leisure industry. Our focus is on sports, however, so we will confine our discussion to this component. This chapter will help you understand the sports industry by analyzing its distinguishing features and showing how it is both similar to and different from private-sector businesses. We will try to gain some understanding of the industry's economic structure, the range of products and services it offers, and how these all interrelate with each other.

ECONOMIC IMPACT

We often think of sports as a diversion from everyday life. This may indeed be the prime function of sports for most people, but economically speaking, sports are not a diversion. For overall, sports and the various business offsprings of sports constitute the twenty-second largest industry in the country, an industry bigger than petroleum, lumber, and air transportation. Total revenues generated by sports in Canada and the United States—from ticket sales to the purchase of running shoes and golf clubs—have reached $88.5 billion per year. Experts expect total spending on sports in North America to double through the 1990s. By the turn of the century U.S. and Canadian companies will spend $13.8 billion per year advertising their products to sports spectators, participants, and fans; this is approximately 3.5 times as much as they currently spend. Globally, corporate advertising associated with sports will likely reach $30 billion by the year 2000. Add to these statistics the fact that newspapers devote several pages per edition to sports and the proliferation of infomercials devoted to the sale of active-lifestyle-related products, and you can begin to understand the importance of sports* to the American economy.[2]

COMPONENTS OF THE SPORTS INDUSTRY

The basic infrastructure of the sports industry—that is, where the production process occurs—consists of five components: Two relate to management (coalition clusters and independent sports units), and three relate to labor (athletes' unions, individual athletes, and sports agents) (see Figure 3.1). Several subgroups support this infrastructure and help the production process. Such groups include umpires and referees. We will refer to this basic configuration as the *primary infrastructure* of the sports industry.

There is also a distribution and service component. From a historical standpoint the prime focus of sports organizations has been on providing sports consumers—the participants and spectators—with a means of consuming the primary product—the physical activity—that may, or may not, come in the form of competition. Providing additional services to the consumption process has essentially been ignored. Sports organizations do not, for example, produce the equipment their consumers need. To fill this void a secondary infrastructure has evolved. This includes all those business activities associated with the distribution and service of the output produced by the primary infrastructure, namely, facility owners, museum curators, book and magazine publishers, camp managers, equipment manufacturers, event producers, television broadcasters, and media personnel.

You will find the secondary infrastructure diagrammed for you in Figure 3.2. There is now some vertical integration of sports organizations into the secondary infrastructure. The Championship Auto Racing Team (CART), and the PGA TOUR, for example, produce their own television programming. This is a fairly recent phenomenon. Most sports organizations have not yet ventured much beyond their primary production function. This distribution and service component plays an important role in the overall sports industry, and we will come back to it later in this chapter. For now, it is sufficient that you simply rec-

---

*Remember, the word *sports* as I use it here also encompasses purposeful physical activity. Thus, when I use the word *sports,* I include fitness and recreational activity as part of the definition.

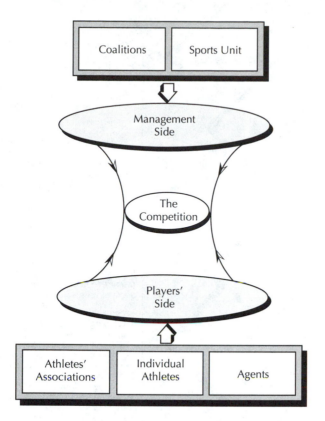

Figure 3.1 Components of the Sports Industry

ognize that a secondary infrastructure exists, that it has a significant economic impact, and that sports organizations are gradually tapping into it in search of new funding sources.

ANALYSIS OF THE PRIMARY INFRASTRUCTURE

The Management Structure

The management structure consists of (a) independent sports units and (b) coalition clusters.

Independent Sports Units

Independent sports units (ISUs) produce the primary sports product. They may come in the form of amateur, recreational, or professional clubs, or they may simply be individual athletes, that is, professional golf and tennis players. Ownership and financial support of ISUs in the United States can come from private,

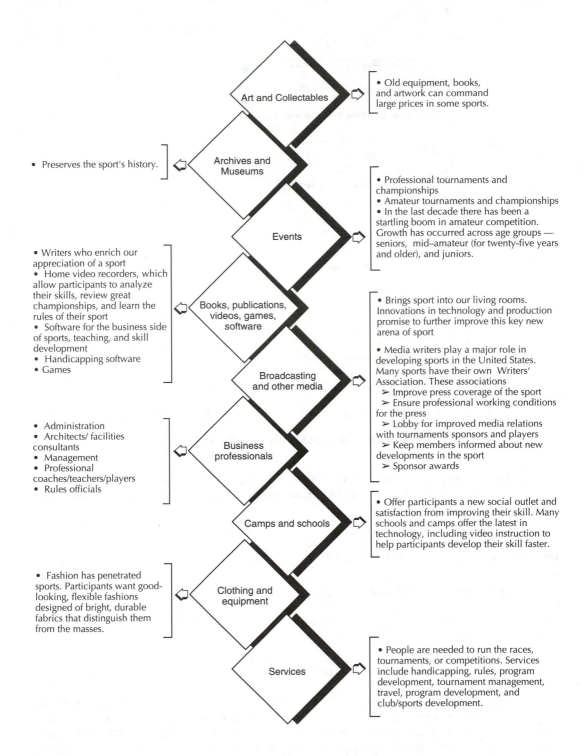

• Old equipment, books, and artwork can command large prices in some sports.

Art and Collectables

• Preserves the sport's history.

Archives and Museums

• Professional tournaments and championships
• Amateur tournaments and championships
• In the last decade there has been a startling boom in amateur competition. Growth has occurred across age groups — seniors, mid–amateur (for twenty-five years and older), and juniors.

Events

• Writers who enrich our appreciation of a sport
• Home video recorders, which allow participants to analyze their skills, review great championships, and learn the rules of their sport
• Software for the business side of sports, teaching, and skill development
• Handicapping software
• Games

Books, publications, videos, games, software

• Brings sport into our living rooms. Innovations in technology and production promise to further improve this key new arena of sport

Broadcasting and other media

• Media writers play a major role in developing sports in the United States. Many sports have their own Writers' Association. These associations
➢ Improve press coverage of the sport
➢ Ensure professional working conditions for the press
➢ Lobby for improved media relations with tournaments sponsors and players
➢ Keep members informed about new developments in the sport
➢ Sponsor awards

• Administration
• Architects/ facilities consultants
• Management
• Professional coaches/teachers/players
• Rules officials

Business professionals

Camps and schools

• Offer participants a new social outlet and satisfaction from improving their skill. Many schools and camps offer the latest in technology, including video instruction to help participants develop their skill faster.

• Fashion has penetrated sports. Participants want good-looking, flexible fashions designed of bright, durable fabrics that distinguish them from the masses.

Clothing and equipment

Services

• People are needed to run the races, tournaments, or competitions. Services include handicapping, rules, program development, tournament management, travel, program development, and club/sports development.

Figure 3.2 Distribution and Servicing Component of the Sports Industry

nonprofit sports groups (predominantly amateur) as well as from for-profit autonomous entities (predominantly professional). In the United States the government has no direct financial or management interest in sports, although government regulations can have an impact on its organization and operation.

As a rule ISUs do not have the same commercial focus as private-sector businesses. Profits, sales, or market share dominate private-sector goals. It is not so easy to delineate the business objectives of ISUs. More so than in the past, ISUs today are concerned with maximizing income. However, sports cannot have profits as their prime goal, for their intent is for the enjoyment of consumers regardless of profits. Thus the focal point in amateur sports is the participants, whereas for professional sports the focal point is the spectators. Even here, sports cannot be structured solely for the profit of the owners or the athletes, although many owners have managed to make their teams work to their financial advantage (see the exhibit that follows). For most ISUs, though, the goal is generally to compete successfully in the athletics arena while remaining financially solvent.

ISU Ownership Structure—Professional Baseball

Private business owners have discovered over that years that baseball clubs can help increase their profits and asset value. August Busch purchased the Cardinals, for example, to increase the sale of his beer. Today you will find it more and more common for broadcasters to own baseball teams. Why? Because it gives broadcasters a source of original programming. Superstations like WTBS, which owns the Atlanta Braves, and WGN, owner of the Chicago Cubs, have used sports programming to break into the national market. Other less ambitious stations have penetrated regional or local markets through sports programming. Baseball has become such an effective market penetration tool for broadcasters that about half of the clubs in baseball are now owned or associated with broadcasters or advertisers.

When teams are owned by a business, it is difficult to determine the ballclub's profitability. For example, the finances of the Cardinals, the Cubs, or the Braves are intermingled with the profits of their parent companies. A club can be made to appear financially weak if the parent company transfers profits from the club to itself. The financial statements of corporate-owned clubs must, therefore, be viewed with suspicion. Some people like G. W. Scully, author of *The Business of Major League Baseball*, argue that part of the profits of Anheuser-Busch Breweries, WGN, and WTBS should really be allocated to the clubs. His reasoning is that the parent companies would have had to purchase these television rights at market value it they did not own the club.

For further details about the ownership structure of professional baseball, see G. W. Scully, *The Business of Major League Baseball* (The University of Chicago Press, Chicago, 1989).

Even if profit were a goal, it would not be reachable for most ISUs. Despite the media attention given to the money paid to or won by certain athletes and to the size of some television contracts, large financial returns for the ISUs themselves are a rarity. Because of the complexity of ownership, profits, if any, are difficult to measure and only a few individuals share it. Most ISUs do not even have a product of sufficient appeal to consumers to ensure their own economic survival. Without some form of subsidization many would fail if they relied on their ability to operate strictly as a commercial venture. This is especially true of amateur federations. The nonprofit ISU in Table 3.1, for example, received $409,850 (69 percent) of its total income from grants. When you add the labor, time, and effort required to manage an ISU, most do not meet the commercial definition of a successful business even though the sports industry as a whole is economically quite large.

Table 3.1   Example of Revenues and Expenses for a Nonprofit ISU

Where the money comes from		
Lilly Foundation Grant	$34,500	
USSS Foundation Grant	57,500	**GRANTS**
USOC Funds	284,910	
USOC Athlete Subsistence	32,940	
Goodwill Games	22,500	
Sports Festival	282	
Membership	81,000	
Life Membership	5,000	
Entry Fees & Sanctions	21,000	
National Camps	1,000	
Contributions & Donations	1,500	
Interest	8,000	
ACEP	1,000	
Clinic Revenue	500	
Merchandising & Books	16,069	
Demonstrations	25,000	
Miscellaneous	1,594	
TOTAL REVENUES	**$594,295**	
Where it goes		
Officers' Expenses	$6,100	
Administrative (includes Olympic athlete support)	347,306	
Technical Equipment	3,330	
Athlete Development	37,424	
Officials	16,450	
Marketing	1,230	
Olympic/International Competition	183,437	
TOTAL EXPENSES	**$595,277**	
	<982>	

Clearly we cannot explain the success of an ISU in terms of profit criteria alone. Owners of professional teams, runners in the 10K race, volunteers who hand out the drinks, and the underpaid or volunteer management staffs, all obtain some degree of psychic benefits that they value but cannot capture in terms of dollars. An association with sports carries a special aura to it. There is an ego gratification associated with something that touches the emotions of hundreds, and sometimes thousands, of people.

The ISU Product.   The ISU creates competition—its primary product.[3] This product has several characteristics that distinguish a professional sports enterprise from a private-sector enterprise.[4] Unlike most products with which you are familiar, you cannot sample a competition, nor can you touch, taste, or see it before you buy it. In other words, if you buy a ticket to watch a competition between two teams or two individual athletes, or you pay an entry fee to run a 10K race and you don't like the outcome, you cannot ask for your money back.

There are other features of a competition product that are important to recognize. First, the product is manufactured and consumed on-site. The athletes comprising the competition, and the spectators watching it, are important sources of their own satisfaction. Participants in a 10K race, for example, produce and consume their own enjoyment, although the event producer can enhance that enjoyment by attending to the environmental dimensions. Second, there is a limit to how many people can consume the original version of the product. A stadium can seat only a certain number of people, and a marathon can handle only so many runners. Third, it is difficult to control quality and consistency of the product. We do not expect one football game to be identical to the next. The mood of the crowd, the health of the athletes, and the skill level of opposing teams all play a role in product quality. Fourth, external elements can play an important role. Running a marathon or watching a football game in bad weather usually reduces the enjoyment most people gain from the experience. Finally, the product is perishable. We cannot store the original version of the competition and use it at some later date. A stadium owner cannot sell the competition at another time. Once the game is played or the race run, the product no longer exists in its original form. It can be reproduced on video, but the real version is extinct.

ISU Marketplace Competition.   A further difference between ISUs and private-sector businesses relates to marketplace competition. Whereas a conventional business entity seeks to outcompete rivals in the marketplace, an ISU must cooperate with its rivals to produce a marketable product. One single team or athlete acting independently cannot produce the product. Instead, one ISU in conjunction with another provides a joint effort that some promoter markets as the competition. This cooperative feature has resulted in a unique industry structure. The objective is to keep other ISUs in business, *not* put them out of business. This is unheard of among competitors in the private sector. So while ISUs use business terminology to describe their activities, they are not commercial operations in the same way that a private-sector business is commercial. Despite its apparent simplicity the business structure of an ISU is deceptively complex. Its structure even varies according to whether it is a team sport or an individual sport (see the next exhibit).

Business Structure of Team versus Individual Sports

Team sports competition is collectively owned by the coalition. Individual sporting events, on the other hand, are generally owned by the individual producing the event. This individual may or may not have some form of relationship to a coalition and takes on the job of paying expenses; promoting the competition; attracting the athletes to play by offering prize money, appearance fees, trophies or medals, and/or status; and selling television and sponsorship rights. Event management has recently become a business in its own right. You can hire a sports management company to do all or part of the jobs associated with the event—from running the event itself, to selling the TV rights, to finding corporate sponsorship.

Individual sports event promoters do not have to cooperate with one another to produce a good product. Many 10K runs and triathlons, for instance, are one-shot deals. But large-scale events are finding it more profitable to package several independent events together. The Grand Slam in tennis (the French, Australian, U.S. Open, and Wimbledon) is a case in point. These are actually four separate events owned and operated by different groups that are marketed as a series. Another example is the PGA TOUR, which links thirty-six different golf tournaments together. Similarly, in 1986 and 1987 boxing linked several individual fights into a tournament-style play-off. The idea here was to increase familiarity and interest in boxing.

Cooperation of this type allows advertisers and sponsors access to a circuit of events that gives them the communication programming consistency they need. It is also more economical for the event manager who is searching for potential sponsors and TV companies. One sales representative can sell several events in the series, so that individual tournament directors do not have to make those same calls. Television producers prefer a series, since programming becomes more consistent and familiar to audiences when a sport is broadcast at the same time each week. Although there are no data to prove it, a circuit of events culminating in an end-of-season championship seems to generate greater fan interest. It is also easier for television to market the entire series to sponsors. In addition, cooperation reduces market competition. Events can be scheduled on different dates, thereby reducing the competition for athletes, television time, and media attention.

Source: Mark S. Levinstein, *An Analysis of Legal and Business Differences between Individual and Team Sports*. (Unpublished manuscript made available to the author, November 5, 1990.)

Coalition Clusters

A coalition cluster is a formal collection of ISUs—clubs in a league, tournaments in a tour, organizations in the United States Olympic Committee (USOC), or universities in the National Collegiate Athletic Association (NCAA). It is often difficult to describe the exact role of a coalition cluster. We know them as cartels, monopolies, joint ventures, and partnerships. In some situations coalitions exist to allocate territory and athletes. In others they simply exist to maximize and allocate revenues. There are three types of coalition structures: league coalitions, athlete coalitions, and custodian coalitions. As you can see in Figure 3.3, a sport may have several different coalitions.

League Coalitions.   A league coalition is a contractual relationship between several clubs or teams of one single sport. The teams within the coalition may organize themselves as a private corporation, public corporation, Subchapter S corporation, ordinary partnership, limited partnership, and even sole proprietorship. A commissioner oversees league operations. There are three categories of operations:[5]

- activities that are predominantly controlled by the teams or clubs
- activities that are based upon collective league decisions
- activities that are governed jointly by the league and the clubs

Individual clubs generally determine the day-to-day operations. In baseball, for instance, the league controls regular season, play-off, and World Series broadcast rights. The clubs, on the other hand, decide ticket prices and keep all their concession profits. Generally member teams agree to share broadcasting revenues, gate receipts, and league merchandising. The breakdown can vary from league to league, however. Teams pay player salaries and facility overhead costs; they also provide uniforms and equipment. The league trains and employs referees and umpires. A key feature of a league coalition is that athletes are analogous to employees in that they receive a salary.

Athlete Coalitions.   Athlete coalitions exist where athletes compete as individuals rather than on teams. Tennis and golf are two examples. To develop a salable product athletes will establish a circuit or tour where they support themselves by competing for prize money provided by event owners. Successful athlete coalitions attempt to organize the prize money so that as many athletes as possible can make a reasonable living. Usually the best athletes have the opportunity to make the most money, although in the case of golf and tennis, lesser-skilled athletes can make more than the best athletes by playing in a larger number of tournaments. The key feature of an athlete coalition is that the athletes are analogous to independent contractors.

An example of an athlete coalition is the PGA TOUR, which is probably the largest sports coalition in the United States.[6] It consists of 250 touring golfers,

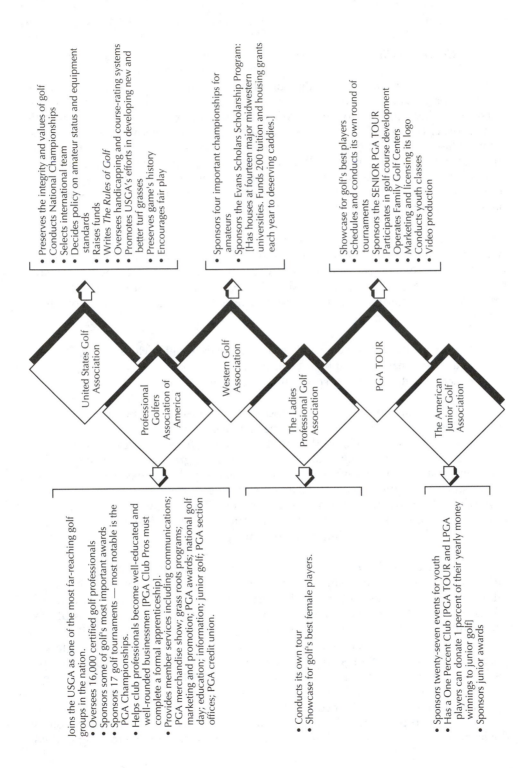

United States Golf Association

- Preserves the integrity and values of golf
- Conducts National Championships
- Selects international team
- Decides policy on amateur status and equipment standards
- Raises funds
- Writes *The Rules of Golf*
- Oversees handicapping and course-rating systems
- Promotes USGA's efforts in developing new and better turf grasses
- Preserves game's history
- Encourages fair play

Professional Golfers Association of America

Joins the USGA as one of the most far-reaching golf groups in the nation.

- Oversees 16,000 certified golf professionals
- Sponsors some of golf's most important awards
- Sponsors 17 golf tournaments — most notable is the PGA Championships.
- Helps club professionals become well-educated and well-rounded businessmen [PGA Club Pros must complete a formal apprenticeship].
- Provides member services including communications; PGA merchandise show; grass roots programs; marketing and promotion; PGA awards; national golf day; education; information; junior golf; PGA section offices; PGA credit union.

Western Golf Association

- Sponsors four important championships for amateurs
- Sponsors the Evans Scholars Scholarship Program: [Has houses at fourteen major midwestern universities. Funds 200 tuition and housing grants each year to deserving caddies.]

The Ladies Professional Golf Association

- Conducts its own tour
- Showcase for golf's best female players.

PGA TOUR

- Showcase for golf's best players
- Schedules and conducts its own round of tournaments
- Sponsors the SENIOR PGA TOUR
- Participates in golf course development
- Operates Family Golf Centers
- Marketing and licensing its logo
- Conducts youth classes
- Video production

The American Junior Golf Association

- Sponsors twenty-seven events for youth
- Has a One Percent Club [PGA TOUR and LPGA players can donate 1 percent of their yearly money winnings to junior golf]
- Sponsors junior awards

Figure 3.3 Coalition Clusters for Golf and a Brief Summary of Their Function

Source: Rhonda Glen and Robert McCord, *The Whole Golf Catalog* (New York: Perigree, Putnam 1990).

more than 800 employees (versus 280 for the NFL), and $52 million in assets that range from golf courses to sportswear lines (Table 3.2). The PGA TOUR, Inc., is a tax-exempt membership organization whose purpose it is to regulate, promote, and improve the business of professional tournament golf. All revenues earned by the TOUR (exclusive of operating expenses, reasonable reserves, and so on) must enhance the profession and the business climate for current and future members. In other words, the TOUR's main job is to help professional tournament golfers earn a better living.

Linking individual events maximizes income for the athletes (see, for example, the previous exhibit). Players assign their individual television rights to the TOUR, which packages these rights and sells them at the best rights fees the PGA TOUR can negotiate (Figure 3.4). The PGA TOUR then uses the majority of those funds (less the amount needed to administer the TOUR) to lure sponsors by offering them events in which the purses are large enough to attract a quality player field and consequently a better television contract. Technically, current players do not own the TOUR or its assets. The TOUR is really an ongoing entity, analogous to a trust that the "trustees" (the Tournament Policy Board) run for the benefit of current and future players.

Custodian Coalitions. The most well known of this form of coalition is the USOC (see the next exhibit) and the NCAA. The ISUs within the cluster each serve a different sport, like the national governing bodies (NGBs) of the USOC, or

---

History of a Custodian Coalition —The U.S. Olympic Committee

The USOC began as an informal group headed by James E. Sullivan, that entered U.S. athletes in the inaugural Olympic Games in Athens in 1898. In 1890 A. G. Spalding, a publisher and sporting goods manufacturer, became the first elected president. In November 1921 the group was officially named the American Olympic Association. Then in 1940 it changed its name to the United States of America Sports Federation, in 1945 changing it again to the United States Olympic Association (USOA). In 1950 Public Law 805 granted the USOA a federal charter enabling it to solicit tax-deductible contributions as a private, nonprofit corporation. Finally in 1961 the USOA became the United States Olympic Committee (USOC).

On November 8, 1978, Public Law 95-606, the Amateur Sports Act, named the USOC as the coordinating body for athletic activity directly relating to international Olympic competition. The act gave the USOC the authority to recognize the NGBs for Olympic (winter and summer) and Pan-American Games sports. This public law gave the USOC exclusive rights to Olympic emblems, the words *Olympic, Olympiad,* and *Citius, Altius, Fortius,* and other Olympic-related symbols in the United States. A grandfather clause permitted anyone using the symbols or terminology before September 21, 1950, to continue using them. The law also required all governance councils of the USOC and NGBs to have at least 20 percent membership and voting power held by "recent or active" athletes. The law further states, "The Corporation shall be nonpolitical and, as an organization, shall not promote the candidacy of any person seeking public office."

The International Olympic Committee (IOC) recognizes the USOC as the guardian of the Olympic movement in the United States. It is the sole agency whose mission is to train, enter, and underwrite the full expenses for U.S. teams in the Olympic and Pan-American Games. Another function of the USOC is to support the bid of American cities to host the winter or summer Olympic Games or the Pan-American Games. It also determines which cities will host the U.S. Olympic Festival and the U.S. trials for the Olympic and Pan-American Games team selections.

This material was adapted from an article appearing in the *Olympian*, January 1990, p. 4.

cluster of sports, like the universities in the NCAA. The prime purpose of this type of coalition is to ensure the survival of a specific form of amateur competition—Olympic sport in the case of the USOC, or collegiate sport in the case of the NCAA. Under certain conditions the coalition provides funding for its ISUs. The key feature here is that like children in a family, athletes require financial, coaching, and moral support during their growth (competitive) years (Figure 3.5).

Whatever the format, the force binding a coalition cluster together is the belief that the whole is much larger than the sum of its parts. That is, the coalition has more power to maximize income than each ISU would have acting as an independent. Although it is sometimes possible to work as an independent, most ISUs must stay within their coalition cluster in order to survive. Members of a coalition cluster abdicate much of their autonomy and power to the coalition. The reasoning is that an optimum product requires cooperation, and an ISU is motivated to pursue its own interests. This would ultimately destroy the sport. The sport needs some form of control in order to curb this self-destructive behavior. In essence, coalition clusters exist to control scarce resources, maximize income, and ensure fair play.

There is one final aspect of coalition clusters you should note. One single sport may have several different types of coalition clusters. Some may act more as a league coalition and others as an athlete or custodian coalition. Golf, for example, has at least six major coalitions each servicing the specific needs of a group of individuals or clubs. Two are athlete coalitions, and the remainder are custodian coalitions (see Figure 3.3, for example).

Table 3.2 Example of Revenues and Expenses of an Athlete Coalition—the PGA Tour

WHERE THE MONEY COMES FROM 1991 Revenues ($189,707,000)		WHERE THE MONEY GOES 1991 Expenses ($189,707,000)	
Television Revenues Network rights fees and television production	$49,958,000 (26.3%)	**Tournament Operations** Cost of field operations for Regular, Senior, and Hogan Tour and cost of operations for the Players Championship, Senior Players Championship, Tour Championship, World Series of Golf, and TOUR Qualifying Tournaments	$9,224,000 (4.9%)
Tournament Operations Membership, qualifying and service fees, sponsor prize money, the Players Championship, Tour Championship, and World Series of Golf	$60,435,000 (31.9%)	**Tournament Players Clubs** Operating costs, interest, depreciation, construction management, and club start-up costs	$53,770,000 (28.3%)
Tournament Players Clubs Operations, royalties and licensing fees, management fees, and membership sales	$60,252,000 (31.8%)	**Tour Reserves** Net revenues over expenses and payments to players and sponsors	$4,634,000 (2.4%)
Marketing Royalties and license fees, promotions, electronic scoreboards, and fitness training vans	$12,417,000 (6.5%)	**Marketing** Operating costs of marketing department, electronic scoreboards, and fitness training vans	$4,466,000 (2.3%)
Other Investment earnings and other fees	$6,645,000 (3.5%)	**Headquarters Support** General and administrative, finance and accounting, executive and communications departments	$8,900,000 (4.7%)
		Payments to Players and Sponsors	$84,433,000 (44.5%)
		Television Costs Costs of broadcast and PGA TOUR productions department and cost of highlights show production	$14,308,000 (7.5%)
		Player Retirement Plans	$5,400,000 (2.9%)
		Other Interest expense	$4,661,000 (2.5%)

Source: PGA TOUR 1991 Annual Report.

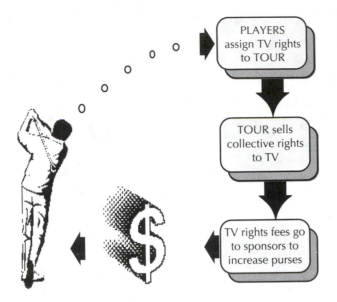

Figure 3.4   An Example of How Athlete Coalitions Maximize Their Income

Figure 3.5   Revenues and Expenses of a Custodian Coalition

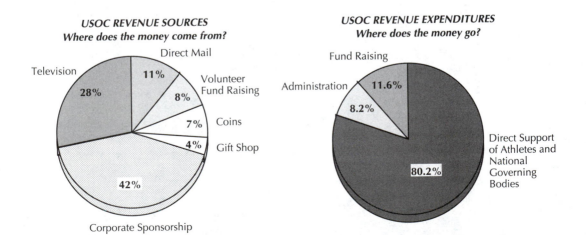

The Labor Structure

Three entities comprise the labor structure of sports organizations and participants. These include (a) athletes' unions, (b) the individual athletes themselves, and (c) the sports agents.

Athletes' Unions

Successful athlete collectives are a relatively recent phenomenon.[7] We presently see them only in professional sports—specifically team sports. Their purpose is to counteract the power of the club or team owners. They are similar to workers' unions, but they are not so easy to define. Athletes' unions deal with a special type of management and serve the needs of a very select group of workers. Although we seldom consider athletes on the same level as doctors, lawyers, or engineers, they are just as highly trained, exceptionally skilled, and relatively few. The odds against succeeding as an athlete, particularly as a professional athlete, are overwhelming. As monetary rewards grow, the odds become even greater, since the sport attracts a larger crop of talented individuals.

A players' union generally has a diverse membership, and this feature distinguishes it from the typical trade union in the commercial sector. Superstars with more consumer appeal and high salaries are mixed with athletes who have average talent, minimal consumer appeal, and lower salaries. The problems faced by the two groups are quite different. Athletes earning several hundred thousand dollars per year are not likely to care much about meal money, travel allowances, or pensions. These are, however, important concerns of athletes earning less money. The short working life of athletes means that their union membership is constantly shifting, making it difficult to fight for perceived rights. Given the diversity and continual state of flux of membership, it is amazing that athletes' unions manage to survive at all.

The Athletes

The athletes are the physical assets of the sports product, and they consist of three types.

Type 1 athletes engage in a specific sport (and sometimes several sports) solely as a pastime. This group includes a wide age range who may or may not participate in structured events. We recognize this group as *recreational participants*.

Type 2 athletes participate for the purpose of developing their skill to a point where they are competitive on a national or international level. Their goal is not to make a living from the sport—just to compete at the highest level possible (although some do make substantial sums of money). We call this group *amateur athletes*.

Type 3 athletes are those who receive compensation for their competitive performance either by way of a salary or prize money. We refer to this group as *professional athletes*, although they are really entertainers.

Although we make the distinction among these three types of athletes, the difference between amateur and professional athletes is often difficult to determine. Some amateur athletes make a substantial income, which they place into a trust account from which they can draw living expenses. There is also a blurring in the entertainment versus skill development distinction between amateur and professional athletes. We consider college football players amateurs, although their prime function is quite frequently entertainment.

From a promoter's standpoint, superior athletic performance affects team sports and individual sports differently.[8] A superior individual performance on a team does not necessarily guarantee team victory. Fans often overlook a superb individual performance if the team loses. In individual sports, however, the best athlete usually wins and gets all the credit. Within one team talent may range from superstar to average. In the major sports like football and men's basketball all have the ability to earn a living, but in an individual sport the average athlete has less opportunity to earn a decent living. Consequently, most individual sports revolve around a smaller number of athletes. Whereas you see more specialization in team sports, individual sports require more all-round talent. In track, for example, the best starter out of the blocks cannot win the race unless the runner is also fast overall. A tennis player with the best serve, a golfer with the best putt, or the heavyweight boxer with the best uppercut will not succeed unless he or she is also one of the best overall performers.

Finally, a spectator's attendance at team events does not depend upon whether or not the superstar is playing. A superstar often enhances fan interest, but the team is generally the prime focus of attention. In contrast, fans tend to go to individual sporting events to watch specific individual athletes. A tennis match between two well-known tennis players, for example, will generally attract more spectator and television interest than a match between unknown players. A top name player is therefore more important to the success of individual sporting events than for team events.

Agents

A breed of commercial sales representative called sports agents market the talents of the most highly skilled athletes. These sports agents may also be attorneys. Their businesses are referred to as *sports agencies* or *sports marketing agencies.*[9]

A handful of agents tend to dominate certain sports. Bob Woolf has extensive influence in basketball, for instance, while Jerry Kapstein is a powerful force in professional basketball. Art Kaminsky reportedly represents one-third of all players in the NHL. In the past Donald Dell has dominated tennis, although his influence in this sport is not quite so dramatic today. Mark McCormack remains a major factor in golf, although he has now expanded his influence into tennis, skiing, and auto racing.

Agents succeed by offering services tailored to meet the special needs of their clientele. A good agent can diversify an athlete's income through endorsements, speaking engagements, and other forms of non-sports-related activities.

Agents also perform many financial tasks for their clients such as investing their money, paying their bills, advising them about retirement, and arranging for adequate insurance, legal services, and tax planning. Some agents like International Management Group (IMG) and ProServ negotiate television and commercial rights for sponsors of sporting events. They have a unique array of integrated services they can offer both the athletes and the business customers. They provide lawyers, insurance specialists, accountants, financial analysts, and investment advisors all under one roof. Such one-stop shopping for planning, executing, publicizing, and televising sporting events is often attractive to corporate clients. This kind of integrated service, along with considerable expertise in a variety of sports endeavors, has given the bigger agencies like IMG and ProServ a powerful competitive advantage over many smaller agents and promoters. In addition, some of the larger sports marketing agencies like IMG have expanded into the production and packaging of pseudo sports programming. IMG, for example, has produced the "Superstars," the "Superteams," "Games People Play," "Challenges of the Sexes," and "Battle of the Network Stars."

The sports agent's role in and influence on the sports industry is unquestionable. As they move into event production and as more top athletes join their client list, sports agents will enter the realm of conflict of interest. Agent domination in a sport puts agents in the precarious role of influencing the entire sport. IMG, for example, has reportedly signed golfers who could establish their own tour in competition with the PGA. Another ISU in which agents dominate athlete representation, the Association of Tennis Professionals (ATP), has recently struggled to regain control over tennis and keep the agents at a safe distance.

THE SECONDARY INFRASTRUCTURE

We have discussed the primary infrastructure in considerable depth since this is important to your understanding of how the core product of sports—the activity—is produced. Now it is time for us to look more closely at the secondary infrastructure. This component of the sports industry is becoming increasingly important to the overall economy of sports. Whereas the primary infrastructure itself may remain relatively stable in terms of job opportunities, the secondary infrastructure is likely to continue expanding. It is within the secondary infrastructure that sports business students like you will likely find your future career. The most effective way for you to fully comprehend the opportunities available in the secondary infrastructure is to do the following assignment.

Making Money from the Secondary Infrastructure

Late last evening you were studying with two friends in the library. You are all exceptionally creative and especially enjoy discussing ideas you have for ways a sports organization can improve its financial status. Until now your discussions have simply been a way to have some fun. However, last night it struck you that it is time to stop having fun and start making some money from your many ideas. You decide to set up your own business—Creative Sports Concepts. Your basic idea is to help sports managers search through the secondary infrastructure of sports for workable new product ideas.

You fully realize that most sports organizations in this country have several deficiencies: little staff, little money, little experience developing new products, and a scarcity of time. You decide to practice on a familiar sport. Your strategy is to devise innovative ways for this sport to integrate into its present product line products typically found in the secondary infrastructure. The goal, of course, is to help this sport raise the money it needs to fund its operations. First, you must go through the process yourself.

You now meet to go through the process. One of you has developed a list of the secondary infrastructure components (see Table 3.3). Look at this list and identify at least five possible products through which a sports manager might generate additional sources of income. You can add categories not included on the list. Your products should be workable for the sports organization you have selected. Once you have your five products, you need to evaluate their potential in terms of five important assessment criteria. These are the criteria:

1. Staff needs: What are the staffing requirements to implement the idea?
2. Start-up costs: How much money does the sports organization need to develop and implement the ideas?
3. Potential for expanding membership in the organization: Membership may include participants, fan clubs, and other support groups.
4. Potential for expanding interest in the sport: This may include improved exposure, more ways for people to learn the sport, and so on.
5. Cost-benefit ratio: How much will the idea cost in terms of time, money, and energy versus benefits to the sport organization?

Use the grid in Figure 3.6 to evaluate your product ideas. Discuss your ideas with your classmates. What do they feel about your idea? Vote on the most creative idea. What suggestions do you have for each other in terms of how you can improve your ideas?

SUMMARY

This chapter introduced you to a conceptual model that will help you place into a logical structure the numerous components of the sports industry that affect your idea. From experience I suspect you will find this chapter quite understandable until you begin to fill out the strategic plan worksheet. It will be difficult for you to see exactly how your idea fits within the structure presented. You may want to shrug your shoulders and assume that the content of this chapter does not concern your specific idea. Of course not all aspects of every chapter will directly relate to your idea all the time. If your idea is to produce a recreational event, such

Table 3.3 The List That You Brought to the Meeting

	Add your extra categories here:

• Art and Collectables
• Archives and Museums
• Events
• Books, publications, video games, software
• Broadcasting and other media
• Business professions
    Administration
    Managers
    Rules
• Camps and schools
• Clothing and equipment
• Services
    facilities
    scoring
    handicapping
    scorecards
    game/tournament management
    program development	

If you need help to generate creative ideas, use the following exercise.

As you search through this secondary infrastructure, look at each of the following words and wait for an idea.

Guest stars	Charity	Family
Photography	Alphabet	Education
Timeliness	Interview	Inert ingredients
Truth	His and hers	Videotape
Testimonials	Outer space	Style
World	Stunts	Decorate
Chart, diagram	Nation	Legalities
Birth	Showmanship	Gauge, scale
Weather	Ethnic	Floor, wall
Zipper	Habit, fad	Push button
Participation	Fantasy	Transportation
Snob appeal	Music	Folklore, magic
Symbolism	Romance	Direct mail
Subconscious need	Calendar	Parody
Summer	Hobbies	Curiosity
Graphics	Holidays	Telephone
Sketch	Security	Religion
Show business	News value	Self-service
Animals	Legend	Efficiency
Catalog	Spectacular	Personalized
Glamorize	Mystery	Code
Optical illusion	Dictionary	Powder
Guarantee	Sophisticate	
Cartoons	Birthdays	
Sex	Sports	

Source: Donald Cantin, *Turn Your Ideas into Money* (New York: Hawthorn Books, 1972). Adapted from pages 34–41.

The Problem Search the secondary infrastructure for products that will meet a need of consumers of a minor sport and will be profitable for the sports organization.

1. Write down several features of each product assessment criterion that will affect your product idea. For example, most sports organizations have a small underpaid, overworked professional staff, a handful of consistent volunteers, and a larger group of volunteers who will help out whenever they can.

2. List the most appropriate products that fit the organization.

3. Rate all alternative products against each assessment criterion (10 fits a criterion best and 1 fits it least). For example, if a product requires a lot of staff time and is too complex for volunteers, you would probably rate this as a 5 or less.

4. Total the scores for each product.

5. Based on these scores, rank the products from the most desirable option to the least desirable option.

Product Assessment Criteria

A	B	C	D	E
Staffing Requirements	Start-up Costs	Membership Expansion Opportunity	Sports Interest Expansion	Cost-Benefit Ratio
1. Write a brief summary of the characteristics of each criterion that will affect the product idea				

2. List Products	3. Rate the products on a scale of 1 to 10 for each criterion Product Assessment Criteria					4. Total Score	5. Rank

Figure 3.6

issues as agents, players' unions, and even ISUs may not appear to concern you. But the general goal of this book is to make you think and learn about factors potentially affecting the success of your idea. Keep in mind that there are always methods of applying material in each chapter toward this goal. Perhaps you are designing computer software that will act as a coach for those recreational weight lifters not familiar with designing their own weight training program. Let's take this weight training program as an example and diagram the primary infrastructure (Figure 3.7).

In place of the competition we will put "weight lifting activity." For "players" we will put "participants"; individual athletes will include those groups that would consider using the weight training coach. Perhaps you are targeting your software to high school football coaches who want to ensure their players are following a sound weight-lifting program. The individual athletes in this case are the football players themselves, and the agents are the coaches, since they will have complete control over the introduction of your product. There are no athletes' associations, although, I am inclined to place the parents here, since weight training may conjure up parental concern about steroid use, which you

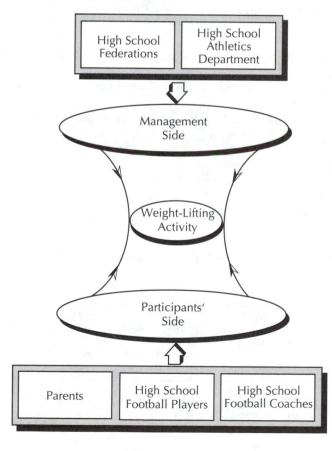

Figure 3.7 Components of the Primary Structure of the Sports Industry, Modeled in Figure 3.1, Adapted to a Computer Software

may have to deal with in some manner. On the management side you would place the high school federations (coalitions), and the ISU is the high school athletics department.

In essence, this chapter tries to make you think more about aspects of the industry structure that may have an impact on the success of your idea. So don't throw up your arms in frustration. Allow your brain to stretch beyond its comfort zone to understand the structure of the sports industry as presented in this chapter, and try to bend the material to fit your needs. The next chapter will introduce another dimension of your business environment.

STRATEGIC PLAN WORKSHEET–CHAPTER 3

What You Should Know about the Sports Industry

Your Goal   ....

To understand the economic structure and the scope of the sports industry and how your venture fits within it

Questions you should answer:

- What is the structure of your component of the sports industry?
- What business are you in?
- What is your specific industry profile—size, geographic spread, market, history, present status, total sales, and profits?
- Diagram your primary infrastructure.
- Diagram your secondary infrastructure.
- What are some products in the secondary infrasture that may help you meet the goals you have for your event?
- Does any specific group of agents have a potential impact on the success of your idea?

REFERENCES   ....

1. Michael E. Porter, *Competitive Strategy: Techniques for Analyzing Industries and Competitors* (New York: Free Press, 1980), p. 5.
2. These figures were obtained from Tom Fennell and D'arcy Jenish, "The Riches of Sport," *Macleans*, April 9, 1990, pp. 42–45.
3. The development of the concepts in this section was influenced by an unpublished paper written by Mark Levinstein, *An Analysis of Legal and Business Differences between Individual and Team Sports*. It was made available to the author on November 5, 1990.
4. For more information on the characteristics of services, see William J. Stanton, *Fundamentals of Marketing*, 6th ed. (New York: McGraw-Hill, 1981), pp. 444–46.

5. Warren Freedman, *Professional Sports and Antitrust* (New York: Quorum Books, 1987), p. 23.
6. PGA TOUR Tournament Policy Board, *Annual Report to the Membership*, 1991 (Sawgrass, Ponte Vedra Beach, FL 32082).
7. For a more detailed review of the function of athletes' unions, see G. W. Scully, *The Business of Major League Baseball* (Chicago: University of Chicago Press, 1989).
8. These differences between team and individual sports have been adapted from Levinstein, *An Analysis of Legal and Business Differences.*
9. For an interesting case study on Sports Marketing agencies see Hartley, R. F. Marketing Successes. John Wiley & Son New York, 1990 p. 202–213.

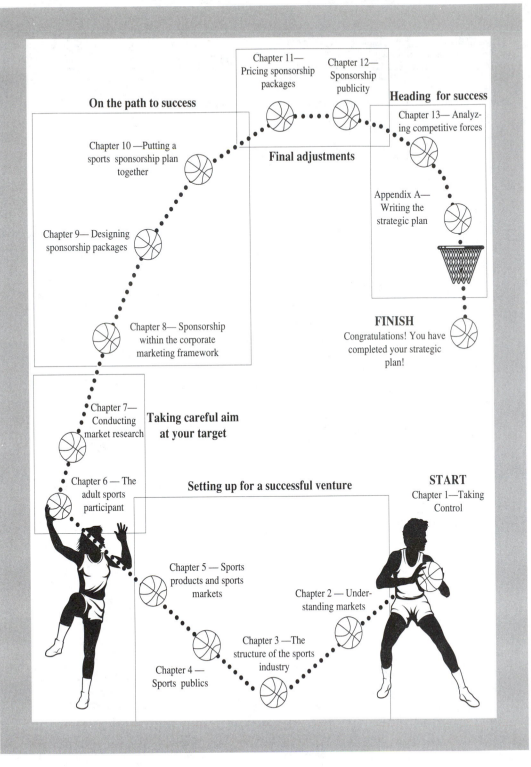

CHAPTER FOUR

Sports Publics

● ●

> It is a general human weakness to allow things, uncertain and
> unknown, to set us up in hope, or plunge us into fear.
> —*Gaius Julius Caesar*
> *(102?–44 B.C.)*

Have you ever seen those late-night commercials for knife sets, cleaning solutions, or Richard Simmons weight loss packages? You know the ones I mean—the kind where you constantly hear, "But wait, there's more!" Just when you think there can't possibly be another free and valuable gift, you hear those words once more, "But wait, there's more!" Well, this is what it feels like when you are organizing a sports event or introducing any form of product associated with sports into the marketplace. So many entities affect your success that just when you think you have everything under control, you will find there is always more. Regardless of the sport, we will find entities such as governments, agents, athletes, sanctioning bodies, media, and competitors having an impact. To stay out of the dark, it is important to understand these forces and how they operate. To see just how complex things can get, read the following case study, which highlights the experiences of Fred Lebow, the mastermind behind the New York City Marathon and the 5th Avenue Mile.[1]

| CASE STUDY | The 5th Avenue Mile |

Fred Lebow is a road racing promoter. He thought of a fantastic event—a mile race down 5th Avenue, the plushest residential section of New York. His friends believed the idea was outrageous. "The mile is always run on an oval track, not a road," they said. "And the merchants and residents of 5th Avenue are so sick and tired of outsiders they have vowed not to permit any more extraordinary use of their streets."

Fred felt this race would be a spectacular event for early autumn. He could envision the race beginning at 82nd Street at the Metropolitan Museum of Art and ending at 62nd Street. What a picture! What a sight for television! The best milers in the world dashing down the middle of 5th Avenue framed on the right by Central Park, on the left by the avenue's most elegant apartment buildings, watched by 100,000 spectators, and televised by network TV. "Excuse me!" his best friend exclaimed. "Are you totally out of your mind! There's no way the city will let you do it. Even if they do, who will be interested in such a race? Certainly not people, definitely not television! What world-class miler would even think about racing a mile on the road? You're nuts . . . you've totally lost it!"

Fred listened to his friend. It was those final few words—"You've totally lost it" that presented the challenge. He would do it! He picked September 26 as the date and called Parks Commissioner Gordon Davis for approval. "I can't give my approval for such a race until you talk with the residents," Davis explained. Fred then called the 5th Avenue residents' association and arranged to make a presentation to them.

Two weeks later Fred relinquished his favorite sweatsuit for his most presentable outfit. He was about to meet the residents' association. He refused to let his nerves get the better of him as he found himself face-to-face with thirty-four somber people, mostly women. They stared at him as if he came from another planet. He checked his shoes to make sure they were the same color—they were. He wondered what it was about him they found so unusual. He made his presentation.

"No way!"a stout woman in the back of the room shouted. "Go somewhere else. 5th Avenue is not the only street in New York City!"

"Ah, but it's the most charismatic street," Fred countered. "The mile is the most charismatic event of track and field. An elegant crowd follows it, not the beer-drinking crowd that follows parades. A mile will tie up your street for only a short time. Please, give me a chance to show you what a great event this will be." To his surprise people in the room started to support him. They discussed it among themselves and finally called for a vote. It was 32 to 2 in Fred's favor.

Armed with their approval Fred headed off to the Police Department the following day seeking police approval. "No, no, no!" said the police chief shaking, his head. "I have most of my men committed to the South African rugby match on that date." Not to be deterred, Fred made another phone call to Commissioner Davis, who agreed to ask the Police Chief to reverse his decision. So far, so good!

That Summer:

Fred was now in Oslo, Norway, where most of the world's top milers were gathering for the Oslo Dream Mile. They loved his idea, especially Steve Ovett, the winner of the Dream Mile and world record holder. Ovett agreed to compete in the 5th Avenue Mile. With Ovett committed, it wasn't difficult to convince twenty-five elite runners from eight different countries to participate. Having landed the athletes Fred now needed a network television contract and sponsors. The travel and hotel bill for all those elite athletes would be expensive. As well, several of the world-class runners had demanded appearance and incentive fees.

As it turned out, it was fairly easy to sell the 5th Avenue Mile to television. Fred simply dangled Ovett, and ABC jumped at the opportunity to schedule the race for "Wide World of Sports." With television and the world's best milers in tow Fred now began his search for a sponsor. That was not difficult either. Pepsi agreed to sponsor the event for $175,000 on the condition that the event be named the Pepsi Challenge 5th Avenue Mile. Fred agreed. He now began work on the print advertising campaign. "Ovett at the Met" is the slogan he decided to use, capitalizing on the fact that the starting line of the race was at the Metropolitan Museum of Art. Things were indeed moving along quite well. Confident, Fred planned a trip to Stockholm, where he would run the marathon.

In Stockholm One Month Before the Mile:

Fred was warming up for the race when he heard his name over the loudspeaker.

"Please come to the officials' table," the voice said. He jogged through the crowd to the starting line. Fred soon discovered that one of his aides from his office in New York was trying to reach him by phone. "The police have canceled the 5th Avenue Mile!" the frantic voice exclaimed.

"What?" Fred responded in disbelief. "Impossible!"

"No, it's not," replied the voice. "One of the newspapers wrote that we expected 1 million spectators instead of 100,000. The police refuse to control a million people for us. They canceled the event."

Within six hours Fred was on a plane for New York. By the time he got there, the police chief had notified all departments that the event was off. The chief absolutely refused to change his mind even though the newspaper had made a mistake. Fred dug deep into his list of New York contacts, cashed in all his IOUs, and eventually took his plea to the mayor's office. The event was reinstated.

A few days later Fred got word from the International Amateur Athletic Federation (IAAF), the world governing body for track and field, that it would not sanction the 5th Avenue Mile. "The 5th Avenue Mile represents gross commercialism," President Adriaan Paulen, an elderly Dutchman, proclaimed to the press in Sarajevo, Yugoslavia. "Athletes who participate will jeopardize their amateur status." Within hours athletes were withdrawing from the race. The whole race was going down the tube. Fred tried to reach Paulen by phone, but he was on his way to Rome for another meeting. Exasperated, Fred caught the next flight to Rome.

In Rome:

Paulen refused to see Fred, who waited around in the lobby of Paulen's hotel hoping to catch him. Finally, Fred spotted him coming through the side entrance. "Mr. Paulen, sir! Please, may I speak with you?" He introduced himself and presented Paulen with a silver apple as a token of New York City hospitality. Paulen accepted gracefully but refused to reconsider his decision. From Paulen's viewpoint the 5th Avenue Mile was a bad joke. Dejected and exhausted, Fred tried to find a hotel room for the night. He would try again tomorrow.

The next day Paulen still refused to discuss the matter. Fred decided to stay one more day and give Paulen one more shot. Then he got the good news— Paulen was out! Primo Nebiolo of Italy was now IAAF president. Fred cashed in a few more IOUs to get a meeting with Nebiolo. "I love the idea of the 5th Avenue Mile," Nebiolo told him. "It will be a great promotional event for track and field." Fred could not believe it. He was back in business.

Fred flew back to New York to learn that Ovett had suddenly canceled due to illness. "What else can happen?" he sighed. The ABC contract hinged on the presence of Ovett. Fred nervously called the people at ABC and broke the news about Ovett. He mentioned that he still had a remarkable group of milers to offer them. They agreed. The contract was still good.

Aftermath:

An estimated crowd of 100,000 and a national TV audience watched the race. The event quickly became an annual race and was part of an international circuit of city-street miles in Rome, Paris, Dublin, and Toronto. Fred traveled from country to country overseeing each race. On one of his trips he got wind that IMG, a sports marketing agency headed by Mark McCormack, was planning a takeover of the mile road racing circuit. This did not surprise Fred. The circuit was very popular with sponsors, and whenever there is the potential for profit, IMG muscles its way in. IMG had already signed many of the top runners. The company had its own television programming capacity and was in the process of tying up an endorsement and financial partnership with the Athletics

Congress, the U.S. governing body for track and field. IMG was danger-
ously close to becoming a monopoly, owning the top marathoners and
the top 10K women. The organization was in a position to dictate which
events their clients would participate in. The whole foundation for road
running could thereby collapse. Fred and his associates around the world
had invested a great deal of time setting up the mile circuit, and now, in
one quick swoop, they were about to lose it all. His adrenaline flowed.
Once again it was time for the great Fred Lebow to move into action.

THE PUBLICS AFFECTING SPORTS

At first glance, the sheer number of entities that Fred Lebow had to take care of,
and the variety of roles they played, seems rather complex. A pattern does, however, exist, and the puzzle fits together quite neatly. Nine different clusters of
groups or publics have an impact on sports and, as such, have a direct bearing on
the economy of sports organizations. Figure 4.1 illustrates the relationship of
these nine publics to a sports organization.

Figure 4.1   The Nine Publics Affecting a Sports Organization

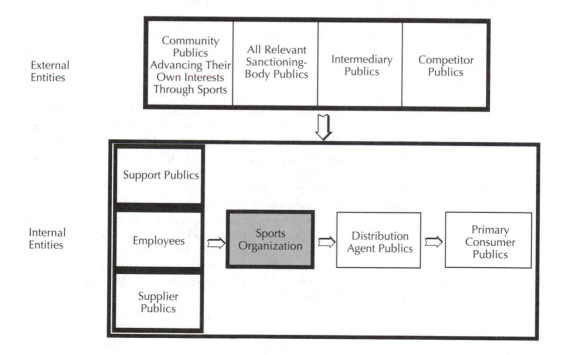

As Figure 4.1 indicates, there are four external and five internal publics. The external publics include.

- Organizations or groups advancing their own interests through sport. These may include a country, a city, a university, or a corporation.
- Sanctioning bodies such as the USOC, the IAAF, league associations, the U.S. government, and the NCAA.
- Intermediaries such as sports agents, sports marketing firms, and sports promoters.
- Competitors involving all forms of leisure and entertainment activities and other like events that vie for scarce resources.

The common feature of external publics is that their impact is largely outside the immediate control of sports managers. Internal publics are more directly under the control of a sports manager. These groups include three input publics, a network of distribution agents, and a primary product consumer. The input publics encompass (1) support groups such as volunteers, directors, local citizens and politicians; (2) employees; and (3) suppliers that provide financial and other necessary resources. These three groups provide the basic ingredients that enable a sports organization to function.

Distribution agents involve all those channels that permit consumption of the sport. First, there are the spectator distribution mechanisms (stadiums, television, and in some instances roads and other public property such as parks); second, participation or athlete distribution systems (clubs, high schools, colleges, events); and third, there are all tangential means of making the sport available to consumers (books, camps, videos). The primary consumers are the actual participants, spectators, or others consuming the sport for its inherent value by watching, participating, or reading about it. They do not seek to profit financially from their consumption.

Each of these nine publics varies in its importance to the economy of a sports organization. Some are more crucial to amateur sports than to professional sports and vice versa. Regardless of the magnitude of their economic effect, though, neglecting any of them could lead to managerial problems. In its own special way, each is a consumer group requiring a specific set of marketing activities. Unfortunately, we know little about the composition of these publics, and how sports organizations can interact with them.

What is the optimum interaction between a sport and each of the nine publics? Are these publics fulfilling important gaps in the economy of certain sports organizations, or is it the other way around? How does the interaction work? Is the interaction symbiotic or parasitic? Answers to such questions require some discussion about the needs of each public and how those needs are fulfilled through sports. This chapter examines these issues so that you can better understand the nature of these nine publics.

THE EXTERNAL PUBLICS ....

Community Publics

Community publics can include a country, city, university, or corporation and use sports to advance their own interests. Each of these communities seeks to improve its own economic conditions, and sports are the conduit to this end. Let's take a look at how each of these four community publics uses sports.

Countries

In the developed world many governments use sports as a showcase for their way of life. The U.S. government is no exception. Olympic sports are an important American asset entrusted by Congress to the USOC, whose job is to ensure that amateur sports function in the best interest of the country as a whole. That means making sure U.S. society is presented to the world in a positive manner, or more directly, ensuring that U.S. athletes win their share of Olympic medals.

Cities

As early as the 1920s Chambers of commerce recognized the economic value of a sporting event. A city wanted to expand by stimulating tourist trade or by making itself an attractive site for companies. In the early years numerous chambers of commerce supported professional golf tournaments. The game supposedly brought prestige to the entire city. In 1926 A. G. Carroll, secretary and general manager of the Los Angeles Chamber of Commerce, said:

> California's $25,000 appropriation for the winter golf season is one of the wisest investments the state ever made. It represents the type of constructive publicity that brings people and money to the merchant, the manufacturer, the wholesaler and the retailer. You can talk of climate and manufacturing, industries and the rest, but there are hundreds of Chambers of Commerce talking the same thing. But talk golf and that takes in [all the above, plus] the very important item—recreation." Source: A. Barkow, *The History of the PGA TOUR* (New York: Double-day, 1989), p. 5.

Sports can have a dramatic impact on a city. A major international sporting event such as the Olympic Games presents a unique opportunity for a city seeking world attention. Japan, for instance, emerged as a world economic power in the early 1960s after the formerly disheveled city of Tokyo virtually rebuilt itself in preparation for the 1964 Summer Olympic Games. Later, city planners in Seoul, Korea, used the Olympic Games to improve the physical environment for its citizens.[2] In these cases, a sporting event focused attention on the fundamental issues in a society.

While their aim is less sensational than the rebuilding of a Tokyo or a Seoul, modern-day U.S. cities use sports franchises for self-promotion purposes.

Economic Impact Studies

Question

You buy two $20 tickets to your college football game. You spend $30 on food and drinks for a tailgate party, $5 to park your car, and $25 on a program, a sweatshirt, and other incidentals. After the game you spend $45 at a local restaurant for dinner. You fill up with $10 of gas and head on home to pay the babysitter $30. What have you added to the economy of the local community by attending the game?
  A. 0
  B. $70
  C. $185
  D. $425.50
  E. Whatever you want it to be.
    Your economic impact (EI) is not easy to assess. If we argue that you have merely diverted to the football game money you would normally spend on something else, then the answer is A. In other words, if you did not go to the game, you would spend the money somewhere else in the community. You may have answered B. That is, you counted tickets, parking fees, and the purchase of incidental items ($70) as the game's added economic impact. However, if you had not gone to the game, would you have eaten out? Would you have spent that money later on during the month on something else, or would you have put it in the bank?
    One problem with most EI studies is that they mix local and out-of-town fans together. Out-of-town fans are more likely to add economic impact than local fans because they bring money from outside the local area. Even if we know precisely how much you have spent, and where you have come from, we still face the problem of knowing just how typical you are.

Direct, Indirect, and Induced

Some EI studies assess economic value any time a dollar passes from one hand and into another (answer C). They assume, for example, that your babysitter will rush to the store and spend the $30 on clothes and that the service station owner will purchase other local goods and services. But we do not know that for sure. Perhaps the babysitter will put your money into her college fund and the service station owner will place a bet on the college team's next game? Each of these scenarios would have a different effect on the game's total economic impact.

Models and Multipliers

Most serious EI studies use a formula to estimate the financial effect of a sports event. EI experts acknowledge that a multiplier effect takes place but disagree on the figure that should be used. We should view multipliers with skepticism if they are above the 2.5 level. Only the biggest metropolitan areas, such as New York, Los Angeles, and Chicago, can support larger multipliers. Even then, anything over 3.0 is too high.

We derived answer D by applying the 2.3 multiplier established by the Department of Commerce's Bureau of Economic Analysis (actual expenditures of $185 x 2.3 = $425.50). When we did this, though, we committed a classic EI error: applying only one multiplier. More precise economic impact models will assign separate multipliers to different categories of expenditures on the statistically proven theory that some types of purchases turn over faster than others.

Other Fudge Factors

Often we will see EI studies that attempt to quantify intangibles such as "major league image" or "increased television exposure" that purport to translate into hard dollars in the form of new businesses and tourists that would otherwise go elsewhere. There certainly is some publicity and image value, and it probably translates into added economic impact, but it's not easy to assess. EI studies also play other games. For example, studies done to determine a team's worth to an area often take a team's payroll into account. However, if an NBA team has a payroll of $10 million, you cannot assume that all of that is going to be spent in the home city.

All these problem areas make it difficult to assess the value of an event to a city.

Reference: J. Barks and E. J. Muller, "The Numbers Game," *Sports Travel*, Nov.-Dec. 1989, pp. 51–55.

Although there remains considerable debate over economic impact studies (see the exhibit above), it is evident that sports can provide an economic boost to a city. When the St. Louis Cardinals football team moved to Phoenix, Arizona, for example, the team's economic impact ranged from $30 million to $50 million each year.[3] The free publicity the team's presence gave the city particularly delighted the Phoenix mayor. The Charlotte Hornets (an NBA franchise) has done wonders for Charlotte's self-image. According to city officials the Hornets put Charlotte in the big leagues, literally and figuratively. People living in the city never considered Charlotte to be a major city. Now the city competes on the basketball court against big-time cities like New York, Los Angeles, and Chicago. This supposedly gives the residents of Charlotte "big city pride."[4] It is for similar economic reasons that cities like Indianapolis have established sport corporations whose sole purpose is to attract sports teams and sporting events to their cities.

Some cities will go to many extremes. The city council in St. Petersburg, Florida, went as far as spearheading a $115 million bond to build a stadium in the city's downtown area. The theory was that major league baseball would take notice and award the city a baseball franchise. Commissioner Peter Ueberroth warned the city that such actions would not sway major league baseball. The city council had the stadium built anyway, and today the 43,000-seat dome hosts a potpourri of events ranging from Davis Cup tennis to tractor pulls. Without baseball, though, the stadium could lose $1.5 million per year.[5]

Universities

Imagine the University of Michigan or Penn State without football. The mission of both universities, and others that have big-time football or basketball teams, is to educate students, further knowledge through research, and provide service to the community. Collegiate sports often seem to overshadow this mission, and universities across the United States use sports extensively for image enhancement and exposure.

Even the most prestigious universities make special arrangements to accommodate athletes who do not meet the necessary academic qualifications for normal admission if they have the potential of contributing to the success of the football or basketball team.

Corporations

Corporations that sponsor sports hope to attract more people to their products. They attempt to match the particular sport they sponsor with the demographics of people who buy their products. The PGA TOUR, for example, attracts companies that sell stocks and bonds, insurance, and luxury cars. In Chapter 8 we will discuss what corporations want to do when they tie in with sports and how they do it. Corporations have become an important source of funding for sports organizations, and it is important to understand the effect they can have. Beer and tobacco companies, for example, are dominant sponsors of sporting events, but not without controversy. Some events, although not many, refuse to have anything to do with alcohol or tobacco sponsors because of the image problem.

In all these community publics—from countries to small-community entities like universities—the relationship between sports and the group can range from parasitic to symbiotic. Parasitic relationships exist when either the sport or the community group feeds off the other without an equal exchange. In many cases the value of the exchange is difficult to assess. How much value, for instance, should an athletics department place on all the free exposure it obtains for the university? What should be given in exchange for this exposure? As sports organizations continue their financial struggles, sports managers will need to turn their parasitic relationships into symbiotic ones. Understanding and placing value on symbiotic exchanges will, therefore, be an important skill for you to develop.

Sanctioning Bodies

Sanctioning bodies include such organizations as the NCAA, the USOC, or the professional leagues like the NFL or the NHL. Government also acts as a sanctioning body protecting the interests of both fans and athletes. We will talk about the role of government as a sanctioning entity first because it has an impact on the governance of sports in this country. Both professional and amateur sports have felt, at one time or another, the rage of government. The following exhibit is

---

Congresswoman Bernice Sisk's Report of the Select Committee on Professional Sports

Mr. Speaker, as chairman of the Select Committee on Professional Sports, I want to report that we have concluded perhaps the most comprehensive study of the professional team sports industry ever conducted. In 28 hearing sessions, we heard from over 80 witnesses and 2,400 pages of transcript testimony. Although our specific mandate was to identify the problems associated with the four major professional team sports, an interesting side revelation of the hearings was the extent of the influence and impact those sports, and almost all other organized sports, professional and amateur, have on the minds and attitudes of the public at large. One evidence of this is the enormous amount of mail to the committee from people connected with other sports who wanted to travel from all parts of the country, at their own expense, to testify about the problems of those sports. A good portion of the mail offered personal evidence of problems with certain sports. Most heartening was the almost unanimous favorable tenor of the communications to the work of the committee.

The overriding theme I am getting at is the widespread concern of the people of this Nation over and about sports. And when things are not right in the sports world, this has an upsetting effect on the public. This was brought sharply into focus by the hullabaloo over the heavyweight championship fight the other night. From all reports, it would appear that three spineless officials were either bought off, sold off, or scared off. Whatever the real story, we can see more widespread evidence of fan disgust with sports.

The reason for the formation of the select committee was the convulsive, unsettled state of the four major professional sports. Little has happened over the last four months to show that we were wrong in our assessment that there was a need for investigations. In fact, some things appear even worse now. All this leads me to believe that the time has come for some type of congressional oversight over all sports on an ongoing, permanent basis. I am totally opposed to any Federal commission to control or dictate sports in this country. I think that would be unwise. But, I have seen the beneficial effects of our hearings thus far. Their seriousness and the evenhanded way they have been conducted seems to have had a restraining effect; the participants have seemed to become more rational, more reasonable.

Congress has a duty to protect the fan interest of this Nation in its sports. Sports provide entertainment and recreation. They are supportive of our Nation's traditional values of sportsmanship and fair play. They are a national asset. If congressional oversight can serve as a conscience for the American sports world, keeping the eyes of those who run sports in America on its important national goal, they have in their care: spiritual and physical integrity, then this is a task we should seriously look into and take on if necessary.

Congressional Record, House, September 30, 1976, p. 34049.

an example of such government intervention.

Amateur sports have also been under the scrutiny of government. Historically, the growth of amateur sports has been one of a disorganized hodgepodge of coalitions each vying for a share of power. The development of programs varied with each organization. Whereas schools and colleges conducted programs that included a broad range of sports, other organizations such as the NGA concentrated on one sport or one aspect of a sport (for example, the PGA TOUR). In contrast, the Amateur Athletic Union (AAU) administered eight sports, including one of the largest, track and field. In addition, many of these coalitions were undemocratic affairs, often failing to represent in their governance the voice of their own athletes, including women and minorities.

The interests of the various sports organizations, together with the unclear jurisdictional divisions, generated struggles for power. In an attempt to preserve power or gain advantage over a rival organization, some amateur groups used athletes as pawns by denying them the opportunity to participate in an event sponsored by the rival coalition. Athletes were a key ingredient to an event; they could therefore be used to frustrate the success of an opposing coalition's event. The NCAA, for example, would threaten to remove scholarships from athletes if they participated in AAU-sanctioned events.

Clearly, U.S. sports organizations were fragmented and unbound by common purpose. Incessant organizational squabbling wasted time and threatened the fundamental rights of athletes. The intent of the Amateur Sports Act of 1978 was to end these squabbles by placing the USOC as the final authority over amateur sports. The USOC was to recognize one national governing body, an NGB, that would be responsible for the governance of each sport. These NGBs had to

Although the Amateur Sports Act certainly helped, Fred Lebow's experiences indicate that conflicts can still arise. People managing a sports organization can affect an event. In Fred Lebow's case the solution to the problem was as simple as a change in leadership. Other conflicts with sanctioning bodies are not so easy to solve, however. The next exhibit presents an incident that occurred to New Zealand runner Alison Roe when Lebow tried to recruit her for the New York Marathon.

The Sanctioning of Athletes

This year we were hyping the prospects for the most dramatic showdown ever in the women's race. In April, Alison Roe, of New Zealand, a statuesque, twenty-five-year-old blonde, had won the Boston Marathon with the second fastest time ever in the world, 2:26:46, a little more than a minute off Grete Waitz's record. Grete had always won easily, but she had never raced against Alison Roe, and with Roe there to push her this year we expected real fireworks.

Roe's presence was in doubt until just before the marathon. She had participated for open prize money at the Cascade Run Off in Portland, Oregon, in June, part of the unsanctioned open circuit set up by the Association of Road Racing Athletes, which was challenging the international amateur policies. The New Zealand Amateur Athletic Association banned Roe from sanctioned competition, but she turned over her $4,000 winnings from Cascade to her association and appealed the ban. The world governing body, IAAF [International Amateur Athletic Federation], was even then trying to come up with a formula for trust funds that would allow athletes to be paid.

For weeks I tried to get clarification of her status from the New Zealand association. In early October she notified us that her ban had been lifted. But Ollan Cassel, executive director of the U.S. association, The Athletics Congress (TAC), insisted she was still banned. It wasn't cleared up until ten days before our marathon.

Source: Fred Lebow, *Inside the World of Big-Time Marathoning* (New York: Rawson Associates, 1984), pp. 142–43.

Intermediary Publics

Intermediary groups include agents, sports marketing agencies, sports promoters, and equipment manufacturers. Of course, agents are not a new phenomenon. Rumor has it that Walter Hagen, the first golfer to make a living by playing golf, hired Bob Harlow to act as his agent. Harlow had a theatrical background and was an avid reader of *Variety* magazine. He reportedly dreamed up many of the comments and pranks that made Hagen a legend in golf. Indeed, Harlow may have been the first to think of professional athletes as entertainers. He became the first official PGA TOUR manager in 1930, designing its structure and administration. Even in these early years people accused an agent like Harlow of conflicts of interest. He was, like the agents of today, a consummate moonlighter—a man with immense energy.[7] Since we have already spent considerable time discussing sports agents and sports marketing agencies we will not go into any more detail now.

Sports promoters are another growth group. Lebow and the New York Road Runners Association are, in reality, sports promoters. They develop a sport by creating events. For example, the triathlon is the product of an event promoter's vivid imagination. Sports marketing agencies like ProServ and IMG are also poking their fingers into the sports promotion business. Other important promoters of certain sports are the equipment manufacturers. As early as 1900 equipment manufacturers like A. G. Spaulding were promoting specific sports. Spaulding, for example, bought Harry Vardon, an Englishman and one of the best golfers in the game, to the United States to promote a new golf ball as well as the game itself.[8] Today the sports equipment industry promotes several sports, including bowling, tennis, windsurfing, surfing, skateboarding, and golf.

Competitors

Many entities vie for the same resources valued by a sports organization. The competition may be for consumer markets, athletes, sponsors, television time, and so on. Lebow ruthlessly prevents any other organization from staging a road race in New York City. He wants his group to be the one single, strong organization in the city responsible for furthering the cause of running. So to appease other organizations like the United Nations Children's Fund (UNICEF) and the March of Dimes, which use road races for fund raising, Lebow organizes one charity event per year, the New York Benefit Run. It is an event in which all charities can take part.

Sometimes eliminating the competition by forming alliances can be more beneficial than directly competing for limited resources. At the present time, for example, each of the NGBs of the USOC must struggle alone in their efforts to compete for television time. Only a handful of Olympic sports is successful. Even then, they are only minimally successful in obtaining small cable television contracts. By joining forces under one umbrella, it is possible to design a more attractive television package, thereby generating new revenue. Thus, you should learn to recognize when cooperative and noncompetitive strategies will work to your advantage.

THE INTERNAL PUBLICS ....

Internal publics are associated with the primary product, that is, the actual sport itself. They consist of those groups involved in the "manufacturing" process (support publics, employees, and supplier publics), groups involved in the distribution process (television, stadiums, high schools, and so on), and groups involved in the consuming process.

Support Publics

Support publics encompass volunteers, ordinary U.S. citizens, and government officials. Without these groups, most sporting events would not take place or would be so expensive that only the very wealthy could afford to consume them. Volunteers are therefore especially important. The New York City Marathon, for example, requires 4,500 volunteers, from ham radio operators, to medical personnel, to block association members who pass out water to the runners. Amateur sports rely heavily on volunteer coaches and parents to run local clubs, and they need people to organize and manage competitive experiences for participants.

The volunteer sector has a special set of needs and wants. Usually volunteers seek psychic benefits, have a deep commitment to some value or ideal, or have an all-encompassing passion for *their* sport. Voluntary activities usually satisfy these psychic benefits, values, or ideals.[9] In the case of sports, such activities satisfy their passion.

Understanding voluntary behavior is particularly critical if you manage smaller sports organizations, since they rely almost entirely on volunteers for their coaches, judges, and officials. The 1984 Summer Olympics held in Los Angeles provides another example of the importance of paying attention to support publics. Before the Games, news stories described all the terrible things that could happen in Los Angeles during the Olympics. Local politicians, local media, and local citizens themselves created much of the adverse publicity. Research pinpointed what kind of information these individuals needed for them to be supportive.[10] With this information in hand, the Los Angeles Olympic Organizing Committee (LAOOC) set about systematically changing the attitudes of local residents and politicians.

On the whole, given the opportunity the American public enjoys being involved in sporting events. In 1990 the Whitbread Round-the-World Yacht Race included a stop in Fort Lauderdale, Florida. Residents had the opportunity to see international relations up close. Indeed, they *made* international relations happen. The sailing competition had been particularly difficult for the Soviet crew, who faced serious financial problems. In a gesture of goodwill local residents housed the Soviets and helped them raise money so they could complete the last leg of the race.

Official government support also has an impact. Without the support of the Department of Parks and Recreation, the mayor, and the police chief, among

the Soviets and helped them raise money so they could complete the last leg of the race.

Official government support also has an impact. Without the support of the Department of Parks and Recreation, the mayor, and the police chief, among others, the New York City Marathon would not exist. According to Lebow, a Berlin road racing promoter had been trying unsuccessfully to bring a marathon to downtown West Berlin, but he couldn't get the cooperation of government.

> I suggested he get through to the heart of the matter: get the chief of police on to his side; make a personal friend of him, invite him to dinner, familiarize himself with the special problems and orientations the police have. And then, I told the director, invite the chief of police to come with him to observe the New York City Marathon—we can set it up so that he can learn everything he needs to know. (Lebow, *Inside the World of Big-Time Marathoning*, p. 180)

Congressman John Danforth's Support of the National Senior Olympics

Mr. President, today I am introducing two bills to allow senior citizens to continue to participate in the U.S. National Senior Olympic (USNSO) games. The USNSO was created in 1985 in order to provide citizens over age 55 with the opportunity to compete in a national Olympiad. The first National Senior Olympics were held in St. Louis in 1987. This event attracted over 2,500 participants, including athletes from Canada and Taiwan. After the conclusion of this successful event, the US Olympic Committee (USOC) informed the USNSO that it could use the word "Olympics" no longer. Despite considerable discussion, the USOC would not modify its position.

On March 29, 1988, I joined 17 other Members of the Senate in writing to the USOC to urge it to permit the USNSO to continue to use the term "Olympics," but it would not permit a national "Senior Olympics." According to the USOC, such games would "compete programmatically or financially with the U.S. Olympic effort." Mr. President, the USOC's decision is wrong. By passing the Amateur Sports Act of 1978, Congress recognized that an effective coordinating body is essential to developing competitive Olympic teams. But, the USOC's mission is not limited to fielding strong teams. The commission is directed by law to establish national goals for amateur athletic activities. This applies to all Americans. The USOC has done a commendable job with the Special Olympics for disabled Americans and the Junior Olympics for young Americans. The USOC permits use of the name "Olympics" because the competition is directed by a member organization which performs an enumerated purpose of the Amateur Sports Act. The Junior Olympics enjoy this privilege as a result of a grandfather clause in the original law passed by Congress to incorporate the USOC. In both cases, Congress acknowledged its support for these competitions in statute. The time has come for Congress to promote a National Senior Olympic competition. The law must be expanded to afford Americans over the age of 55 the opportunity to participate in an official Olympiad.

The USOC has the authority to permit the USNSO to use the Olympic name. To date, the USOC has refused. The Supreme Court has upheld the plain meaning of the Amateur Sports Act which grants the USOC complete authority over use of the name "Olympics." Negotiations between the USOC and the Senior Olympics have not resolved this issue. The only solution is to change the law to reflect the importance of a National Senior Olympic competition.

The first bill that I am introducing amends the Amateur Sports Act of 1978 to authorize the USNSO to use the name "Olympics" in order to promote athletic competition among our Nation's senior citizens. The second bill will permit USNSO to register "National Senior Olympics" as its trademark under the Lanham Act. Mr. President, these are modest measures, but they are important to the Senior Olympics. Elderly Americans should have the same opportunity as disabled Americans and young Americans to participate in official Olympic games. I urge my colleagues to support these bills.

Congressional Record, Senate, April 3, 1990, pp. 3856–57.

Employee Publics

We know very little about the personalities of individuals who staff sports organizations. General observations indicate that these individuals enjoy power and are good politicians, creative thinkers, and well organized people. In the past many were men and women in their twenties and thirties who were passionate advocates and participants of their sport, working long hours and travelling frequently. More recently, though, this has been less true. U.S. Synchronized Swimming and U.S. Rowing, for example, have both had executive directors who did not participate in the sport they governed. Most are well educated in diverse fields—lawyers, teachers, engineers, bankers, actors, and so on. Many left better paying jobs in the private business sector. Indeed, compared with employees in other business sectors, the average sports employee is poorly paid. Typically, employees initially get involved as volunteers, and some stay long enough to eventually get hired.

Deane Beman, commissioner of the PGA TOUR, however, probably still typifies most employees of sports organizations. Beman had won the U.S. Amateur Championships twice (1960 and 1963), had won the British Amateur once (1959), and had played on four United States Walker Cup and World Cup Amateur teams. He joined the TOUR in 1967. Beman studied business in college and was a successful insurance agent before turning pro. In addition, he had served on various golf committees. Individuals such as Beman are believed to be better managers of their sport because they know the players, have had personal experience with the travel and conditions of competition, and know the game intricately.[11]

Supplier Publics

Supplier publics provide all the necessary resources, usually financial, so that a sport can exist. Suppliers range from corporations, to private individuals, to non-profit groups such as chambers of commerce. We know very little about how sports can foster a supplier base. All we can do here is to provide you with some examples of how sports organizations can interact with suppliers.

- The Atlanta Olympic Committee (AOC) made many of its trips pitching the city to Olympic officials courtesy of Delta Airlines. Of the $7 million the AOC spent on its bid, $500,000 came from the Atlanta Chamber of Commerce's economic development department. The rest came from corporate supporters.[12]
- When the Galbrath family, owners of the Pittsburgh Pirates, had the team up for sale, the city of Pittsburgh feared losing the team. It raised $20 million through a bond issue, and executives from ten of the city's corporations, including Westinghouse, ALCOA, and PNC Financial, had their companies provide $2 million each. This, along with another $2 million each from three private investors, brought the total to $46 million to purchase and finance the team.[13]
- Numerous food companies provide the United States Olympic Training Centers with the food needed to feed the athletes.

Apart from anecdotal examples such as these, we have no data to help us understand the range of suppliers available to sports, the composition of suppliers, restrictions suppliers impose, and what they expect in return. However, we do know that professional sports groups are generally better able to develop a supplier base than amateur sports groups. Despite the Amateur Sports Act, corporate executives perceive amateur sports as fraught with jurisdictional disputes and managerial incompetence. The potential for private-sector funding of amateur sports, is nonetheless, bright, if the groups can rectify their organizational and managerial weaknesses. In addition, future government assistance may also depend on how well amateur sports put their organizational and managerial houses in order. While the U.S. government will not finance amateur sports directly, there have been many initiatives, including commemorative Olympic coins, a check-off box on federal tax returns, an excise tax on admissions to professional sporting events, and a modified lottery system. For various political reasons, many of these initiatives have yet to be implemented.

Of course, we cannot overlook the innumerable "watch dogs" who ensure that public tax dollars do not go to sports. When Los Angeles Olympics' promoters maneuvered to bring the 1984 Games to the city, voters changed the city charter to make sure the city would not be stuck with any of the big deficits for

sure that public tax dollars do not go to sports. When Los Angeles Olympics' promoters maneuvered to bring the 1984 Games to the city, voters changed the city charter to make sure the city would not be stuck with any of the big deficits for which the Olympic Games are famous. The following exhibit provides you with the arguments used by those opposed to using federal dollars for the Los Angeles

Americans Are Generally Against Governmental Funding of Sports

Letter to Jimmy Carter, November 8th, 1979— Charles H. Wilson (House)

Dear Mr. President: I understand that your staff will be meeting with officials from Los Angeles concerning the possibility of committing federal funds for the construction of permanent sports facilities for Los Angeles and the 1984 Summer Olympics. While I fully support the city hosting the Summer Olympics, I believe it would be a serious mistake for the federal taxpayer to assume financial responsibility for the Olympics. Consequently, I am opposed to federal funding for the L.A. Olympics.

It is important to realize from the very outset that I support the concept of Olympic competition and the need for our international sports teams to be competitive. Our mutual agreement on this is certainly not in dispute. However, federal funding specifically for the 1984 L.A. Olympics has no bearing on (1) the competitive ability of our team since the funding is for facility construction, nor (2) the need for federal funds in order to have the Olympics in Los Angeles. The Olympic Games in 1984 can go on without the spending of federal tax dollars.

I urge you to be cautious in the midst of the present rush by individuals seeking to have federal tax dollars committed in the fiscal year 1981 budget which you will present to Congress next spring. Please take into consideration some of the problems with committing federal tax dollars to the 1984 Olympics— which I have briefly outlined below.

First, the elected officials of the City of Los Angeles, and the people of Los Angeles, made a pledge and voted for a city-wide referendum limiting the use of Los Angeles tax dollars to support the 1984 Olympics. The City also reaffirmed its commitment to this referendum by prohibiting the use of city funds to be added to the $141,511,356 application for federal funds for matching grant purposes.

Are we to assume that the Los Angeles community will not differentiate between the use of their local tax dollars as opposed to their federal tax dollars? Are we to assume that for some reason it is proposed to use federal tax dollars in order to circumvent the prohibition of the use of local tax dollars? I think not. It is clear that the Los Angeles public does not want the use of any tax dollar to subsidize the Olympics. The State of California has recognized the public's feeling by refusing to commit state money to the Olympics. Mr. President, a public referendum against using tax monies, coupled with the State of California's refusal to spend state tax monies, cannot justify the use of federal tax monies.

Second, the Los Angeles Olympic Organizing Committee has, in its financial plan, estimated that it will have a profit of over $21,000,000. This does not include any federal funding at all, which is true to the Committee's pledge of running a "spartan" Olympics. Yet, this profit of over $21,000,000 does not tell the whole story. In addition to this figure, the Committee has figured in $48,000,000 they are willing to commit to construction and improvement costs, and there is an additional $39,000,000 the Committee has placed in a contingency fund which equals 15% of the Committee's expenses. This is a total of $108,000,000 either committed or ready for utilization over and above the anticipated, budgeted expenditures for operating the Olympics.

Also in the financial plan of the Committee is the affirmative commitment that existing venues or facilities can be adequately utilized and that the sports which cannot be accommodated with existing facilities be provided with temporary facilities. Mr. President, the Olympic Committee has devised a plan for putting on the Olympics. It is public record that the Olympics in Los Angeles can be a financial success through the involvement of private business and with the support of the public. There is no need for any federal funds. The central question is whether the Olympics can be held under existing financial arrangements. The answer is yes, perhaps not with all of the luxurious trappings that government supported Olympics of the past have had (and resulted in cost overruns I might add), but the Olympics will go on.

Third, the City of Los Angeles has proposed an initial request of over $141,000,000 to construct permanent facilities for the Olympics instead of effectively utilizing the plan of the Organizing Committee to use temporary facilities. I can understand the City's desire to have the federal government finance its recreation facilities. And that, Mr. President, is what the City's request comes down to. It is a private relief request for the City of Los Angeles' recreation program. Take a look at what the City is requesting, yet remember that there has been no discussion of the transportation or security arrangements, which will be part of an additional request from Los Angeles. In addition to the rowing, yachting, bicycling, and archery facilities which have a limited value for post-Olympic utilization, there is the renovation of the Los Angeles Coliseum.

As we all know, the Los Angeles Rams will be leaving the Coliseum facilities to go to Anaheim which is presently redoing its stadium facility at local public expense. Because the professional football team is leaving, every effort is underway to have another team move from an existing franchise to Los Angeles. I find it interesting that almost 40% of the Los Angeles request is to renovate the LA Coliseum to provide for such expenses as putting in a new scoreboard, enlarging and renovating dressing rooms, putting in additional seating in a stadium that already seats over 97,000 people, the addition of private boxes, and the installation of a new playing field.

A number of prospective football teams have expressed an interest in moving to Los Angeles, but the NFL would not allow them to move unless the

Coliseum was renovated. It should not be the policy of the federal government to subsidize the National Football League, or in the case of Los Angeles, to subsidize the renovation of a stadium for a city to lure an existing professional football team from another city.

The federal government has always been a booster of Olympic competition and has encouraged the American public to support our Olympic teams. This is a national effort, and in the case of Southern California, an event that it can be proud of hosting. If Los Angeles really needs help in siting Olympic events because of their lack of facilities, cities such as San Diego have offered to assist the Olympic Committee by holding events in facilities provided by San Diego. Certainly this cooperative effort should be encouraged but with the federal government electing to provide funding to just the City of Los Angeles, the whole atmosphere is changed. Are we to assume that the cooperative effort of the Southern California area is less viable than federal funding for a program only for Los Angeles? The object is to put on the Olympics, and utilizing existing facilities is far better than building duplicative and unnecessary facilities in Los Angeles.

Congressional Record , House, November 14, 1979, p. 32372.

Olympic Games.

Distribution Agent Publics

Distribution channels provide consumers with easy access to a sport or a sporting event. Although not necessarily equally important across sports organizations, two distribution systems are of concern: participant distribution systems and spectator distribution systems.

Participant Distribution

Consumers cannot participate in a sport unless it is accessible to them. They need facilities and equipment. As well, the cost of participating must be reasonable. When it comes to participant distribution channels, some sports like football, basketball, track and field, and swimming, have it fairly easy, since they already have a wide network of participant distribution channels through the school system. Yet others, like gymnastics, work through a private club system. Sports like synchronized swimming, rowing, water polo, and handball, however, lack these *built-in* distribution channels and must find ways of developing them. In almost all sports, though, there are insufficient clinics, seminars, training camps, competitions, technical publication, handbooks, equipment, and international experiences for athletes, coaches, and officials. In addition, unless the equipment

to the beginner, and there are a scattering of opportunities to learn windsurfing, water skiing, and other such less popular sports. Such lack of participant distribution channels limits the growth of a sport. Solutions to this problem require creative thinking.

Spectator Distribution Systems

Establishing spectator distribution channels involves searching for methods to close the spatial gaps that exist between the sports organization and the spectators. Spatial gaps occur because potential spectators may be spread all over the country and thus unable to view a sporting competition in person. Television serves to fill this gap, and as such it is a valuable spectator distribution system for a handful of mass consumption sports. Most sports, though, do not have mass appeal.

Understandably, television executives concentrate their efforts on sports that are profitable to the television business. Also understandably, most sports organizations have considered how they can appeal to television. An unexciting sport to television executives or a sport that has small market appeal is relegated to the lower ranks of sports society, where survival depends on subsidization and the occasional handout. The challenge to agents and organizations of these sports with small markets is find creative ways to develop aspects of their product so that it has value to defined segments of society. In other words you should hone your niche market strategy skills to meet this requirement of a sports organization.

Consumer Publics

Consumer publics are the primary consumers of sports and consist of two broad groups:

- participant consumers
- nonparticipant consumers

Participant Consumers

As we have already discussed, participants are the key to all sports organizations. Without them, sports would not exist. Yet many sports managers operate as if the participant is inconsequential. They have given little thought to developmental programs needed to improve opportunities for participants, programs that provide (a) identification, recruitment, classification, and education; (b) improved communication; (c) increased participation opportunities; and (d) an overall developmental plan for the introduction of consumers to the sport. However, a wide disparity of problems exists in these areas from sport to sport. For example, team handball has acute problems in expanding its grassroots programs, whereas soccer does not. All sports need to take steps to improve opportunities for women, minorities, and the handicapped, and many need developmental coaching programs.

Nonparticipant Consumers

Remaining are those publics that encompass all those nonparticipant groups that consume sport in some way, but not by way of participation. Researchers need to spend more time defining the intangible and tangible dimensions of sports so that managers can find ways to broaden consumer appeal. Sports products can include everything from packaging its entertainment dimension to merchandising, logos, licensing, promotional packages, videos, publishing, and sponsorship packages. We develop products by linking a tangible dimension such as the athlete, the team, the competition, or the sport itself, with one or more intangible dimensions, such as prestige, fantasy, aesthetics, or style. Examples of markets for these products include stadium, television, corporate, and affinity consumption.

Stadium Consumption. Combinations of the sport of football (the tangible dimension) with university tradition and the associative festive atmosphere with bands, tailgate parties, and social interaction (the intangible dimension) is an example of a product designed specifically for stadium consumption.

Television Consumption. Television producers now attach minicameras to the front of a bobsled, a skier's boot, and even a hockey puck. Their objective is to let television viewers experience the competition. We now see microphones being used extensively to enhance the viewer's involvement. In essence, television producers are attempting to create a distinctive experience for the television audience, one that is different from the stadium experience.

Corporate Consumption. Products for corporate consumption are designed specifically for those corporations using sports as a communication, targeting, or differentiating vehicle. Sports with mass consumer appeal are particularly desirable.

Affinity Consumption. Affinity consumption products include items such as sports clothing, video highlights of games and athletes, and the numerous sports books, magazines, and games that allow the sports follower to fantasize about team ownership or about being team coach, until his or her heart is content.

Television and other media such as newspapers, magazines, and radio have always had an interesting relationship with nonparticipant consumers. The media have used sports to sell more newspapers or attract more viewers and listeners. In turn, sports organizations use the media for free exposure, publicity, and as an inexpensive method of sharing the drama, suspense, tension, and raw emotion with their fans.

More often than not, the sports-media relationship is a positive one. However, recent events require that sports organizations pay more attention to how the press portrays their sport and athletes. Few of us are under any delusion that sports offer an escape from the drugs, gambling, dishonesty, sexism, and racism now rampant in our society. The problem faced by sports organizations is that the media tend to magnify these issues in sports. The spatial gap between the athlete and the public continues to narrow, and athletes are no longer on a pedestal. Stories depicting them as drug addicts, gamblers, steroid users, rapists, and dumb or violent individuals sell newspapers.

This proliferation of negative images of sports in the press is having serious consequences for struggling Olympic hopefuls. After the Ben Johnson incident during the 1990 Olympics, for example, Carol Ann Alie, a Canadian who won the world board sailing championships five times, found the task of attracting sponsors for the financial support she needed to train for the Barcelona Olympic Games almost impossible to obtain (personal communications).

SUMMARY

This chapter set out to establish some order to the various entities affecting the economic conditions of a sports organization. You discovered that the tasks associated with marketing a sport are multifaceted with the nine distinct publics requiring their own specific market strategies. Although the actual "product" being marketed varies depending upon the needs of each public, your goal, you have learned, is to determine the needs and wants of each public and to undertake the necessary actions that will satisfy these needs and wants. Again, as noted in the previous chapter, you may have to bend the model to suit your specific idea. Your objective is to account fully for all those groups that may affect its success.

Let's see how you might go about this process with a recreational event. Assume your event is a three-on-three basketball tournament entitled Hoops Madness. The tournament will appeal to the competition needs of recreational basketball players on your campus and raise money for your department. One of the first things you must do is conduct an audit of the impact each category of publics can have on your proposed event. In Figure 4.2 you will find a grid that lists the nine publics and several important impact categories.

Across the top of the grid in Figure 4.2 you will find listed all the publics that may or may not have an impact on your ability to produce the tournament. As you now know, each public can involve more than one entity. For the purpose of this practice example, select one important entity from each public category. On the left hand side of the grid are eight impact analysis criteria. Examine the impact criteria for each public to decide how that public will affect your event. For example, the community benefiting from your event will be your department. What benefits will it seek? What is its profile in terms of interested faculty, alumni interest, public relations assistance, and so on? One of the competitors will possibly be your recreation department, especially if it owns the facilities you must use to stage your event. Your important consumer public will be recreational basketball players. What benefits do recreational basketball players seek from an event such as this? How will you obtain your labor to run the event? If

Public Analysis	Community Publics	Sanctioning Bodies	Intermediary Publics	Competitor Publics	Support Publics	Employees	Supplier Publics	Distribution Publics	Consumer Publics
			[Identify an important public from each category]						
Economic Importance									
Impact on the event									
Benefits Sought									
Profile									
Goals									
Risks associated with each public									
Opportunities offered									
Potential product design									

Figure 4.2   Sports Public Audit Worksheet

you use the most popular players from your men's and women's basketball teams for publicity purposes, what rules must you worry about? In other words, go through each block on the grid and determine the impact each of the publics will have (both positive and negative) on such an event as Hoops Madness.

STRATEGIC PLAN WORKSHEET–CHAPTER 4

What You Should Know about Sports Publics

Your Goal ....

To assess the impact sports publics can have on the marketability of your venture.

Use the Sports Public Audit worksheet (Figure 4.2) to determine how the following nine entities will influence your ability to conduct your event or introduce your idea to the marketplace.

External Entities ....

    Communities advancing their own interests through sports

    Sanctioning organizations
    Intermediaries
    Competitors

Internal Entities ....

    Nonpaid support personnel
    Paid employees
    Suppliers
    Distributors
    Primary consumers

For your actual strategic planning simulation you should assign one or two students in your group the job of interviewing each public to find out how it will affect your idea. Make a list of everything this public will require for it to support you.

REFERENCES ....

1. This scenario is based on experiences described by Fred Lebow in his book *Inside the World of Big-Time* *Marathoning* (New York: Rawson Associates, 1984).

2. John McBeth, "Games: Good News and Bad," *Far Eastern Economic Review*, September 8, 1988, p. 62.
3. Steven Bergsman, "Pro Football Boosts in the Valley of the Sun," *Hotel and Motel Management*, November 28, 1988, pp. 3–4.
4. Reported in *Nation's Business*, March 1990, p. 33.
5. Reported in *Financial World*, March 19, 1991.
6. Al Barkow, *The History of the PGA TOUR* (New York: Bantam Publishing, 1989).
7. Ibid.
8. Ibid.
9. David H. Smith, "The Impact of the Voluntary Sector," in *America's Voluntary Spirit*, ed. Brian O'Connell (New York: Foundation Center, 1983).
10. John Fransen, "Public Relations Captures the Gold," *Public Relations Journal*, September 1984, p. 14.
11. Barkow, *History of the PGA TOUR*.
12. *Adweek*, September 24, 1990.
14. Michael Winkleman, "The Sporting Life," *Public Relations Journal*, January-February 1987, p. 2.

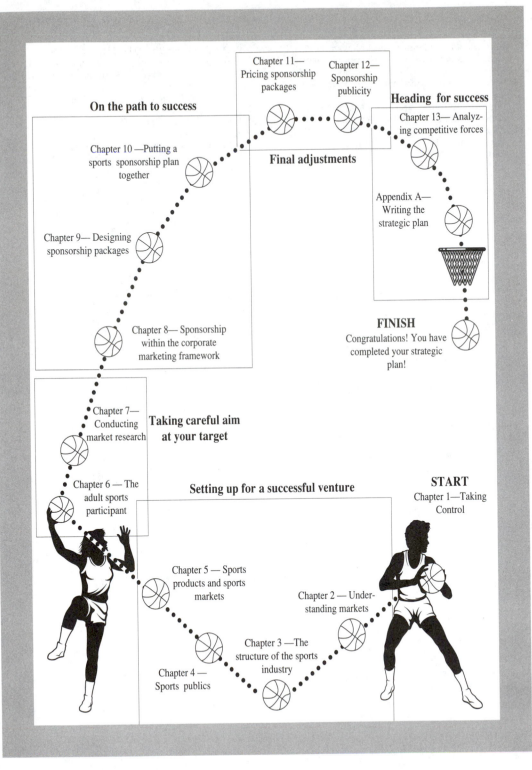

CHAPTER FIVE

Sports Products and Sports Markets

∙∙∙

> He had been eight years upon a project for extracting sun-
> beams out of cucumbers, which were to be put into phials and
> hermetically sealed, and let out to warm the air in raw in-
> clement summers.
>
> *Jonathan Swift (1667–1745)*

The challenge facing sports managers today is to devise innovative products and market expansion strategies so that their sports can gain a presence. This requires that they understand quite a bit about the assets available to them. Following that, they must creatively rearrange these assets into products that are of value to homogeneous segments of consumers. The main purpose of this chapter is to clarify the kinds of markets available to sports managers and to introduce you to a sports product planning tool. You can employ this tool to stimulate innovative product and consumer market ideas.

Some people have a knack for coming up with salable product ideas. In the following case studies you will meet the type of people who are the creative talent in the sports industry.

∙∙∙

CASE STUDY | *Triathlon Today!* **A Magazine for the Masses**[1]

In 1986 Bill Zolkowski, a folk-art retailer turned freelance stagehand, and lawyer Lew Kidder began publishing *Triathlon Today!* By 1988 the magazine had 50,000 subscribers. In its original Greek meaning, *triathlon* refers to a three-event athletic competition. The standard version includes successive swimming, bicycling, and running segments, with typical distances a 1.5-kilometer swim, a 40-kilometer bicycle ride, and a 10-kilometer run. However, many variations have emerged. For example, some triathlons substitute skiing or canoeing for one of the usual events. At the time Zolkowski and Kidder were designing the format for *Triathlon Today!* two slick monthlies were already on the market. These focused on the superstars. As you read these magazines, you would never guess there were tens of thousands of ordinary people participating every year in hundreds of races. In contrast, *Triathlon Today!* ventures beyond the superstars to the thousands of triathletes who are the mainstay of the sport. The magazine is a newsprint tabloid format that gives its readers race results within a few weeks of each race. It focuses on the men and women of all ages, from all over the country, who enjoy training for and competing in triathlons.

Before they launched their magazine, Zolkowski and Kidder tested a pilot edition. It was an instant success. Athletes particularly liked the idea of having complete results, by age group, more quickly than was currently available. The enthusiastic reception from triathletes told Zolkowski and Kidder that they had a sound idea. They rented an office and started working on a second issue.

....

....

| CASE STUDY | The Birth of an Event[2]

The Players

Jack Kramer. Wimbledon champion in 1947 and first executive director of the Association of Tennis Professionals (ATP).

Donald Dell. Former Davis Cup player and now a Washington lawyer. He owned a sports marketing company, ProServ, and had a prestigious client list including Arthur Ashe, Ivan Lendl, and Jimmy Connors. Experts credit Dell with laying the foundation for the riches that were to flow into tennis.

Phillippe Chatrier. A strange, complex man, a dreamer, thin-skinned, moody, and very French despite his fluent English.

The Innovation

The first of a whole series of meetings between this formidable trio took place in Chatrier's old apartment just off the Avenue des Ternes in the

17th arrondissement in 1969. The talks lacked structure; they involved just three friends arguing passionately about how the game of tennis should develop. During one of these talks Kramer produced the basic structure for the Grand Prix. It was based on the motor-racing Grand Prix. Players earned points according to the overall level of the prize money in the tournament. At the end of the year the top eight finishers qualified for the Masters and the top thirty earned graduated levels of bonus money. Eventually, the Grand Prix became the event that rocketed tennis before the public eye.

CASE STUDY | A Board with a Sail[3]

In August 1965 *Popular Science* ran a feature on a "sailboard" designed by Newman Darby—a sport so new that fewer than ten people had mastered it. The shape was primitive, with a square-rigger type of sail. Two Californians—Hoyle Schweitzer and Jim Drake—developed the prototype. The latter was an aeronautical engineer who invented the articulated rig. This led to the universal–joint mast foot system. Windsurfer with a capital W is the brand name of the board that resulted from the work of these two men, and windsurfing or boardsailing is the generic name for sailing it.

On 26 April 1969 at a technical symposium on sailboat design, Drake presented a paper entitled *Windsurfing—A New Concept in Sailing*. In that presentation Drake revealed that he had already tested a number of designs. A year later Schweitzer had his designs in limited production.

In just over a decade windsurfing has become one of the most successful new sports of the century. From its birth through people experimenting with surfboards in California, it has grown into a multi-million-dollar industry enjoyed by Americans, Europeans, Asians, and Australians. In 1984 it became an Olympic sport.

CASE STUDY | Unusual Adventures in Uncommon Comfort[4]

Ray Benton, president of ProServ, Inc., a successful sports management company, made a living traveling the world, representing famous athletes, including Arthur Ashe, Jimmy Connors, and Michael Jordan. At age forty-seven Benton decided that he needed a change in his life. He quit ProServ and began what he referred to as "a sabbatical," where he could recharge his batteries and define his goals for the next stage of his life. A casual cyclist, he and his son ventured on a leisurely bicycle tour through France. He had one of the best experiences of his life, and he returned with a new business idea. Within weeks he bought small bicycle touring companies in the United States and Europe and formed Travent, Ltd. This company is now a leading packager of luxury bicycle vacations. The slogan is "Unusual adventure in uncommon comfort."

Benton felt that there was a market of adults who wanted to get away from jet planes, freeways, theme parks, and tourist traps and instead combine a health fitness activity with a more intimate experience that combined people with the countryside. He designed his luxury bicycle vacations to meet that need.

| CASE STUDY | The Video News Release[5]

How does a company get its sponsored sport on television when the sport is a minor one like tennis or waterskiing? Leonard Zelick found a way for television producers to place a sports event into a news program with a minimum of effort. He created the video news release, in which he would package clips of the event suitable for television stations. Before the modern era of satellites Zelick would fly the video clips to the networks in New York. Now he rents time on the satellites and transmits the video directly to television stations all over the country. All television producers need to know is the satellite and the feed time. Zelick also provides the announcer with a suggested voice overlay as the video clip is being broadcast to viewers.

These five examples feature some creative individuals who have found a market niche for themselves in the world of sports. Their ideas seem simple enough—a magazine for triathletes, a tournament, a surfboard with a sail, a bicycle tour, a video news release—but coming up with any idea, specifically new product ideas, is not as easy as it seems.

Unfortunately, we get little help from researchers. They have paid sports products and sports markets little attention; so we lack crucial information, making it difficult to design and package product lines for sports markets. Compounding the problem is that people usually "consume" sports without knowing precisely which element is important to them. When you ask consumers to explain why they watch or play a specific sport, they will usually respond, "I don't know, it's just fun!" However, whereas consumers might be unaware of their consumption process, sports marketers must know what their various markets want from sports. Marketers must also have a clear notion of how people consume sports so that they can more clearly determine how to design suitable products.

This turns out to be a formidable task. Despite their apparent simplicity, sports are a complex product to package and sell. Confusing the issue is that the final form of a product is ultimately in the consumer's mind. We may design and package a sports product for a specific market that, from our standpoint, makes sense. The consumer, however, may view our package from an entirely different perspective. Take synchronized swimming, for instance. This is a sport that combines water, music, athletic talent, and some amazing lung stamina. The participants love the combination of these elements packaged as a competition. Unless they understand the sport, however, the majority of spectators do not watch synchronized swimming with the idea that it is a sport. To most, it is simply a form of water art. Yet athletes find the spectators' appreciation of the creative, rather than the athletic, dimension annoying. However, after years fighting the spectators' perception, those responsible for marketing this sport now realize that they can develop profitable products if they think in terms of art as well as sports. The lesson here is that there is no avoiding the active role of the consumer. The ultimate value of any sports product is a combination of both the sports manager's input and the resulting consumer's perception.

WHAT IS A PRODUCT?

At this stage in our discussion let us pursue the meaning of a "product." When people think of a product, they usually think of it in terms of its physical attributes. When you buy a car, for instance, you take home a physical shape that we all recognize as a car and not as a plane or tractor. You can touch it, clean it, and sit in it. If you delve deeper into the reasons behind your purchase, though, you would discover that the car offers more than the physical object. True, the tangible dimensions such as color, size, and shape probably influenced you. The style, brand, sound, quality, service, price, warranty, and prestige probably weighed heavily in your ultimate choice. These are the intangibles. In other words, this product—a car—is a bundle of tangible and intangible features combined in just the right dose to meet your particular needs in a car.

WHAT IS A SPORTS PRODUCT?

It is easy to recognize a car. What is sport? Is tennis a sport? What about walking or aerobic dance? Some of you will contend that walking and aerobics are not sports. Others will argue to the contrary. To prevent such arguments we need some definition so that we all have a similar image of sports in our minds. As we established in the outset of this book we define a sport as any form of physical activity that pits one's talents against an opponent's. This definition of sport is quite broad. It encompasses an individual out in the middle of a lake waterskiing for fun, a neighborhood baseball game, and mountain climbing, as well as a professional football game.

As a product, a sport is no different from the car or, for that matter, any consumer product. It has both tangible and intangible features. The final sports product itself is a composite of these interrelated tangible and intangible elements.

The Tangible Elements

There are four tangible elements in the core sports product (Figure 5.1). They include

- the sports type—football, basketball, gymnastics
- the participants (athletes, coaches, and environment)—beginning or advanced players and coaches, challenging golf courses, difficult mountains
- the team— Notre Dame, Michigan, Dallas Cowboys, Australian Olympic Team
- the competition— The Bear (golf course), friends, rivals, world class, NCAA championships, the Super Bowl, local and regional championships

The Intangible Elements

The intangible dimension covers the psychic side of sports such as emotions and experiences and is an internally generated component. These psychic elements embrace such things as

- the *high* we get from running our best marathon
- the *thrill* of winning our age group in the local 10K run
- the *satisfaction* of overcoming the challenge of a difficult golf course
- the *pride* we feel when our team wins. Figure 5.2 presents a model of the tangible and intangible components of the core product.

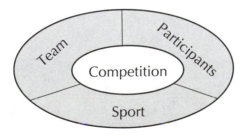

Figure 5.1   Tangible Dimensions of the Core Components of the Sports Product

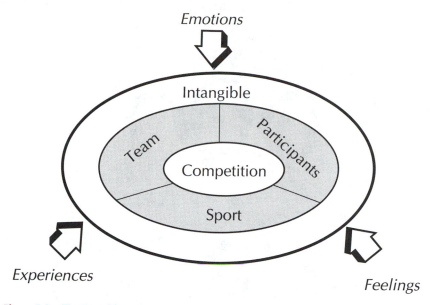

Figure 5.2   The Tangible and Intangible Components of a Sports Product

SPORTS MARKETS

From this core notion of sports, as shown in Figure 5.2, we can now model our consumer markets. We begin with our core product, and from there we build our markets. When we do this, we find there are six distinct broad consumer markets for sports, three at a primary level, three at a secondary level (Figure 5.3).

In using the term, *primary level*, my intention is simply to convey the idea that these markets consist of the immediate consumers of sports. Spectators, participants, and volunteers are examples of primary consumers. The secondary-level markets are consumers who use sports for some auxiliary purpose. Corporate marketers who place advertising messages in stadiums, for example, are a secondary market. Corporate sponsors are another group of secondary consumers. Sports interest these consumers only because they attract clusters of people either as participants or spectators. A third secondary market is the affinity market. This market consumes the images associated with sports.

The Primary Markets

The primary markets consist of participants, spectators, and volunteers.

The Participant Markets

Participants are the actual producers of sports, and as such they are the single most important component of the core product. Without the engine the car will

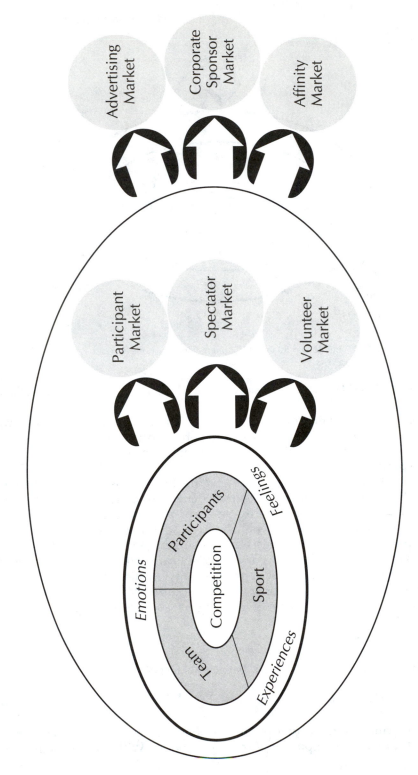

SECONDARY MARKET

Advertising Market

Corporate Sponsor Market

Affinity Market

PRIMARY MARKET

Participant Market

Spectator Market

Volunteer Market

Emotions

Participants

Feelings

Competition

Team

Sport

Experiences

Figure 5.3 The Primary and Secondary Markets for Sports

not work; without participants a sport will not exist. This is an important consumer market and we will discuss them further in Chapter 6.

The Spectator Markets

The spectator market includes television viewers, stadium attendees, radio listeners, and press readers. Spectators consume the core tangible product (the sport, participants, team, and competition) and experience it in the intangible realm. Research on how spectators consume the core sports product and what intangible elements are important to them is still in the formative stages. Preliminary research using University of Michigan undergraduates uncovered three clusters of consumption items that are important to spectators.

Cluster 1 The first cluster relates to the tangible core product. Spectators want to watch those who have mastered a sport test their skills against each other. They want to see highly developed skill and talent; the best athletes in action; exciting and exhilarating competition. This really tells sports managers what they may already know, namely, that they must concern themselves with the quality of the contest, the quality of the participants, and the team record.

Cluster 2 The second cluster relates to a feeling of ownership or team adoption. Here our subjects mentioned such elements as contributing to the spirit of the university, absorbing the pride of belonging to the university when the team wins, and being a part of Michigan tradition. This ownership cluster may explain why there is a sudden surge of support of American athletes during a major world event like the Olympic Games. It also explains why people start watching "their" team during playoffs after ignoring it all season. It is an unfortunate fact of life for sports managers that most Americans love winners and abandon losers. Even those who call themselves "true fans" do not want to "own" a core product that is not the best. So the ownership consumption element, and its use in marketing strategy, depends on the quality of the core product.

Cluster 3 A part of the satisfaction a spectator obtains from sports comes from the environment. The third cluster contains these environmental factors—the exciting and fun atmosphere and the chance to have a good time with friends. Sports marketers are gradually moving more of their efforts on packaging environmental consumption elements. Quality competition, top athletes, and winning records are difficult to control. One can, however, have a major impact on the environmental experiences for spectators. A typical Bulls (NBA) game, for example, has every minute packed with some form of action to create an electric atmosphere for spectators.

The Importance of the Consumption Clusters

The chart in Figure 5.4 shows the relative importance of these three consumption clusters to University of Michigan undergraduates. A zero on the scale indicates a low interest in the element. An 8 indicates the highest interest. All three clusters fall between the range of 3–5 suggesting that, on average, people seek approximately similar amounts of each consumption cluster.

Although exciting competition is one of the most important consumption elements for both men and women, the data indicate that women prefer the social and atmosphere elements more than the skill and talent elements. However, these gender differences seem to relate to knowledge about sports. Unknowledgeable spectators, both men and women, evaluate their spectator experience from environmental factors. It just so happens that most of the women in our sample were unknowledgeable about sports.

This is preliminary research, and considerable work remains before we understand the relative importance of these consumption clusters across different types of sports. Do basketball fans show a different consumption pattern than football fans, for instance? Our data indicate the level of "fandom" is the key, and not the actual type of sport. That is, both male and female avid fans are much higher on the core product dimension than more casual spectators across all sports.

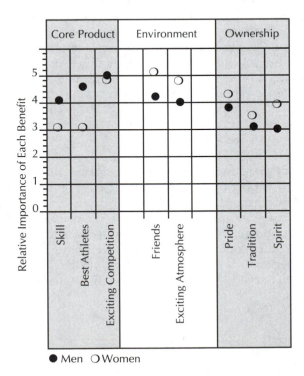

Figure 5.4   Relative Importance of Three Spectatorship Consumption Clusters

Capturing the Competition

The emphasis both men and women place on exciting competition presents a problem for most sports managers. For the most part, sports are designed for participants, not spectators. Only a handful of sports can easily package the competition for broad spectator appeal. The competition element of the core product is too slow (track and field), too repetitive (synchronized swimming, gymnastics), or lacking in viewing capacity (golf, auto racing).

This has not stopped skilled sports marketers, though. We commonly see examples of sports that are successfully repackaged to give greater spectator appeal. The PGA, for example, gives spectators more access to players by landscaping special viewing sites into key competition courses. In another instance, Sportsband network introduced an innovative product to golf spectators in 1986. Sportsband has a twenty-one-person production staff, as many as six on-course roving reporters, two anchors, and various personalities who do features and interviews with players during the competition. Spectators can rent a foam ear piece about the size of a nickel and a tiny receiver, the size of a pager. (Most spectators choose a favorite spot on the golf course and stay there.[6]) This idea was conceived by two Dallas oil executives when they became frustrated with not being able to see what was happening elsewhere on the course.

Television is an intimate medium, and producers provide us with remarkable examples of bringing normally boring competition to their audiences in a dramatic and exciting way. The on-board action of Dennis Conner and his crew during the America's Cup races, for example, was thrilling to watch and fairly inexpensive to do. In this case, television brought the normally inaccessible competition among sailors right into our living rooms. The future for television viewers promises exciting innovations that will put the viewer inside the game. In the next exhibit you will see a fantasy view of what the television baseball viewer

---

A Fantasy Look at the Future of Baseball

The development of interactive communication between the home and the studio gives the fan a chance to second-guess the manager. If your skipper brings a lefty from the bullpen, you can key in the right-hander of your choice. Your home computer, armed with up-to-the-second data from the network feed, analyzes the game situation. While you watch the manager's lefty being shelled, you learn that your reliever would (probably) have retired the enemy without incident.

Pinch hitters, defensive substitutions, even infield and outfield overshifts are in your power—at least in so far as knowing the probabilities if the real manager had done it your way. Home control takes another step as viewers can tap into a control room with a high-speed switcher to pick camera angles on each play or replay. The process, called ACTV, can give you as many as fifteen different views of the same play. "Super slomo" and zooming allow you to check if a runner is safe or out, while high resolution lets you count the stitches on the baseball. . . .

For the TV viewer, increased use of stereo and more mikes installed in unusual places, such as on players' and managers' uniforms, bring the sounds of the ballpark into his home. And a seven-second delay bleeper lets him sanitize dugout language for the youngsters.

Fact is, the advantages of watching at home so outweigh those of actually going out to the game that crowd noise now has to be electronically augmented. Nevertheless the stands are always packed. With robots.

From ''Baseball Television 1999: Through a Glass Brightly,'' *The Whole Baseball Catalogue*, ed. John Thorn and Bob Carrol (New York: Simon & Schuster, 1990), p. 178.

The Volunteer Market

The third primary product market consists of those individuals who love the sport so much that they spend almost all their leisure time devoted to helping it grow. They coach the youngsters, drive the courtesy cars at competitive events, hand out water during a marathon, act as social hosts and hostesses, and generally look after all the incidentals that allow the competition to exist. Without these volunteers, most sporting events are only marginally profitable.

You will find volunteers at every level of sports. You will see them at local fun runs and at the Super Bowl. They are the referees at the local tennis tournaments and the line watchers at the ATP tour events. Many take vacation time to help, and they use their own money to get to the competition site. They come in all shapes and sizes, both young and old. Their common love of their sport and their loyalty is unmatched in any other industry. Imagine the employees of Chrysler volunteering to help with a car exhibit! Even now, when so much has been streamlined in this multi-million-dollar age for sports, amateur volunteers still play a valuable role. Like a faithful spouse, whether you win or lose, go through good times or bad, they remain staunch supporters. Capturing and packaging a sport so that it satisfies the needs of volunteers to keep them psychologically attached to the sport is crucial to long-term financial survival.

The Secondary Markets

Secondary markets consist of people and organizations that consume sports tangentially. There is another motive behind their consumption besides the sport itself. Specifically, their interests are in one or both the spectators (or participants) or the images associated with the participants, the team, the sport, and the competition. Again, three markets emerge from the tangible (spectators or participants) and intangible (images) dimensions (see Figure 5.3). They include the advertising market, the corporate sponsorship market, and the affinity market.

The Advertising Market

Sports are an important advertising medium because traditional media are expensive and cluttered. Corporate advertisers are constantly searching for ways to more effectively reach people who might buy their products. Sports provide an efficient way for advertisers to target and communicate with large groups of people. By selling banner space in the stadium and making advertising time during your event available, you are providing a valued service to advertisers.

The Corporate Sponsorship Market

Sponsors are different from advertisers. Advertisers only want easy access to spectators. There is no more contact between the advertiser and the sports manager. Corporate sponsors not only want access to spectators; they also wish to differentiate themselves and their products from all others in the marketplace by using the images associated with sports to their financial and emotional advantage. They are, in other words, purchasing two things: (a) the right to target and communicate with ready-made clusters of consumers and (b) the right to use positive images affiliated with sports for their commercial benefit.

The controversy over the tobacco and alcohol industry's sponsorship of sports relates directly to this issue of image enhancement. Antismoking and alcohol advocates claim that these companies are misleading the public by trading in on the health, the prestige, and the image of athletic competition. There are, though, many examples of less controversial uses of sports images. Subaru and the National Ski Team, Volvo and tennis, and Cadillac and golf are such examples. Ideally the company and the sport become so closely intertwined with each other that they sometimes become synonymous.

The Affinity Market

Sports have personalities. A well thought out symbol, logo, or trademark can portray that personality. Merchandising properties use this personality to create consumer demand for an otherwise fairly ordinary product. For example, a T-shirt is simply a T-shirt until it has the America's Cup logo placed on it. Now this T-shirt represents an image or character that represents something important to its wearer, and as such it is part of the affinity market. Properties in this kind of market consist of three groups: popularity properties, prestige properties, and metamorphosis properties.

Popularity Properties Some sports receive such wide exposure on television and through other media that they achieve a high level of public recognition. Baseball is an example of a popularity property. This sport has a huge market for its logos and trademarks. Nearly 400 firms have a license to use official baseball logos under eight categories.[7]

- The Diamond Collection—merchandise actually used by major league players
- Apparel—T-shirts, sweaters, night shirts, travel bags, and other items bearing team logos
- Headgear and sporting goods—including hats, caps, towels, and even baseball golf bags
- Accessories—from ties and watches to beach umbrellas
- Household products—sheets, linens, aprons, clocks, and telephones
- Gifts and novelties—mugs, key chains, baseball parking signs, buttons, plus autographed and painted baseballs
- Toys, games, and school supplies—featuring a variety of games and toys, including figurines of active players
- Extra innings—trading cards and stickers, posters, photographs, reproductions of newspaper headlines about baseball, and foods served in containers emblazoned with baseball logos

To serve the rocketing national demand for baseball items, Major League Baseball plans to continue opening stores across the country.

Prestige Properties Some sports may not have a mass following but they have prestige. Polo is an example of a prestige property. The U.S. Rowing NGB believes that rowing is, like polo, a prestige property. Products take on value when they are linked with certain prestigious sports symbols.

Metamorphosis Properties In some instances a famous athlete can enhance the value of a product if the public transposes that athlete's ability or stature to the product. Michael Jordon is an example of a metamorphosis property. When you attach the Jordan name to an ordinary basketball shoe, it becomes a very special shoe to many consumers. Youngsters believe that the Jordan shoe, and only that shoe, can help them jump higher, dunk better, and run faster.

Companies use popularity, prestige, or metamorphosis properties to create consumer pull for their own products. *Sports Illustrated* marketers, for example, use NFL videos to sell subscriptions to their magazine. To maximize your opportunities with the affinity market you must understand the consumer's perception of your sport, understand how the equity you have in your image can be packaged into products, and develop the concept so that there is enough meat on the bone to attract consumers.

What Makes a Person Creative?

Innovative ideas come from creative, highly motivated people who dare to step outside traditional modes of thinking. Keniche Ohmae, a Japanese business strategist, contends that creative people "have an idiosyncratic mode of thinking in which a company, customer and competition merge in a dynamic interaction out of which a comprehensive set of objectives and plans for action eventually crystallize.''[8]

Psychologists have identified a list of traits associated with creativity.[9] One set of traits suggests artistic creativity; the other, scientific or technical creativity. The people we find developing product ideas for sports markets are certainly artistically creative, but they also have a sense of how technology can meet sports market needs. They are both artist and scientist blended as one.

You may not be as creative as you might like to be, but there are things you can do that will help stimulate ideas. Try the following assignment to see if you can come up with a product idea that you will not normally have thought about.

The Sports Product Market Wheel

Choose an existing product. Then using Figure 5.5, do the following:

1. Write your product in the center circle.
2. Now think about a change you can make to this product so that it becomes a different product. Write this change in one of the second-ring circles in Figure 5.5.
3. In the outer ring of circles write in potential markets for your new product.
4. Repeat steps 2–4 three more times until you have four new products derived from your original product.

You should now have four products and as many as twelve new markets . Your work has just begun. You will need to determine the answers to such questions as these:

- How big is the market?
- How does it behave?
- Who are the existing competitors?
- What response will this market have to your new product?

SUMMARY

This chapter focused on providing an understanding of the nature of sports products and sport markets. We began by reading case studies about people who had introduced some rather innovative ideas to sports consumers. Then we pursued the notion that a sports product consisted of tangible and intangible dimensions. As a sports manager you must attempt to understand these intangible and tangible dimensions and adjust the mix to meet the needs of your consumers. Needs will vary according to the type of consumer markets you are pursuing. We discovered that there are six distinct markets for sports: Three of these markets (participants, spectators, and volunteers) are the immediate consumers of sports. The remaining three (sponsors, advertisers, and the affinity market) are interested in

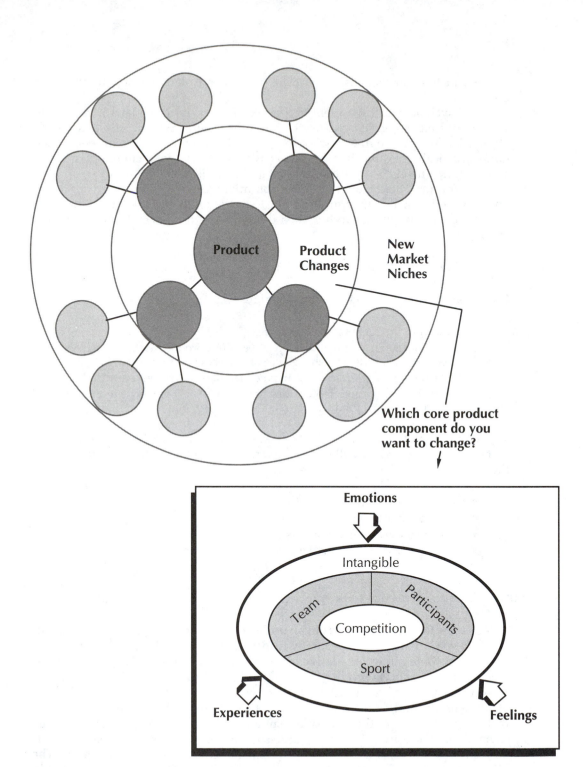

Figure 5.5 The Sports Product Market Wheel

sports only because they attract clusters of people who might buy other products unrelated to sports.

Now that you have acquired a perspective on what a sports product means and the markets that are available, you are in a better position to examine one of the largest and most exciting markets for sports products—the adult sports participant. The following chapter elaborates on how and why adults participate in sports.

STRATEGIC PLAN WORKSHEET-CHAPTER 5

What You Should Know About Your Products and Markets

Your Goal ....

To understand the product you are offering consumers in terms of its structure, its fit in the marketplace, and how you can search for new markets

Product Description ....

- What is your product (its components)?
- How does your product fit consumer needs?
- What are its special features?
- What are its unique capabilities?

Competitive Advantage ....

- What advantage does your product have over competitors?
- What weaknesses do your competitor's products have?
- How do your products differ from those offered by competitors?

Product Adaptability ....

- What can you do to adapt your product to expand markets?

Service ....

- How can you provide additional services to your consumers to put you at a competitive advantage in the marketplace?

REFERENCES ....

1. Reported in the Ann Arbor *Observer*, September 1988, p. 17.
2. Reported in Richard Evans, *Open Tennis 1968–1989*. (New York: Stephen Greene Press, 1990).
3. Jeremy Evans, *The Complete Guide to Windsurfing* (New York: Facts on File, 1990).
4. Reported in David Chauner and M. Halstead, *The Tour De France* (New York: Villard Books,1990), pp. 156-57.
5. Personal communications with Leonard Zelick, November 1991.
6. Rhonda Glenn and Robert McCord, *The Whole Golf Catalog* (New York: Perigee Books,1990). p. 106.
7. Reported in John Thorn and B. Carrol, eds., *The Whole Baseball Catalogue*. (New York: Simon & Schuster, 1990).
8. Ohmae Kenichie, *The Mind of the Strategist* (New York: McGraw-Hill, 1982), p. 2.
9. Morris I. Stein, *Stimulating Creativity*, Vol 1 (New York: Academic Press, 1974), pp. 58–61.

The ideas presented in this chapter were also influenced by the following authors:

Cooper, R. G. "New Product Strategies: What Distinguishes the Top Performers." *Journal of Product Innovation Management 2* (1984): 151–64.

Crawford, C. M. "Protocol: New Tool for Product Innovation." *Journal of Product Innovation Management 2* (1984): 85–91.

Urban, G. L., and J. R. Houser. *"Design and Marketing of New Products."* Englewood Cliffs, N.J.: Prentice-Hall, 1980.

Crawford, C. M. "Defining the Charter of Product Innovation." *Sloan Management Review* (Fall 1980): 3–12.

Corey, R. E. "Key Options in Market Selection and Product Planning." *Harvard Business Review* (September–October 1978): 119–128

Levitt, T. H. "Marketing Myopia." *Harvard Business Review* 38 (July–August 1960): 45–86.

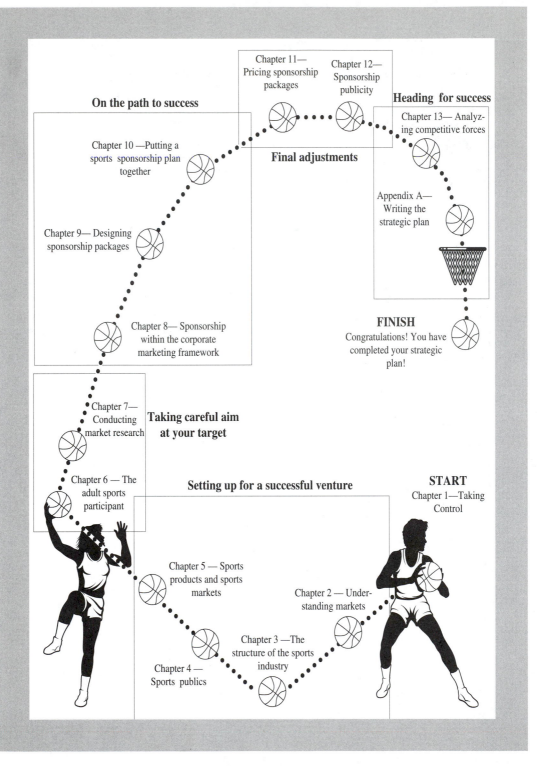

CHAPTER SIX

The Adult Sports Participant

• •

All human actions have one or more of these seven causes:
chance, nature, compulsions, habit, reason, passion, desire.
— *Aristotle (384–322 B.C.)*

Promoting sports among adults is a challenging task, for effective promotion of sports and physical activity demands more than an expertise in sports programming. It also requires sensitivity and familiarity with what people like and want to do. This chapter presents this kind of information. First we will examine the motivation processes driving active lifestyle behavior. Second, we will examine the images people have about the different types of sports available to them, as well as the impact these images have on their participation. Third, we will analyze how adults initially become involved in a sport, what motivates them to keep participating, and the needs they might be satisfying by doing so.

ACTIVE LIFESTYLE MOTIVATION

Why do some adults—even a handful over fifty or sixty years of age—spend their free time climbing cliffs, competing in a grueling ironman triathlon, skydiving, or working out in the local gym? When we see people pursuing physical activity with such intensity, we really can't help wonder what motivates them. The first thing you need to know about motivation is that there are several interlocking pieces to the puzzle, with each piece playing a role in influencing our behavior. Culture, social environment, thoughts, perceptions, needs, and biological drives all have their impact.[1] As well, a central element is that participants perceive that an active lifestyle will likely result in certain rewarding outcomes. The satisfaction derived from these rewards strengthens or weakens future commitment to the activity.

Figure 6.1 shows how the interlocking pieces of the motivation puzzle fit together. There are six components: sociocultural environment, psychological states, sense of competence, sense of commitment, expectations, rewards received, and satisfaction. By understanding the six components of this model, you will gain better insights into the active lifestyle consumer. This, in turn, may help you to develop and promote your specific active lifestyle product more effectively.

Pieces of the Active Lifestyle Motivation Puzzle

Sociocultural Environment

Let's begin with sociocultural environment, for this really shapes who we are. Our culture and the people around us have a significant influence on our choice of lifestyle. As well, specific cultures value certain things in their environments and teach their members that those things are worth working for. In other words, social and cultural factors act and interact with our personal attitudes and needs to influence our behavior. It is for this reason that marketers find demographics, socioeconomic status, and social stratification useful market segmentation strate-

Figure 6.1   A Model of the Factors Influencing Active Lifestyle Behavior

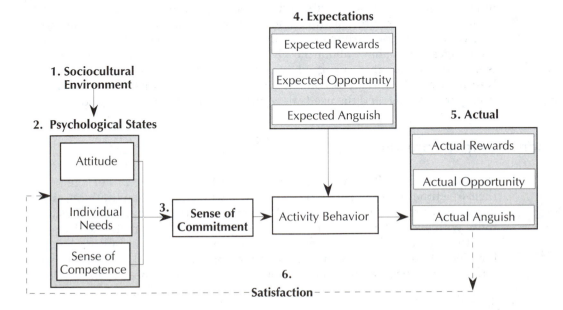

gies. With some theoretical justification, they assume that people who come from the same backgrounds will react to their products in similar ways.

Psychological State

Psychological state represents what is going on in the minds of consumers —how they think and how they feel about activity. A state of mind consists of three elements: attitude, needs, and sense of competence.

Attitude   Experience has an impact on attitude formation and contains both personal and impersonal elements. The personal element has to do with an intrinsic emotional sense of how we feel about the specific activities. Psychologists call this *affect*. Some people like to jog, hate lifting weights, and are ambivalent about bicycling. They are not sure why—they just have those feelings. The impersonal element has to do with the characteristics associated with the activity itself. These associations are expressed as beliefs. For example, some people believe weight lifting is unfeminine, that members of health clubs are already in good shape, or that skiing is dangerous. These beliefs influence attitude and in turn affect not only the type of activity people will do but where they will do that activity.

Here is a comment from a forty-six-year-old male who was thirty pounds overweight and had just started to exercise. His statement reflects his beliefs about health clubs, which, in turn have had an impact on his attitude toward them.

> I don't go to a health club because there are too many people. From what I've seen on TV, health clubs seem geared for people in great shape. They also seem to be social hangouts. I don't want to socialize when I work out. I want to go, I want to work out, I want to sweat, do what I've got to get done, and then leave. I don't want to go to the juice bar or flex in front of people to see how I'm doing. I don't need mirrors. And I'm out of shape still, so I don't want to feel bad because I don't look the way the other guys look.

Individual Needs   Abraham Maslow originally proposed the theory that there were five levels of needs that directly affected our behavior. They range from the most basic biological needs like the need for food and water, up through the desire for security, social relationships, and self-esteem, and finally to the need for personal growth or self-actualization. Although the jury is still out on the arrangement of the need categories, there is enough evidence to suggest that they are a part of each individual's need structure. Certain unmet needs will wipe out the possibility of any other need becoming important. If you are hungry, for example, very little else other than satisfying your hunger will motivate you. Fear is often the reason that keeps people from taking up some sports. In essence, their basic need for security is challenged.

The needs driving people to active lifestyles are often varied and difficult to determine. Many who are involved in a purposeful daily exercise program will claim they are trying to improve their physical appearance. In essence, they are working on their self-esteem needs. In fact, it turns out to be much more complicated than that. Although self-esteem needs are often the reason given, we frequently find biological needs displacing self-esteem needs as the primary motivation in older consumers. Take, for example, the following statement:

> For at least ten years I haven't done much in the way of exercise and consequently my weight is out of control. Over the years I've gradually changed to a sit-down position rather than an active position. I woke up one day and realized I couldn't do many things I wanted to do. I felt like I needed to get back to the point where I could do things. I have it in my mind now that I'm going to exercise each day. I am going to reclaim control of my body—right now the poor physical state of my body controls my life. That is no longer a satisfactory state of affairs for me.

In this case the subject is focusing on correcting the biological state of his body. His physical appearance is not the prime motivating factor. It is his inability to perform what he feels are normal everyday tasks that bothers him.

Sense of Competence   Generally people will not pursue sports or activities they do not believe they can perform adequately. There is a field of psychology called *attribution theory*. Very generally, attribution theorists deal with the perceived causes of sense of competence and incompetence. They answer such questions as *Why do I feel successful? Why do I feel a failure? How do I reach those conclusions? How do I know I'm incompetent? What are the consequences of these thoughts on my behavior?* From where does the *I can't, I am not physically capable, I don't have the skill, or I look stupid doing aerobics*, which invariably leads to perceived incompetence, come? Because sense of competence is an essential element of active lifestyle behavior, we need to understand more about it.

Competence affects active lifestyle behavior in many ways. People often avoid working out with others because they feel embarrased at their own physical condition. Many also feel nervous about trying a new activity or experiencing an unfamiliar environment. They worry about whether they can keep up with the instructor, whether they will look stupid, whether they will have to *give up* in front of others, and whether they will experience too much psychological and physical pain. Therefore, they generally choose an activity that they know they can do. Experience becomes an important element in their selection. Those afraid to venture outside what they know will usually choose activities that require very little skill, such as walking, riding a stationary bike, or using a rowing machine. Some even elect to do nothing.

Sense of Commitment

People have various levels of commitment to pursue an active lifestyle. As the model in Figure 6.1 indicates, attitude and needs both affect commitment. The stronger the needs, the stronger the commitment. People must also believe that activity is the pathway to their needs satisfaction. Without this belief they will find other ways to satisfy their needs. It is not really clear why and how people reach the point where they say, "Enough is enough. It's time to commit to exercise!" There does, however, appear to be a threshold that must be reached before any action will occur.

Expectations

An active lifestyle has certain expectations associated with it. There are three expectations: opportunity, anguish, and rewards.

Expected Opportunity This reflects availability of the sport or activity to those interested in participating. If, for example, we want to join an aerobics class but find that there is none available at a convenient time or at a convenient place, then this lack of opportunity inhibits participation. If we would like to lift weights but find the fees for using the local gym are too high, then this, too, inhibits participation. People generally choose to do the things that meet their time, accessibility, and cost requirements.

Expected Anguish When an individual pursues a new activity, a certain level of learning, physical pain, or intimidation is inevitable. Some activities are difficult to learn. Windsurfing is an example. You don't just step on a windsurfing board and sail off into the sunset. You must first learn how to balance on the board, and then how to hold the sail and steer without a rudder. You spend most of the first five or six hours of learning inelegantly falling off and climbing back on the board. The feedback for such low-level windsurfing skill is immediate and heartless. Similarly, golf and tennis require a considerable learning period just to develop the basic skills.

If people have some reasonable expectations of how easy or difficult it is to learn a sport, then there is a better chance they will continue to participate. Adults do not generally like to learn a new activity that will make them look stupid or clumsy. They especially do not like to feel intimidated. For some, physical pain is part of the challenge; others want to avoid it at all costs. For some, overcoming a difficult activity is enjoyable; for others it is miserable.

Many adults will try to foresee possible anguish to eliminate it from their activity. They will not go to an exercise facility if they expect to feel intimidated, for example; nor will they exercise with others if they expect to lose control of their level of exertion. Furthermore, they will seldom try an activity if they expect that it will be too difficult to learn. Many times the anguish associated with participation inhibits further participation. Consider this comment made by a thirty-four-year-old woman who joined an aerobics class:

> **Before:** I don't know anybody so I'm kind of nervous. Plus, I don't think that I'll do very well because I haven't done this in ages. I hope the instructor doesn't kill us. I'm going to stay in the back so I don't make a fool of myself.

After the experience she said: I'll go back after I get in better shape. I felt tired and a little stupid. But, I don't think I was the worst one out there. The staff were not very friendly. Some of the people working out were friendly, others were not. The ones I got along with were the ones who were dying out there. The ones in good shape wouldn't talk to me. I really didn't feel like I belonged.

Expected Rewards There are two types of expected rewards, extrinsic and intrinsic. *Extrinsic rewards* come from outside the individual. These include tangible rewards such as weight loss, body toning, and muscular development and intangible rewards such as respect, social approval, and affiliation. Many people participate in triathlons, for instance, because the grueling image this sport projects gives them a certain degree of perceived respect and admiration from others. *Intrinsic rewards* are more difficult to explain, since they arise from simply experiencing the activity. There are three categories of intrinsic rewards:

- simple enjoyment (or affect , as psychologists call it).
- potency—derived from a sense that we can do something physically challenging.
- mission—derived from the sense that we are accomplishing a higher-level goal that is longer range than the immediate task. Good health in old age is an example of a mission reward. Here, the task itself may or may not be immediately rewarding, since the motivating factor is potential well-being in old age.

We often see a combination of expected rewards. Frequently, extrinsic reasons, weight loss or improvement in physical appearances, for example, are the motivating factors. However, intrinsic rewards are also motivating. Here's a case in point:

I want my body to be as close to the optimum weight that it can be. I want to feel good about myself, to have good self-esteem. If I want to do something on the weekend, I want to be able to do it and be strong completing what I'm doing. I want to be able to play eighteen holes of golf in August when it's 90 degrees and feel good. If I was just in this to lose weight, I would just walk. But I'm in it for a lot more than that.

Rewards Received

These are actual intrinsic and extrinsic rewards received as a consequence of participation. In some cases the anguish experienced becomes in itself a reward, as is the case with this subject:

At first I thought people might say,"Look at that guy. He's fat and he's running." But the more I come down to the track and I see the same people I feel more comfortable. I even get some cheering now. One guy said, "Hey, I've been watching you and you're doing good." That's motivating in itself. Lately I don't see it as people thinking, "Hey look at that fat guy run." It's more like "Hey, I'm doing it and they're not!" At least they see the fat guy working out rather than the fat guy not working out. I feel like I have a lot more energy to do things during the day than I did before. Before I would feel run down half way through the day, but now I feel a lot better. I can appreciate what athletes feel like again. I haven't felt this way in a long time. I'm happy because of it. I'm tired at the end of my workout, but I feel good—like I've accomplished something. I feel motivated. I feel good about myself.

Satisfaction   When expected rewards match the rewards received and the anguish factor has not made things too uncomfortable, there is a certain level of satisfaction. In Figure 6.1 satisfaction feeds back to the individual's psychological state. An unpleasant experience will negatively affect this state perhaps deterring any future commitment to the activity.

Practical Considerations

People create their own activity. The active lifestyle promoter simply provides the environment and the ability for that activity to take place. Your job, whether it's running an exercise facility, instructing an exercise class, providing active lifestyle equipment (machines, golf clubs, windsurfing equipment, and so on), or managing events (marathons, triathlons, masters competitions, and so on) is to ensure that your consumers satisfy their needs through their chosen activity. If you forget the complexity of the active lifestyle motivation process and don't take into consideration that the reasons people are active are as varied as the activities they do, then you will fail to provide a motivating environment for more than a handful of people. On the whole, people want to be more physically active; they want to do something to improve their health and to accomplish something that improves them as people. It's just a matter of finding the right motivating opportunity and environment so that they can do it.

As active lifestyle promoters, you should make it your goal to discover what in the environment you can change to lead consumers naturally to an active lifestyle. This means creating a climate of trust, confidence, and relaxation. If you are not careful you can lock people out of active lifestyles by presenting the wrong image and by providing the wrong environment.

There are no simple, pat answers to why some adults are active and others are not because we are dealing with the broad field of motivation, satisfaction, achievement, performance, and results. Each of these has an impact on active lifestyle status. All we know is that there are many reasons why people do or do not pursue an active lifestyle. The biggest mistake you can make is to assume that everyone wants the same thing and is driven by the same needs.

ACTIVE LIFESTYLE IMAGES

"Skiing is a sport for the younger crowd. I don't think I will fit in very well on the slopes." This is a comment made by Patricia, a fairly inactive forty-six-year-old. An occasional walk in pleasant weather was the state of her activity. What should intrigue you is how Patricia knew that skiing was for the younger crowd. How did she know she would not fit in? How do people form such perceptions or images? We will now focus on images and what impact they have on active lifestyle participation.

First, let us revisit Patricia to find out more about her images of skiing.

> Skiing looks as if it would take too much coordination and skill that I lack. All I see are young, physically fit people on television. I never see older and less-experienced people. The way those young people fly down the slopes scares me. I don't think my body can withstand that sort of activity.
>
> But then I keep thinking about my younger brother and his wife, who took up skiing last year. They are pestering me to try skiing. They tell me it really isn't that dangerous. I keep reminding myself that my brother and his wife are no more physically active than I am. If they can ski and survive, then I should be able to.
>
> But what I see on television is having an effect on me. The idea of skiing gives me goose bumps. The sport really scares me.

Everyone has a mind's eye view of sports, exercise facilities, and other active lifestyle products. A good image means acceptance. A bad image almost certainly leads to rejection. Exercise facility owners potentially face a composite problem. Consumers may not only have a bad image of the activities offered; they may also have a poor image of exercise facilities generally, and even a poor image of the type of equipment in the facility.

Before you can develop a marketing strategy and certainly before you can set communications goals, you must have an understanding of the image consumers have of your active lifestyle product. Then you need to decide if this is the image you want. Your goal is to present your product to them in an enticing but reasonable manner.

The corporate arena has used image research for many years. In the sports industry, however, image research has been slower to develop. This is unfortunate because as you will discover when you read this section, we can draw certain general and useful information from images consumers have of active lifestyles and related products.

Image Formation

Very few people have all the right information and sufficient, if any, experience with the specific type of sport you offer. They depend on hints they can pick up from other sources. In addition to the sport itself, with all its features and symbols, various stimuli from numerous mediums—bombard consumers. Out of this maze of information, consumers select a subset of stimuli—perhaps a few physical attributes, the information from an advertisement or two, the expectations from family members, and one or two other selected stimuli. From this subset they develop an emotional reaction toward the sport, beliefs about it, and evaluations of it. Although part of an image is based on the physical aspect of the sport itself, symbols, the communication mix, and the environment also play a role. Figure 6.2 graphically demonstrates for you the image formation process.

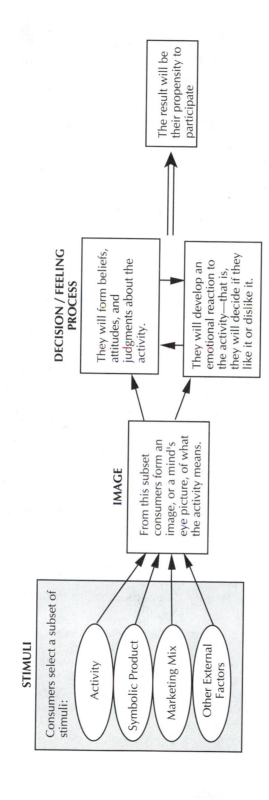

Figure 6.2 The Image Formation Process

(This model is adapted from a model appearing in Richard P. Bagozzi, *Principles of Marketing Management* (Chicago: Science Research Associates, 1986), p. 154. Reprinted with the permission of Macmillan College Publishing Company. Copyright © 1986 by Macmillan College Publishing Company, Inc.)

STIMULI

Consumers select a subset of stimuli:

- Activity
- Symbolic Product
- Marketing Mix
- Other External Factors

IMAGE

From this subset consumers form an image, or a mind's eye picture, of what the activity means.

DECISION / FEELING PROCESS

They will form beliefs, attitudes, and judgments about the activity.

They will develop an emotional reaction to the activity—that is, they will decide if they like it or dislike it.

The result will be their propensity to participate

It is difficult to guess what image consumers have about specific kinds of active lifestyles. When you do guess, you are likely to be quite wrong. It is much better to have some hard data upon which you can more accurately gauge the actual images consumers have. This means venturing forth from your office and into the marketplace. Ask your potential consumers, What do you think? Do you like what we have to offer? What feelings do you get when you think about skiing? Or walking? Or biking? Will you participate? If they will not, you need to consider what you could do to make your sport more interesting to them. Only after you have answers to such questions can you design active lifestyle products that will fit the needs of specific consumer segments. Only then can you choose a communication mix that will attract their attention.

The Role Images Play

Active lifestyle images seem to serve at least one of four main purposes. They express how consumers define their fit in the active lifestyle world; they help consumers preserve their egos; they help consumers integrate the knowledge that they have about active lifestyles; they also help consumers rate the potential rewards that they may receive from an active lifestyle.

Consumer Fit   Each consumer holds a distinctive view of his or her active lifestyle personality and athletic talent. The images people hold of certain types of active lifestyles help them decide if they fit the lifestyle, given their personality and ability. Intentionally or not, many sports and activity promoters present images of outgoing, daring, and athletic young people who are physically fit. Anyone who has ever read a windsurfing magazine or watched a body-shaping program on television knows that youth and beauty are the external wrappings. Older consumers see these images and conclude that it's too late for them to participate.

Consumer Egos   Fragile egos cause us much grief. Whenever possible, we ward off the feeling of inadequacy, embarrassment, and humiliation by avoiding what we believe we cannot do competently. For our own protection we dissociate ourselves from activities that make us feel stupid. If consumers perceive that the sport or activity demands more than their present physical condition or athletic ability will allow, they will generally decide not to even try it.

Consumer Knowledge   Images help a consumer store knowledge about active lifestyles. If consumers have had very little experience with the activity, they will evaluate the images they see and group the activity with something familiar. If they perceive skiing as a high-speed and youth-oriented sport, for example, they may group it with all the products associated with high speed and youth.[2] That may generate positive or negative feelings depending on how the consumer values high speed and youth. The consumer may label this as dangerous—something to avoid—or he or she may label it as exciting and adventurous—something to try.

One aim of any communications program is to instruct and inform consumers so that they can store positive, rather than negative, images. Thus when consumers do eventually decide to participate, they will have adequate positive knowledge. Even if they elect not to participate, it still pays to ensure that consumers have positive images.

Reward Value   Images serve to inform the consumer about the potential rewards associated with active lifestyle products. When consumers see positive rewards, they will tend to like the idea of participation. One way for consumers to rate potential positive rewards is to try the activity. We find we can change people's perception of an activity if we can persuade them to give it a try. For example, when Patricia finally tried skiing she said the following:

> **On the slopes:** On the first run I was so nervous that I didn't really think about anything. I am getting much better already. I think about trying to keep my balance and go straight. Also, it's kind of hard to steer, so I try not to get near other people. The first few times I went down the slope my brother was with me. Now he is off skiing somewhere else, and here I am.
>
> Skiing isn't as dangerous as I thought it was going to be. I have fallen twice, and it really isn't that bad. Of course, I'm going down the smallest hill, but I'm having a great time.
>
> There are people of all ages, and they are very nice. I have only been here for a while, and I have met three people. One was out here for the first time also. This is a much different crowd than I expected. I was expecting a lot of great skiers who would be laughing at me. I wish I had started skiing years ago.
>
> **Later in the day while she was relaxing in the lodge:** I really enjoyed myself. This was a shock to me because I thought that this experience was going to be painful and scary. Skiing is a lot of fun. Even when I fell down there was no pain. I would just stand up and do it again.
>
> There were a lot of good skiers out there. However, there were also a lot of people like me who were having a good time. The people I met on the slopes and in the lodge were very friendly. Almost everybody was willing to help and wanted to get to know you. I'm coming again as soon as possible.
>
> **The next day:** I am very sore. However, the pain is not that bad and it's worth it for the amount of fun I had. Being sore will not stop me from going again. The impression I got from television about skiing was wrong. The ski slopes are very different. Everyone out there is not an expert. There are a lot of people of all ages who are exactly like me. I'm so glad I tried skiing, or else my opinion of it would never have changed.

People often do not see rewards in most activities until they try them. They tend to focus on all the bad things that might happen and overlook the good.

The Images People Have

Focus groups and in-depth interviews with potential consumers often uncover images people have of certain types of active lifestyles. To give you an idea of the kind of data you can gather and how useful they can be, a group of students like you conducted personal in-depth interviews with a convenience sample of 250 inactive adults. The students selected ten activities and asked their sample what came to mind when they thought about each activity. They also asked the subjects what activity they would select if they were to adopt an active lifestyle and to explain why they made that particular selection. This type of personal interview study is very labor intensive, and this usually limits the number of people you can include in the sample. However, if you are careful you can design the sample so that it adequately represents your target market. In this case it was inactive adults from eighteen to seventy-five years of age. Keep in mind that this study does not replace the homework you will have to do on your own consumer group. You will need to do a similar study geared toward your specific consumer needs.

Each member of the sample was asked to express what came to mind for each of the following:

Jogging
Aerobics
Free weights
Machine weights
Swimming
Snow skiing
Windsurfing
Bowling
Golf
Walking
Health clubs

Responses were grouped according to categories that conveyed the essence of the image associated with each subject. Fourteen categories captured all the responses (Table 6.1). The grid in Figure 6.3 provides a summary of the images this group of deconditioned adults associated with the activities they had selected. The shading on the grid represents images associated with at least 5 percent of the sample.

All of the activities have three or four specific images associated with them. Almost 40 percent of the sample perceived jogging as painful and boring. About 10 percent had no significant positive or negative image; they simply indicated a nominal word like *exercise* or *workout*. The sample viewed aerobics as a feminine activity, had feelings of dislike, or focused on nominal words.

You can look across the grid in Figure 6.3 and quickly obtain a picture of

	Health Clubs	Jogging	Aerobics	Free Weights	Machine Wts	Swimming	Snow Skiing	Windsurfing	Bowling	Golfing	Walking
Physical Sacrifice											
Money											
Clothing/equipment											
Environment											
Body parts											
What it does for body											
Nominal words											
Activity difficulty											
Boredom											
Intrinsic/like											
Intrinsic/dislike											
Sex											
Age											
Lifestyle											

Key: The shading provides you with some idea of the number of people with the specific image of each activity.

30-40% 20-30% 15-20% 10-15% 5-10%

Figure 6.3   Overview Summary: Deconditioned Adults' Images of Certain Physical Activities

Table 6.1   Categories of Images

Physical Sacrifice: Pain, sweat, exhausting, intense, shinsplints, struggle, tiring, sore, grueling, agony,
  bad knees, knee pain, intimidating
Money: Expensive, waste of money, rip-off
Nominal words: exercise, workout, jumping, moving, recreation, bouncing
Clothing / equipment: Stairmaster, nautilus, spandex, water
Environment: summer, fresh air, social, trendy, meat market, pick-up-joint
Body parts: muscles, bulky, big muscles, thin legs
Effect on the body: lose weight, tone, strengthens, fitness, stress reliever, cardiovascular
Activity difficulty: difficult, complicated, frustrating, hard, dangerous
Boredom: monotonous, boring, routine, slow
Intrinsic like: satisfying, exhilarating, enjoyable, fun, awesome, refreshing, exciting
Intrinsic dislike: Yuck, hate, gross, cheesy, worthless, wimpy
Sex: masculine, feminine
Age: young, old, old timers
Lifestyle: drinking, beer, fat people, lazy people, out-of-shape

---

how each activity is being perceived by this sample of deconditioned adults. As you analyze the grid, you should ask yourself, Is the active lifestyle industry adequately communicating the benefits of these activities to the consumer? What features are consumers focusing on? Is this what we want them to focus on? Are these the images we want people to have? Are these images detrimental to consumer participation?

If you were a sports promoter, the nominal word category might concern you a bit. Imagine how upset Mercedes marketers would feel if people responded "car" or "transportation" when faced with the word Mercedes. These marketers have spent millions of dollars trying to convince us that Mercedes means "high class," "success," or "status." Like them, you can use advertising, packaging, and slogans to create an image. The goal is to encourage consumers to associate certain positive attributes with your sport. These attributes may be relatively concrete and objective (type of workout, what it does for the body), or they may be abstract and subjective (makes me feel good).

What They Want and Why

The members of the sample were also asked what type of activity they would choose if they were to adopt a more active lifestyle. Then they were asked why they chose that specific activity. In this instance deconditioned adults were most likely to choose walking, weight lifting, jogging, and aerobics. Walking is a particularly popular choice. The reasons for their choices fell within one of eight categories:

> Ease of access to the activity
> Effects on the body
> Low physical sacrifice
> Intrinsic liking
> Type of workout

Difficulty level
Environment
Familiarity

You will find an explanation of the type of responses placed in each category in Table 6.2. The data are presented for five age groups, with the shading indicating where the bulk of the responses fell. With only minor exceptions, the data suggest that this group of consumers was looking for fairly consistent features: what the activity could do for their body, whether it was enjoyable, and the type of workout it offered them. They also suggest that consumers over sixty years of age avoid physically stressful and difficult activities.

Table 6.2 The Reasons Adults Choose an Activity

	AGE				
	18–29	*30–39*	*40–49*	*50–59*	*60+*
Opportunity • easy; accessible; little equipment needed; fits schedule	10.1%	5.0%	40.4%	31.5%	17.5%
What it does for the body • burns calories; improves muscle strength; cardiovascular; keeps me young; feel more energetic; I feel better	40.5%	45.0%	31.0%	11.4%	27.5%
Physical sacrifice • not stressful on joints/body; not strenuous	4.5%	17.5%	9.5%	14.3%	27.5%
Intrinsic/phychic • fun; enjoyable; I like it; satisfying	31.5%	32.5%	16.7%	34.3%	27.5%
Type of workout • full body workout; good all-round workout; quickest way to get into shape	34.9%	20.0%	26.2%	22.9%	15.0%
Difficulty level • something I can do; too out of shape to do anything else; I can do it without dying; don't have to be in any kind of shape; sensible for a beginner; safest for a beginner	14.5%	17.5%	11.9%	11.5%	30.0%
Environment • can be outside; be with nature; good social activity; can do it with my friend	14.6%	5.0%	11.9%	22.8%	17.5%
Familiarity • done it before; already know how to do it; had fun doing it before	10.1%	12.5%	9.5%	8.6%	7.5%

Note: Columns do not add to 100 percent because some people gave more than one reason.

Implications

As you decide how you should design your communications strategies, the key question you should ask is, How can I communicate the benefits of my sport to my targeted consumer? According to this study you would need to communicate at least three important features, namely, the effects on the body, the type of workout consumers are getting, and the intrinsic qualities. At the same time try to evaluate perceptions people have and find ways to reduce any negative feelings. You can't persuade people to do an activity if they have a bad image of it. Although it may be impossible for you to develop a complete picture of how people perceive your sport or exercise facility, you should be able to determine its greatest strengths and weaknesses. As you have seen, many of these dimensions become measurable in consumer reaction. From a marketing perspective the trick is to present an image people can relate to, and then provide consumers with enough information to make an informed choice.

Let us focus for a minute on price. By price we mean the physical sacrifice and intimidation features of activity. As you can see by the data, these features play a role in deterring active lifestyle consumption. Although only the individuals in the oldest category specifically selected an activity based on low physical stress and on their belief that they could do that activity, these two features seem to have an impact on all age groups even when not specifically mentioned. If people perceive an activity to be physically stressful, or difficult to learn, they will generally not select it. People rate an activity enjoyable or satisfying because generally they feel it is something they can do and something that does not cause them a great deal of physical stress.

As a market strategist you will need to spend time and effort determining the type of image that will turn your consumers on. A hard physical workout packaged in a youthful, glamorous wrapping might seem like the image that will attract consumers. Certainly such images make a strong visual statement of high performance, high style, and ego enhancement. You must be absolutely sure, though, that this is the image your targeted consumers want. Don't get caught up in your own enthusiasm and excitement about your active lifestyle product. Go to the consumers and ask, What do you want? Then design your product specifically for them.

Actionability

The purpose of research is to give you some idea of what actions you can take. For example, what could you do to change the image consumers apparently have about jogging? Well, you could do one or all of the following:

1. Change the meaning of an existing jogging attribute, that it is painful, for example, by helping people understand that pain usually derives from lack of knowledge about shoes and about how to start a jogging program. Educate people on how to select suitable equipment and how to begin a safe jogging program.
2. Introduce a new product attribute the consumer has not considered important be-

fore. For example, you might educate consumers on how muscles use fat and why jogging is an efficient fat-burning activity. Show them how dieting without exercise generally leads to failure.

3. Change consumer interpretations or evaluations of jogging from nominal words to more powerful motivating images.

HOW ADULTS BECOME INVOLVED IN SPORTS AND WHAT NEEDS THEY ARE SATISFYING ....

We know very little about the breed of adult who challenges body and mental tenacity through sports participation. We are going to explore some of these issues using a specific group of adult sports participants—triathletes. These individuals are part of a rapidly expanding phenomenon in physical activity known as cross-training. The triathlon popularized the concept of cross-training. This is a hybrid sport that links three sports, the most common combination being swimming, biking, and running. The information obtained from triathletes may help you understand more about active lifestyle consumers, as the following exhibit demonstrates.

The Sample

The triathletes sampled for this study were designated by *Triathlon Today!* Magazine as being among the top ten to twenty in their age group. Table 6.3 describes the demographics of the sample. These individuals were mailed a survey consisting of open-ended questions. Respondents answered in their own words—the more detail they could give the better. The questionnaire took about forty-five minutes to one hour to complete. About 60 percent, or approximately 1,000, of those eligible to receive the survey returned it. Given the nature of the questionnaire, this was an exceptional yield. As well, the very detailed manner in which respondents answered the questions was unusual for a survey of this type. These individuals clearly have a tremendous passion for their sport.

In this section you are presented with an analysis of the responses this sample of triathletes gave to the following two questions:

- We would like to learn a little about the way you became a triathlete. Think back to when you first began participating. Briefly explain the reason why you began participating in triathlons.
- What is it about triathlons that makes you continue to participate?

Just over 970 triathletes eighteen years of age and older gave usable responses to these two questions.

To capture the richness of details provided, responses to each question were grouped according to categories that conveyed the essence of the factor contributing to beginning or continuing the triathlon. Many respondents gave more than one reason why they began or why they continued. Three hundred, for

Table 6.3 Selected Demographics of Triathletes

	n	%
Sex		
Men	581	59.8
Women	391	40.2
Age		
18–24	113	11.6
25–34	323	33.2
35–44	264	27.1
45–54	152	15.6
55–64	85	8.7
65+	36	3.7
Occupation		
Professional	448	46.4
Managers/Administrators	83	8.6
Clerical/Sales	87	9.0
Craftsmen/Labor/Service	80	8.3
Proprietors	66	6.8
Not in the workforce	209	20.8
Homemakers	29	
Retired	41	
Unemployed	2	
Professional triathletes	27	
Students	110	
Total in sample	973	100

example, described two factors that contributed to the way they became a triathlete. A handful (twenty-three) gave three factors. Four hundred attributed two reasons for why they continued with the sport, and 300 gave three reasons. None gave more than three reasons. Thus, for each question, up to three factors were coded.

Why They Began to Participate

Adults began their triathlon participation for four reasons (Table 6.4):

A. They had a specific need and searched for a way to satisfy it.
B. Someone they knew influenced them.
C. They saw a race or read about the sport, and it had an intrinsic appeal.
D. The activity they were doing failed them in some way, and so they searched for a replacement.

Table 6.4   Reasons for Initially Becoming Involved with the Triathlon

		Percentage of sample mentioning this reason
A. Had a need and searched for a way to satisfy it		33.8%
• Wanted to improve mental well-being	1.8%	
• Wanted to get into shape	9.3	
• Wanted to erase self-doubts	21.7	
• Wanted to experience success	6.4	
B. Influenced by someone they knew personally		24.3%
• Personal friend, boyfriend, girlfriend, husband, wife, other family member	24.6%	
C. Intrinsic appeal (saw it and liked the idea)		19.4%
• Exposed to a tri through an ad, race, TV, etc.	10.1%	
• Just looked like fun	11.9	
D. Old activity failed them in some way and searched for a replacement		42.2%
• Wanted to keep active after an injury	14.0%	
• Was doing one or more of the three sports separately—not satisfying enough	21.2	
• Wanted more variety in physical activity	11.4	

Why They Continued to Participate

Five clusters of reasons why adults continue their triathlon participation became evident from the data (Table 6.5). These included the following:

A. They liked the makeup of the sport.
B. There were tangible measures of success.
C. There was intrinsic gratification from the physical effort.
D. There was intrinsic gratification from the sport and the event associated with it.
E. They liked the tangible benefits related to health and well-being.

Needs and Motivations

Familiarity with needs and how physical activity can satisfy those needs will bring you a step closer to providing the type of programs consumers will welcome and appreciate. The more acquainted you are with the differences that occur among people, the more effectively you will be able to talk to them about sports and physical activity, develop programs they will want, and choose the price they will pay in terms of money, time, and effort.[3]

Table 6.5 Reasons for Continuing with the Triathlon

		Percentage of sample mentioning this reason
A. Liked the makeup of the product		19.4%
• Liked the combination of events/variety	19.4%	
B. Tangible measures of success		43.7%
• See improvement and achieve success	23.8%	
• Can win/be the best, achieve recognition	6.4	
• Love the competition	22.2	
C. Intrinsic gratification from the physical effort		46.3%
• Love the challenge	29.3%	
• Thrill of accomplishing	29.7	
D. Intrinsic gratification from the sport and event		42.3%
• The fun and enjoyment	13.4%	
• The atmosphere, friendships	34.7	
• Travel	5.7	
E. Other tangible benefits		19.8%
• Health and well-being	19.2%	
• Family relationships, fulfilling retirement	2.3	

The Needs Assessment Profile

Psychologists claim that there are fifteen needs that motivate our behavior (Table 6.6)[4]. Figure 6.4 presents a needs assessment profile of this sample of triathletes. Achievement, diversion, and security were the three most frequently mentioned reasons. Of these three, achievement was the most frequently mentioned motive for involvement in the triathlon. Approximately 78 percent of the sample discussed various challenges they were hoping to meet and overcome. Achievement needs were mentioned less frequently with increasing age. However, even among the oldest age category, over 65 percent indicated that they were using the triathlon to satisfy achievement needs.

Almost 68 percent of the sample indicated that they were triathlon participants for diversionary purposes. They sought fun, enjoyment, and recreation. Age was not a differentiating factor here.

Sixty-two percent of the sample mentioned security needs. Thus, a sizable portion of individuals sought to improve health and fitness, to avoid injury by varying the type of activity they were doing, or to overcome some form of compulsive behavior. The two youngest age categories were significantly less likely to mention security needs than were triathletes over the age of thirty-five.

Table 6.6 The Fifteen Needs that Motivate Our Actions and How They Were Identified in a Sample of Competitive Triathletes

Need	Definition	Response Summary
Achievement	The desire to meet and overcome challenges	• Qualify for the Ironman and other major events • Improve performance • Overcome the challenge of a triathlon • Achieve athletic success not possible in
Independence	The desire to be free from the influence of others	• Want to train self, want to make own decisions • I can accomplish on my own • Want to stand on my own two feet • Learning determination and discipline
Exhibition	The desire to be noticed, to win the attention and interests of others	• To win, to be the best, be recognized as an all-American
Recognition	The desire to be acclaimed, receive social rewards or notoriety	• Be competitive in own age group • To receive prestige, credibility, and respect
Dominance	The desire to show strength and prowess by conquering others	• To beat well-known athletes • The chance to compete, love to compete
Affiliation	The desire to be accepted, to enjoy satisfying relationships	• Participating due to encouragement by others • Provides social opportunities • Reinforces family relationships • Makes you a better person
Nurturance	The desire to support and help the progress and development of others	• Help the sport of triathlon in some way • Set an example to others
Succorance	The desire to receive support, encouragement, or reassurance	• Want supportive family and friends • Use a coach for inspiration, motivation,
Sexuality	The desire to establish one's attractiveness	• Seeking the perfect body • Keep in shape, lose weight
Stimulation	The desire to experience events and activities that stimulate the senses	• To do unusual triathlons or endurance events • Experience the inner thrill of accomplishing
Diversion	The desire to play, and have fun, to break from routine and relax	• Participate, have fun, enjoy life • Have recreation • Enjoyment of activity
Novelty	The desire for change and diversity in life; to learn new skills and do new activities	• Triathlon discovered as a new extension of present activities • Search for variety and ways to reduce boredom • Enjoy travel • Like the variety of the combination of the
Understanding	The desire to learn and comprehend	• Use a coach for technical help • Use the triathlon to learn goal and success process
Consistency	The desire for order and to avoid uncertainty	• Preference for sports they have done for a long time • Preference for sports they can do forever • Indications that they want to continue with the
Security	The desire to protect, to have an adequate supply of what one needs, to be invulnerable to attack, avoid accidents	• Improve and maintain health and fitness • Avoid injury from overuse of muscles and joints • Overcome compulsive behavior and mishaps

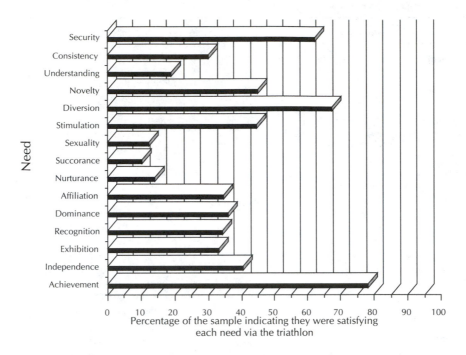

Figure 6.4   Needs Assessment of Competitive Triathletes

However, there was no difference in the frequency of occurrence of security needs among triathletes over thirty-five years of age.

About 45 percent mentioned novelty, stimulation, and independence needs, with independence needs cited more frequently among respondents under twenty-five years of age. Novelty and stimulation were equally mentioned across age categories, however.

Between 30 and 40 percent of the sample mentioned recognition, dominance, affiliation, and consistency needs. Recognition was clearly more important to triathletes under thirty-five years of age than for those over thirty-five years of age. On the other hand, consistency appeared to be more important to triathletes over thirty-five years of age. Consistency indicates a preference for familiar sports and sports that one can continue into old age.

The final four needs, understanding, nurturing, succorance, and sexuality, were mentioned by less than 20 percent of the sample.

Needs Assessment Summary

Although this research is in a very early phase of development, the findings to date add some intriguing insights into this group of physically active adults. Figure 6.5 presents the survey of the most frequently mentioned motives for triathlon participation. Needs and age categories are arranged in a matrix to pro-

Six of the needs had significant χ2 across age categories. These are presented below.

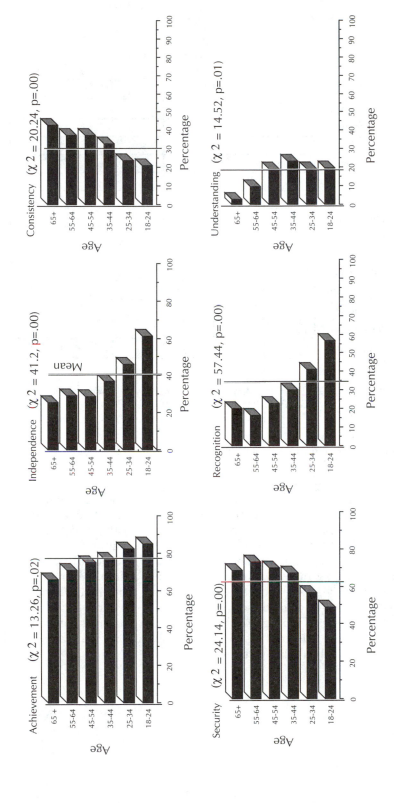

Figure 6.4 (Continued)

125

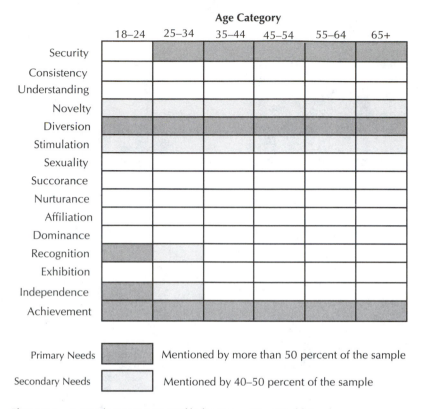

Figure 6.5   A Needs Assessment Profile for Competitive Triathletes

duce a map of needs segments. The segments to which the need is prevalent are shaded. At a glance, Figure 6.5 shows that the majority of this group of physically active adults are motivated by five needs: security, novelty, diversion, stimulation, and achievement. These needs are remarkably consistent across age categories. Only recognition and independence are additional needs for the two youngest age groups. Security needs are not a dominant motive for participants under twenty-five years of age. The advantage for identifying the most important needs associated with the different forms of physical activity relates to promotional activities. To promote physical activity you must have a reasonable idea of what needs people are satisfying and be able to articulate those needs clearly and precisely in advertising campaigns.

SUMMARY

This chapter analyzed the factors that might motivate an adult to participate in sports. These factors included sociocultural environment, psychological state (attitude, needs, and sense of competence), sense of commitment, expectations (opportunity, rewards, and anguish), actual outcome (rewards, opportunity, anguish), and satisfaction. You also found that the images people have of your sport also plays a role in whether or not they are willing to give it a try. The final topic discussed was needs. We analyzed a group of very intensive adult sports participants (triathletes) and tried to understand what motivates them, by studying the needs they were satisfying through their participation.

Now you are ready to undertake a research project of your own. You will see how to do this in the next chapter.

STRATEGIC PLAN WORKSHEET–CHAPTER 6

What You Should Know about Adult Sports Participants

Your Goal

To understand your participant consumer so that you can design your event specifically for this market

The information you need is laid out for you on worksheets 6.1–6.3

Check when completed

- Worksheet 6.1: Market Opportunities
- Worksheet 6.2: Interested nonparticipants
- Worksheet 6.3: Target market profile

WORKSHEET 6.1

Market Opportunities

Have these markets been maximized?

List Existing Events Programs Products	Present Markets Served	Yes	No	Don't Know	Potential New Markets
		☐	☐	☐	
		☐	☐	☐	
		☐	☐	☐	
		☐	☐	☐	
		☐	☐	☐	
		☐	☐	☐	

List Existing Events Programs Products	Variations for Present Markets	Variations for New Markets

WORKSHEET 6.2

Interested Nonparticipants

	Yes	No	Yes	No	Yes	No	Yes	No	Yes	No	Yes	No
Past Exposure to the Sport	☐	☐	☐	☐	☐	☐	☐	☐	☐	☐	☐	☐

Demographics
Age
Education
Income
Sex

Helpful Lifestyle Variables

How They Would Prefer to Participate

Other Assorted Insights

Segments (Describe briefly)

WORKSHEET 6.3

Target Market Profile

Do You Know:	Yes	No	Marketing Application of the Information
How your present participants became involved in your sport	☐	☐	
Their long-term ambitions in the sport	☐	☐	
If there are any disabilities or obstacles your participants have overcome	☐	☐	
Their use of a coach, trainer, or professional	☐	☐	
What it is about your sport that keeps them involved	☐	☐	
How participation in your sport contributes to accomplishment of major goals in their life	☐	☐	

REFERENCES

1. For introductory reviews in the psychological literature see Arnold L. Glass, Keith J. Holyoak, and John L. Santa, *Cognition* (Reading, Mass.: Addison-Wesley, 1979); for treatments in the marketing literature see J. A. Howard, *Consumer Behavior: Application of Theory* (New York: McGraw-Hill, 1977).

2. For an interesting discussion of how people form word associations see J. A. Howard, *Consumer Behavior: Application of Theory* (New York: McGraw-Hill, 1977).

3. For an overview of this line of thinking see F. T. Juster and F. P. Stafford, eds. *Time, Goods and Well-Being* (Ann Arbor: University of Michigan, 1985).

4. This presentation of needs has been adapted from R. B. Settle and P. Alreck, *Why They Buy: American Consumers Inside and Out* (New York: John Wiley, 1986), pp. 24–27.

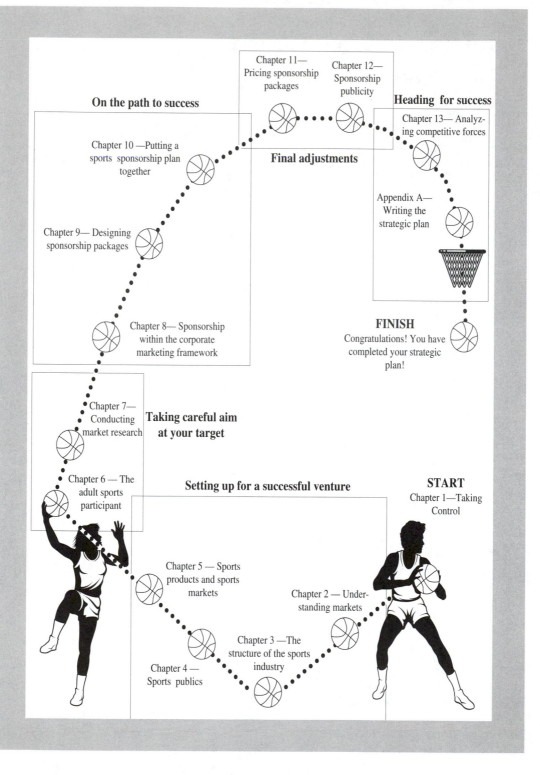

Chapter 11—
Pricing sponsorship
packages

Chapter 12—
Sponsorship
publicity

On the path to success

Heading for success

Chapter 13— Analyz-
ing competitive forces

Chapter 10 —Putting a
sports sponsorship plan
together

Final adjustments

Appendix A—
Writing the
strategic plan

Chapter 9— Designing
sponsorship packages

Chapter 8— Sponsorship
within the corporate
marketing framework

FINISH
Congratulations! You have
completed your strategic
plan!

Chapter 7—
Conducting
market research

Taking careful aim
at your target

Chapter 6 — The
adult sports
participant

Setting up for a successful venture

START
Chapter 1—Taking
Control

Chapter 5 — Sports
products and sports
markets

Chapter 2 — Under-
standing markets

Chapter 3 —The
structure of the sports
industry

Chapter 4 —
Sports publics

CHAPTER SEVEN

Conducting Market Research

••

> Knowledge is of two kinds. We know a subject ourselves, or
> we know where we can find information upon it.
> —*Dr. Samuel Johnson (1709–1784)*

The goal of this chapter is to foster in you an appreciation of market research, and help you be a wise buyer and user of it. Generally, many students find that mastering the technical details of research alone is of little use without knowing how to apply this information. With an informed practical perspective you can better decide which types of sports problems can benefit most from market research.

There are many points of view about market research. What this chapter attempts to do is present you with some of the more general ideas and formats for conducting research. It will give you a solid grounding in the fundamentals of market research. Your journey through the market research process begins with a summary of some jargon. Then you will do some "hands-on" exercises, preferably using real sports consumers as subjects.

MARKET RESEARCH

Market research—these two words simply describe a method used to learn about the marketplace. It is a process of discovery. You might do research for a number of reasons, including

- to measure market potential
- to perform market forecasts
- to study the effectiveness of advertising
- to study the effect of prices
- to study the needs of the consumer
- to find out who the consumer is

Why should you spend time learning about research? This is an important question because in this chapter you will learn about such things as focus groups, sampling, interviewing, bias, and variables—things that seem fairly distant to providing your consumers with sports opportunities. You will ultimately discover that market research not only is relevant to the modern sport manager but holds the answers to *effective* management, marketing, and growth strategies.

As you go through this chapter, you will realize that you already know quite a bit about the research process, since you conduct research in your own life all the time. Research is really about gaining new knowledge. You can gain knowledge in two ways: Someone else provides you with the information, or you gain information through your own personal experiences. Unfortunately, your experiences and what other people tell you are invariably tainted by perceptions and interpretations. What you finish up *knowing* may, or may not, be a true representation of reality. Research offers a special approach to the discovery of reality; it is the process of "finding out" what might be real, and not your *personal* perception of what is real.

The research process begins with defining the problem. The researcher asks why, how, what, and who questions:

> Who are the consumers of sports?
> What are their needs?
> How do they make decisions about pursuing a sport?
> Why do certain forms of sports interest people more than others?

Your information needs quite often guide the problem definition. Prior research, for instance, might indicate that adults who participate in the triathlon like this sport because they are easily able to see constant improvement in their performance. Assume for a moment that you have designed a product that will help triathletes improve their performance. You might decide that the triathlon market is too small for you to make a profit. What can you do to expand your potential sales? In this case you might decide to do more research to find out if improved performance also motivates adults who ski, sail, or play tennis. If so, then these would be possible markets for your product.

One of the problems you will face in research is defining exactly what it is you are trying to measure. For example, how would you define the words *healthy lifestyle*? Make sure you come up with an answer. Now read the following to see if other people might agree or disagree with you.

Measuring Concepts

A large corporation has hired you to run its exercise facility, and your boss has invited you to lunch so she can get to know you better. Since your boss is paying, you select the most expensive meal on the menu. During lunch your boss tells you what a great job you are doing and asks if you would conduct a research project for the company. As you discuss the project, the following occurs:

Your Boss:	Okay, you're the expert. We can measure anything we want about the active lifestyle behavior of our employees, right?
You:	Hmmm, I'm not really sure about that.
Your Boss:	Of course we can. Give me something we should know that will help us understand our employee active lifestyle behavior better, and I'll tell you how to measure it.
You:	Okay, let's see—a healthy lifestyle. Employees who have a healthy lifestyle are important to us. If we could measure a healthy lifestyle, we might be able to figure out how to develop that feature in more people.
Your Boss:	Excellent idea. But I'm not sure what you mean by *healthy lifestyle.*
You:	I've heard people talk about pursuing a healthy lifestyle.
Your Boss:	Give me an example of it.
You:	Well, I know this one guy who works out in the weight room every day.
Your Boss:	Wow, really! Yep, I'd say that indicates a healthy lifestyle. Okay, let's find out if our employees pursue a healthy lifestyle by asking them if they work out in our weight facility every day. If they do, we'll count them as employees who have a healthy lifestyle, and let's see how many we have in the company. Then we can try to persuade more employees to work out in the weight facility every day, and maybe they will become more concerned about pursuing a healthy lifestyle.
You:	Hold on a sec! Aren't we going to miss a number of employees who pursue a healthy lifestyle? I know of people who consider themselves to be pursuing a healthy lifestyle, and they do other forms of physical activity.
Your Boss:	Hmm . . . that's true. I know of this woman who jogs every morning before work. Now I call that a healthy lifestyle. We'll find out how many employees we have who pursue a healthy lifestyle by checking people who exercise every day. Then we'll find out how they became regular exercisers and try to use that information to encourage more employees to exercise.
You:	That won't do it either. At least three of my friends are fanatics about their health, but they don't exercise every day. They watch what they eat, follow a stress reduction program, and don't smoke or drink alcohol. As well, they all walk two or three times a week.

	You'll miss these types of people if you just research those who exercise daily.
Your Boss:	You're right. You know what? I think we've discovered something we can't measure. I know there are people who do certain things that indicate they are pursuing a healthy lifestyle. I'd sure like to measure whatever that is so we can cultivate it in people who are not pursuing a healthy lifestyle. But I'm not sure it's possible. Perhaps we can't measure anything we want to measure after all!
You:	Of course we can.
Your Boss:	For crying out loud! Here *(tossing you the check)*, you pay for lunch.

This discussion illustrates a few problems we have as researchers. First, there are some things we would like to measure that are difficult to describe. A healthy lifestyle is one of those things. The words *healthy lifestyle* exist, and we frequently use them to describe a certain type of behavior, but a healthy lifestyle as a concrete, tangible object does not exist in the sense that a chair exists, or this book exists. We know that there are certain kinds of people who exhibit behavior that tells us they will do things that are good for their health. Some follow a ritual of jogging every morning. Others buy a health club membership. Others will watch what they eat, avoid alcohol, and cigarettes, and get an annual medical checkup. Over time we have developed a label for the behavior these kinds of people exhibit—we call it a healthy lifestyle. Our problem is how to define a healthy lifestyle.

Second, you and I might disagree on what behaviors indicate a healthy lifestyle. For illustrative purposes, let's take another word, *active*. Let's assume you are setting up a blind date for your friend, Susan. When Susan asks you to describe this person (Tom) you want her to date, you think for a moment. Flashing through your mind are images of Tom—he loves to grow his own vegetables, he does all the maintenance around the apartment building, he's involved in the local pro-abortion movement, and he spends his summers building homes for the poor. You finally say, "He's a very active person." Susan thinks back on people she thinks of as active. She sees images of a well-defined body toned through years of lifting weights, sun-tanned from outside activities like sailing and bicycling. She also imagines a dare-devil personality that thrives on fast-paced winter sports like downhill skiing. When Susan finally meets Tom, she is disappointed. Later she asks you why you described Tom as active.

You:	Well, Tom is outside in his garden a lot, and he does all the maintenance in the apartment building.
Susan:	Activity is fun-type stuff. Gardening and maintenance are not fun. That's labor!
You:	He's also involved in the pro-abortion movement.
Susan:	I call that activism.
You:	What about all the building he does for the poor during the summer?
Susan:	That tells me he's a socially conscious person. It doesn't describe an active person to me.

As you can see, words can have very different meanings. The term *active lifestyle* can mean very different things to different people depending on how they interpret the word *active.*

If you and Susan decided to conduct a research project in your community to determine how many adults fit into the category of having an active lifestyle, you would have to decide how you were going to define active lifestyle. Suppose you agree to limit your study to physical activity. You both quickly agree that this includes sports and exercise. What about walking to the shops? Should that be on your list? Should you include yoga? What about calisthenics? How about degree of activity—if I run five miles a day, does this suggest I have a more active lifestyle than someone who bikes ten miles a day? The two of you would have to come to an agreement about what behaviors indicate an active lifestyle. What you must do is agree to a conceptual meaning of the word *active.* Figure 7.1 traces why we have such a problem with labeling.

You and Susan eventually decide to ask adults in your community about all forms of physical activity that have some impact on their cardiovascular system. You decide to choose several types of physical activity and will attempt to assess the level of exertion for each activity. When you have the data, you will classify adults into low, medium, and highly active lifestyles. The measures you use are called indicators. Keep in mind, though, that if two of your friends are doing the same project, they might come up with totally different indicators of a physically active lifestyle. Other people who read your study will decide if they agree with your indicators or not.

Two Research Approaches

Once you have defined the problem, you can follow one of two general research approaches. The first is the deductive approach and the second the inductive approach. Both approaches occur during a research project to some degree (Figure 7.2).

The Deductive Approach   When you use this approach you begin with some theory or hypothesis. Then you would design a project that would prove your hypothesis true or false. For example, in thinking about why older women do not use weight room facilities, you might suspect (hypothesize) that these women find the weight training room environment intimidating. To see if this was true, you would gather information on how older women perceive weight training room facilities. You would then decide if your suspicion was true or false.

The Inductive Approach   In this case you do not have any suspicions about existing relationships among variables, but you would like to *discover* any relationships that might exist. You begin with a set of loosely gathered, fairly unstructured data with the idea of *exploring* or *discovering* potential hypotheses

STEP 1. Many different types of behaviors seem to represent something more general than the simple content of any single behavior.

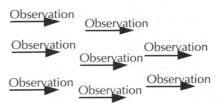

STEP 2. Since it is inconvenient to list all the specific behaviors whenever we want to refer to the general image or concept they portray, we give the collective behavior a label.

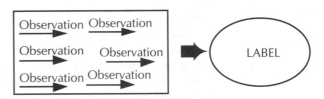

STEP 3. Over time we begin to ignore the individual behaviors and think of the label as something that really exists. We forget that the label is just a summary reference for several concrete behaviors.

STEP 4. Now we begin to debate whether the specific behaviors we have selected are "really" sufficient indicators of the concept.

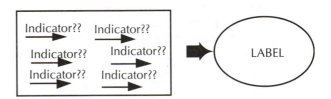

Figure 7.1   Putting Labels on Behaviors

(Adapted from Earl Babbie, *The Practice of Social Research* (New York: Wadsworth Publishing Co., © 1986, p. 101. Used with permission from Wadsworth, Inc.)

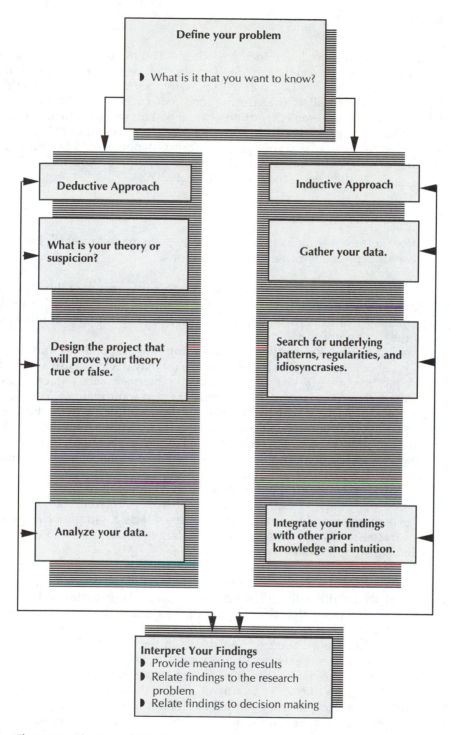

Figure 7.2 The Research Process

(Adapted from Richard P. Bagozzi, *Principles of Marketing Management* (Chicago: Science Research Associates, 1986), p. 279. Reprinted with permission of Science Research Associates, an imprint of Macmillan Publishing Company. Copyright © 1986 by Science Research Associates.)

rather than testing a predetermined hypothesis. You might be curious, for example, about why people compete in the triathlon. You would collect some information from local triathletes that will tell you why they compete. You would then look at the data you collected, searching for a pattern, recurring themes, and regularities that best represented your observations. You would then arrive at some possible conclusions. Your conclusions are only tentative, though, because your observations are a source of your pattern. Your task now would be to find a logical explanation for the pattern you discovered. Eventually you might decide to test your explanation using the deductive approach.

Research Methods

The three most frequently used research methods in market research include surveys, experiments, and open-ended explorations.

Survey Research   A survey asks people to express their thoughts, ideas, beliefs, feelings, intentions, and so on. For example, you might ask consumers how much they liked participating in various activities. Surveys of this kind are one of the most popular methods of research.

In a typical survey, you select a sample of respondents and ask them questions about the topic that interests you. You may decide to use a self-administered questionnaire, or you may conduct the interview face to face. Once you have collected the data, you will summarize them in some manner. You may simply *describe* the characteristics of your sample (for example, 60 percent of the men surveyed preferred playing golf over tennis), you may test a hypothesis (whether attitudes towards a sport relate to intentions to participate in it), or you may try to make predictions (for example, 5 percent of the residents of a town would join a health club if it had a weight training facility).

Surveys are an excellent way to observe large populations directly; public opinion polls such as Gallup, Harris, and Roper are well-known examples. The researcher generally knows the variables, selects a sample of respondents with characteristics resembling those of the larger population, and constructs a questionnaire that provides the necessary data.

Experimental Research   This research technique is generally associated with what we traditionally call structured science. An experiment typically involves your first *doing* something to your subjects and then observing how the subjects respond. A true experiment randomly assigns subjects to either a *treatment* or a *control* group. You expose subjects in the treatment group to your action, whereas those in the control group are not exposed. For example, you might expose a group of overweight women to a motivational message about starting an exercise program (this is the treatment group); then over the following two to three months you compare their participation rates in exercise to a group of overweight women not exposed to the message (this is the control group).

You generally use experiments to explain behavior or test ideas. Let's assume, for example, that you want to study women who dislike weight training. You want to discover a way to reduce their dislike. We suspect (hypothesize) that if they acquired an understanding of weight training, their dislike would be reduced. You can test this hypothesis experimentally. First you might test the level of dislike of weight training among a group of women and select only those who dislike this activity the most. Next you might show these women a videotape that describes weight training in a fun and entertaining manner. It describes the basic muscular benefits to them, explains the jargon, introduces them to the equipment, and graphically illustrates what muscles of the body this equipment trains. After the video, we measure the level of dislike for weight training among our women and determine whether the video had reduced dislike.

All the situations we have discussed so far are experiments that require a laboratory setting. However, we can also conduct an experiment in a natural setting. This is a *field experiment*. Assigning subjects to treatment and control groups in a field setting is usually quite difficult to do, since we are taking advantage of natural occurrences. For example, assume you want to know if holding events such as marathons, triathlons, and other highly energetic sporting events influences the exercise behavior of people living in those towns. You might survey the exercise behavior of people who live in two types of towns, those towns in which such sporting events are held and those in which these events are not held. In this case you are taking advantage of a natural experiment that would have been impossible to arrange. Unfortunately, because you must take things as they occur, natural experiments raise many validity problems. Perhaps, for example, the level of physical activity within some towns attracts promoters who want to take advantage of the physical activity behavior of the residents. Here, it is not the holding of the event that raises the level of community exercise participation; it is rather, the community's interest in exercise that attracts event promoters. There are usually many other unknown forces at play that may make the apparent positive influence of events on community exercise behavior a spurious or accidental one.

Exploratory Research   On occasion we need a research strategy that allows us to *discover* or *stumble across* new knowledge. We call this strategy exploratory research. This is a relatively unstructured research strategy. Focus groups, in-depth interviews, participant observation, and projective techniques are all examples of exploratory research strategies.

Focus Groups   A focus group consists of six to twelve people who sit around a table and talk about healthy lifestyles or exercise from their personal perspective. The interview is unstructured and is led by a moderator, whose task is to keep people talking about the topic of interest to the researcher. People express whatever is on their mind, and discussions may wander in any direction, even tangential to the topic of the session. The free environment and relatively long period of the interview (about one and a half to two and a half hours) allows people time to reveal deep consumer needs, motives, beliefs, values, and feelings. The focus group session is usually tape recorded (or videotaped) for later analysis.

Depth Interviews   Similar to focus group interviews, in-depth interviews are conducted on a one-on-one basis. The interviewer's objective is to induce the interviewee to express his or her thoughts, emotions, and values. This is a particularly useful method if you suspect certain topics will embarrass people.

Projective Techniques   Use this technique to detect deep-seated psychological forces in consumers. A subject responds to a vague or ambiguous stimulus. The stimulus might be a word, statement, object, or picture. The subject is asked to describe what the stimulus means or suggests. The researcher then interprets the interview in the hope of discovering underlying causes of behavior.

Phase 1: Understand Your Topic

You are about to embark on the first of four phases usually followed when you conduct a market research project. You will complete the following tasks in this project:

1. Conduct a focus group and write a report.
2. Write a questionnaire and test it.
3. Collect the data.
4. Write the research report.

Note that you should choose a sports consumer who is of special interest to you. The consumer in the following assignment is an example. You should substitute the consumer of your choice for the words that are in the square brackets [ ].

Focus Group Simulation—The Active
Sports Consumer

You are the director of a [corporate aerobics program]. [Aerobics classes] have been very popular among women even though the classes are not only for female employees. There is a handful of men enrolled in the classes, and you would like to attract more. You have absolutely no idea why women have been signing up for classes while the men have not. Your assignment is to conduct a focus group consisting of six employees. Three of your respondents should be male and three should be female. One of each sex should be active in sports and dislike [aerobics] as an activity; one of each sex should be fairly inactive and never have been involved in an [aerobics class]; the remaining two respondents should have participated in an [aerobics class] at some point.
    There are five practical questions you want to answer:

1. What is the role of physical activity in the employee's life?
2. What type of person likes [aerobics] as a form of exercise?
3. Why do people prefer certain types of physical activity?

4. Are there any special feelings about [aerobics] on the part of the males?
5. Is there a difference between the sexes regarding their feelings about [aerobics]?

To answer these questions, you need to probe for the whole range of the employee's feelings about [aerobics]. Encourage maximum spontaneity and probe any area that seems likely to be significant. Get your group talking freely about all their feelings about [aerobics].

Try to delve into the following areas:

Spontaneous Associations. Encourage maximum free association with [aerobics], probe everything that comes into an employee's mind when he or she thinks of [aerobics]. Ask for sensory impressions, smell, appearance, and so on.

Kind of Aerobics. What are their impressions about different types of [aerobics]—high intensity, low intensity; difficulty in attending classes; how one should design an [aerobics program], and so on.

Exercise Atmosphere. What type of atmosphere are they looking for? When is exercise most wanted, best liked?

Best Physical Activity. What is the best type of physical activity they have ever done, when, how, and so on.

Childhood. What was their experience with physical activity in childhood? When did they become conscious of the need to exercise?

Friends. Ask for comments about what the attitudes of their friends would be if they were to participate in [aerobics classes].

Frequency. How active are they in their daily lives?

Health. What are their feelings about exercise and health? [Aerobics] and health? Food and health?

Before you do your focus group, you should test your knowledge about focus groups by completing Table 7.1. There are five clusters of questions. Answer all of them, since they hold clues that will help you conduct your own focus group. Your interview should last about one hour. Tape record your focus group and transcribe the tape word for word. If possible conduct at least two focus groups. On the basis of these two focus groups, write a focus group report. If you need guidelines about writing a report, see Table 7.2.

NOTE: For the purpose of this assignment you should do your own focus group moderation. When you have completed your focus group assignment, move to phase 2, Writing the Questionnaire.

Phase 2. Writing the Questionnaire

You are now ready to move to phase 2 of the market research process, writing a questionnaire that will provide you with the data needed to answer your problem. You should apply the knowledge you have learned from your focus groups to this phase of your research. Before you begin to tackle this phase, though, you need some background information.

Table 7.1   Test Your Knowledge about Focus Groups

Answer these questions before proceeding with your focus group assignment. If you are unsure of the correct responses to the questions, you may seek advice by turning to the asterisk (*) to locate additional information.

Group 1 Questions—*Understanding the meaning of "focus groups."*
➤ A focus group is an example of a qualitative research technique.   T   F
➤ Why are open-ended questions on a survey a poor substitute for a focus group?

_____

➤ What are three advantages focus groups have over quantitative research?
1. _____

2. _____

3. _____

➤ Focus groups can be used to provide a description of the elements
   that drive perceptions, attitudes, and behavior.   T   F
➤ Quantitative data provide the _____while qualitative data provide an understanding
   of _____

If you need advice for group 1 questions, see the next exhibit

---

Quantitative versus Qualitative Studies

A quantitative study usually has two fundamental objectives:
   To provide an estimate of the percentages of people who think, feel, and act in certain ways.
   To provide a description and an understanding of the emotional, rational, and behavioral forces that give rise to perceptions, attitudes, and behavior. In short, to answer the question "Why?"
   A quantitative study can achieve the first objective but to obtain the second, open-ended questions are generally necessary. Open-ended questions, however, have several drawbacks. Behavioral forces are complex. Most people need an interviewer to help them probe the forces behind their behavior. Quantitative studies encourage brief, superficial responses. Even when an answer is thoughtful, interviewers seldom capture the texture of the response.
   Focus groups and individual depth interviews can overcome some of the problems inherent in open-ended questions. The qualitative format of these strategies gives respondents time to think. A skilled interviewer can probe for further detail whenever necessary. Everything that the respondents say can be captured on tape for later review.

Table 7.1   (Continued)

Focus groups and depth interviews should be used to provide a description and an understanding of the mix of behavioral elements contributing to that behavior. The results of both the quantitative and qualitative phases can be integrated fully into a single report. The quantitative data provide the objective framework explaining the behavior or attitudes. The qualitative data add depth of understanding of the forces that produce the behavior.

The integration between quantitative and qualitative research offers a more instructive, useful, and satisfying set of findings.

Group 2 Questions —*The role of the moderator.*
➤ What are the disadvantages of doing your own focus group research?

_____

➤ An outside moderator can be more objective than you.	T	F
➤ Focus group moderation is a learned skill.	T	F
➤ An outside moderator is helpful in designing the focus group research.	T	F
➤ A lack of knowledge about the topic can be an advantage to the research.	T	F

* If you need advice for group 2 questions, see the next exhibit.

Should You Moderate Your Own Focus Group?

Focus groups are expensive, and it is tempting to cut these costs by conducting your own focus group interviews. Not only can you save money but since you are more familiar with your consumers, you may feel that you will better be able to ask the right questions. However, moderating your own focus group is usually a mistake. In the end you will generally obtain more useful qualitative data if you assign the task to a professional who has specific skills in focus group moderation. Here are some important reasons you should not do your own focus group:

An outside moderator can sometimes be more objective than you.

Focus group moderation is a learned skill, and an experienced moderator knows how to benefit from the group dynamics, can handle the dominant person, can draw shy individuals into the conversation, and has many tricks such as word association, conceptual mapping, and attitudinal scaling to extract the maximum amount of information possible.

An outside moderator usually brings experience from different research situations.

Table 7.1 (Continued)

An **outside moderator** can be more objective in interpreting the results. Often you can benefit from the professional insights of the outsider.

You can generally gather more insight about your consumers by observing the group rather than being a part of the process.

Group 3 Questions — *Identifying a good focus group moderator.*

➤ There is an accreditation process before you can become a moderator.	T	F
➤ An effective moderator should be able to suggest different ways to achieve your objectives within the focus group framework.	T	F
➤ A good moderator should prepare a moderator's guide.	T	F
➤ A good moderator should do more than just ask simple questions.	T	F
➤ A good moderator should help you recruit the participants who will be a part of the focus group.	T	F

*If you need advice for group 3 questions, see the next exhibit.

Choosing the Right Moderator

There are no accreditation requirements for focus group moderators. Anyone can become one. As a result, you could possibly hire an inadequate moderator — so choose carefully. Here are some things you should look for:

1. Find out how long the individual has been doing focus groups. You don't want to be the test client for an inexperienced moderator.
2. An experienced moderator can suggest different ways to achieve your objectives. A specific line of questioning, strategies for probing difficult questions, or even techniques other than focus groups are possibilities.
3. A moderator's guide forces you and the moderator to think through the content of the focus group. Will this be provided?
4. It is not necessary for the moderator to be an expert on your consumer, but some knowledge about the topic generally results in higher-quality data.
5. Can the moderator help you interpret the results and make some marketing recommendations?
6. Does your moderator use modern interview strategies such as personality association, conceptual mapping, or attitudinal scaling to delve deeper into the minds of your consumers?
7. Who recruits the participants? This is sometimes delegated to the field service. What guarantee do you have that the participants are typical consumers?
8. Many moderators run out of steam about halfway into the second group simply because they are not really enjoying the process of interacting with the participants.

Table 7.1   (Continued)

Group 4 Questions — *Avoiding biases in qualitative research.*
What is bias?

Bias can be introduced during the recruiting phase.   T   F
Does the facility impact bias? If so, how?

How does the moderator introduce bias?

How can you avoid bias in reports and debriefings?

If you need advice for group 4 questions , see the next exhibit .

Bias and Qualitative Research

The bias problems of quantitative research are also relevant to qualitative research. Bias is introduced into the qualitative process during recruiting, during the research interview or focus group, and also during the analysis.

Recruiting. White middle-class individuals appear in qualitative research projects in numbers disproportionate to their presence in the marketplace. Be careful not to sell the study to your recruits as an easy way to make a little extra money.

Facility. Formal decor, physical discomfort, or cramped seating may make it difficult for respondents to relax and share their feelings.

Interview or group process. The greatest potential for distorting the research process can occur during the interview. The moderator must take care not to prejudice responses. Respondents may look for clues in the moderator that will influence how they respond. Emphasize honest opinions and that it's all right to disagree with others or to say things that are controversial. You might want to check the following in your moderator:

Table 7.1 (Continued)

- Does the moderator have strong reactions or opinions about the topic?
- Does the moderator expect to hear certain things?
- Does the moderator seem awkward with difficult questions?
- Is the moderator affected by the characteristics of the respondents—their dress, race, or education?

Interview structure. Question order or interview approach may cause systematic error.

Analysis. How does the moderator report the results of the focus group? Is the focus group taped, or does the moderator rely on memory? A major source of bias occurs when the moderator tries to recollect what was said or is influenced by his or her point of view when presenting the findings.

Group 5 Questions—*Projective strategies*

Art therapy allows you to probe the unconscious.	T	F
When using art as a strategy, you should encourage people not to use stick figures.	T	F
A typical drawing exercise will last about one hour.	T	F

List the types of things you should pay attention to in people's drawings.

1. _____
2. _____
3. _____
4. _____
5. _____
6. _____
7. _____

* If you need advice for group 5 questions, see the next exhibit.

Projective Techniques

By having participants draw pictures, you can tap the unconscious. Sometimes consumers might be unable to express their feelings verbally, but they may be able to express themselves in a drawing. For example, in trying to understand the images of weight training facilities, a group moderator asked a group of women to draw a picture of a weight room. Weight rooms described as intimidating were

Table 7.1 (Continued)

frequently drawn with free-weight equipment and big muscle-bound men. A weight room described as more friendly was shown with machines, smaller weights, and smaller people.

The moderator should reassure participants that this is not an art class so that they are not embarrassed if they cannot draw very well. Ask them to use as many colors as they like and to avoid stick figures if possible. As we found in the weight training exercise, the size of the body parts may be clues to what the drawing says.

Drawings usually generate group discussions and are a useful way of getting participants involved. Allow about ten minutes for the drawing. Each participant should explain the drawing to the group. The moderator should cue in on key features, saying, for example, "I see you have given all your men in the weight room big muscles. Why?" Here are some other features to ask about:

- What feelings does the picture evoke in the drawer? In the group?
- Is there anything unusual about the use of color? Why are all your men brown?
- What is different about the people or the environment? Are all the women blonde, skinny, overweight?
- What equipment is included?
- What or who is missing?
- What is in the central feature of the drawing?
- What is big and what is small?

Take time later to do additional interpretation of the drawings. Pin the drawings on a wall and study them for a few days while you are analyzing the focus group data.

NOW CONDUCT YOUR FOCUS GROUP.

What Do You Want to Know?

One of the chief problems with research is selecting the types of questions to ask, their level of precision, and their level of measurement.

Types of Questions You Can Ask. Suppose you are studying the effect high health club fees have on membership. You want to find out how people feel about health club fees. Here are some angles you might consider using to tackle the issue:

Do people think that health clubs are overpriced?
How much do they think a health club membership should be?
How certain are they that health clubs are overpriced?
Do they feel that overpriced health clubs are a problem in society?

Table 7.2 How to Write a Focus Group Report

Suggested Length: This depends on the nature of the focus group topic. Usually three to five pages are sufficient.
Objective: To provide your client with the highlights of the most significant findings of your focus group research

Topics	What You Should Accomplish	Details
Research Objectives	In general terms, briefly describe the type of information the focus group was designed to provide.	
Focus Group Overview	Briefly discuss the value of a focus group.	You may want to tell your readers that focus groups are useful in providing input into the quantitative survey that will follow and that they help in providing a context that should make interpretations of the survey results clearer.
Methodology	Briefly discuss the methodology you used.	Tell the reader how you selected the focus groups.
Major Findings	Discuss primary findings.	Organize the findings in some type of order. Answer the following questions for each finding: ➢ What does it mean? ➢ What impact does it have?
Summary	Briefly summarize your general impressions of the data you gathered from the focus groups. Inform your reader that the results are useful in developing the questionnaire for the survey and helping interpret the eventual results.	Stress that the results are interpretive and impressionistic and that confirmation of the findings awaits the results of the survey of a truly representative sample of the population segments that are of interest.
Moderator's Guide: This should include a detailed outline under four headings.	Provide the Moderator's Guide you used. I. Introduction (10 minutes)	Who are you and why are you doing this research. Stress that everyone is an expert, you want to hear from everyone, and there are no right or wrong answers.
	II. Preliminary Topics (5–10 minutes)	Have participants introduce themselves. Have them briefly state their feelings toward [your topic].
	III. The Main Topic (60 minutes)	
	IV. Conclusion (10 minutes)	Allow participants a debriefing period. Thank them for their participation.

What do they think causes overpricing of health clubs?

Do they think high health club fees are inevitable?

What do they think should be done about high club fees?

What are they willing to pay personally for a health club membership?

How certain are they that they would join a health club even if the price were not a factor?

Clearly, we could attack each issue from many different directions. You must be quite certain of the type of information you want to obtain from your study. You may measure what people think health club fees should be instead of what they *feel about* health club fees. Go back to the objective of your project and select questions that pertain only to that objective.

Required Precision   How much detail do you want to obtain? If you are measuring age, for example, do you want the exact age of your respondents, or will categories of age do? Be careful when you answer this question. If you are conducting a survey among company employees, for example, you may decide that collapsing all employees into two age categories (eighteen to forty-five and forty-six and older) will be sufficient. You might want to know what factors affect exercise behavior for the age categories eighteen to twenty-four, twenty-five to thirty-four, and so on—information you will lose by collapsing the data into two age categories. Similarly, if respondents are single, do you want to know whether they are divorced, separated, or never married? There is no simple answer to how precise you need to be. It depends on the purpose of the data and how you intend to use the information.

Level of Measurement   Questions may be open-ended or closed-ended.

Open-ended—the respondent provides his or her own answer to the question. For example, you may ask, "What is the prime reason you compete in the triathlon?" The respondent will give you an explanation, which you will record in detail. You must code open-ended questions before you can enter the data into the computer.

Closed-ended —the respondent selects from a list that best represents his or her response. For example: Which of the following best represents the most important reason you participate in triathlon races?

Select one

1[ ]To improve my looks

2[ ]To lose weight

3[ ]To have fun

4[ ]To improve my health

5[ ]To feel a sense of accomplishment

6[ ]To test myself against others my age

7[ ] To be with my friends

8[ ]Other (please specify)

Closed-ended responses such as these assume that you have identified the domi-nant reasons people participate in triathlon races. For this type of response you must do considerable exploratory research by way of focus groups and depth in-terviews to ensure relevancy. The danger of the closed-ended question is that re-spondents might feel that two of the categories equally represent their reasons for participating. It is beneficial if you include a statement that directs respondents to select the *one best* answer. The advantage of closed-ended questions is that you can enter them directly into the computer.

Other Considerations   Make your questions clear and unambiguous. If you are not completely familiar with the topic, your questions are likely to be vague. Avoid double-barreled questions and beware double-barreled statements like, "My company should stop spending so much money on exercise facilities and spend more money on improving the work environment." A respondent might agree fully with a reduction in money spent on exercise facilities. On the other hand, he or she might totally disagree that the company should spend more money on improving the work environment. If you use the word *and* in a ques-tion, make sure it isn't double-barreled. Ask yourself if your respondents are ca-pable of answering your questions reliably. In assessing physically activity behavior, for example, we commonly ask people to estimate how often they did such-and-such an activity during the previous twelve months. Those who never participated in the activity or those who participate on a regular schedule, for ex-ample, they jog three times per week, can be quite accurate with their response. All those individuals in between have a difficult time estimating whether it was twenty-five times or thirty-five times that they did the activity. Also make sure you ask questions that are relevant to respondents. Finally, you should try to keep your questions short and to the point.

Writing a Questionnaire Assignment

Select one research question from your focus group research and then write a one-page to two-page questionnaire that will provide you with the answer to this question. Write a paragraph clearly stating your research objective. Test your questionnaire on six to twelve people. Do they have any comments on how you might improve your questionnaire? When you have finished testing your ques-tionnaire and are satisfied that it will provide the information you need, move to the next phase.

Phases 3 and 4. Data Collection and Writing the Research Report

After you write your questionnaire, you will generally hire a market research firm or some other qualified data collection agency to collect the data. You will likely have hired this company early in the research process. For this assignment, though, you should now select a sample and collect data from a group of con-sumers. The questions in Table 7.3 will give you a basic understanding of the survey process. Once you have your data, you must write a research report. If you are unfamiliar with report writing, consult the outline provided in Table 7.4.

Table 7.3   Test Your Knowledge on Surveys.

Answer these questions before conducting your survey. If you need help with the answers consult the exhibit indicated by the asterisk (*).

Group 1 Questions: *Judging the quality of a survey.*

➤ With random samples you can make generalizations about a population based on data collected from a few people.   T   F

➤ What is a sampling frame?

_____

➤ What is the relationship between response rate and reliability of the data?

_____

➤ Describe briefly what is meant by a sampling error.

_____

➤ Describe briefly what is meant by a nonrandom error.

_____

*If you need advice for group 1 questions, see the next exhibit.

Judging the Quality of Surveys

Survey quality varies considerably. For example, a poll of employees who voluntarily fill out a health-risk appraisal is not a valid survey of the entire employee population. This method self-selects people. Only samples where every member of the population has a known chance of inclusion in the survey can be projected to the larger population. The accuracy of a sample is only as good as the source from which the sample is drawn. This is known as the *sampling frame*. A sample from a list of employees in one company is a reasonable sampling frame for a survey of employee physical activity behavior in that specific company. However, it cannot describe employee physical activity behavior in all companies.

Table 7.3 (Continued)

Sampling can get complicated, especially when the sample has a stratified design. Stratified designs are often used to capture a relatively rare group. Stratification by race, geographical area, and household type are common. In instances where a comprehensive, accurate list of the population you want to target is not readily available, other forms of sampling are necessary, like *cluster samples*. Cluster samples are based on physical elements such as cities, blocks, or schools. Most use a random sample of elements, such as city blocks. This is called stage 1. Further sampling is usually needed before an accurate list is ready. This is called stage 2. Although cluster designs are cost effective, they are less efficient than most other sample designs. The sampling errors are larger. Also, many software packages do not adjust for sample design effects.

The percentage of people who answered a questionnaire, the *response rate*, is also important. Surveys range from response rates of 95 percent to 40 percent or lower. The higher the response rate, the more reliable the data.

There are two types of survey errors: (1) *random* or *sampling errors* and (2) *nonrandom error*, otherwise known as bias. The difference between a sample estimate and the true value in the population is a random error. If the average age of a population is twenty-five but the average age of people in the sample is twenty-two, you have a random error. It is possible to estimate the size of random error. In contrast, a nonrandom error, which is systematic, can arise from a poorly designed questionnaire, coding errors, or an incomplete sampling frame. Unfortunately, a nonrandom error cannot be detected or adjusted using statistical procedures; it is a hidden error that often leads you to the wrong conclusion. You will need to study the questionnaire and interviewing instructions in order to detect nonrandom error.

Group 2 Questions: *Optimum sample sizes.*

➤ The cost of a research project is related directly to the sample size.   T   F
➤ Research buyers do not always act rationally.   T   F
➤ Briefly explain why some samples may be larger than necessary.

If you need advice for group 2 questions, see the next exhibit.

Table 7.3   (Continued)

Optimum Sample Size

Establishing an optimum sample size is one of the most difficult things to decide. The cost of a research project is often directly related to the sample size. For this reason, you will usually want to keep the sample size to a minimum.

But it's not quite as easy as that. There will be times when larger samples are needed simply because of the type of analyses you want to do. Emotional factors also come into play. Some of the consumers of your research will frequently have a set sample size in mind. If you are below that level, they will have little faith in your data. Textbooks are helpful in discussing the concepts and theories involved in determining sample size. However, these discussions often ignore reality. The questionnaire length, budget, schedule, subject attitudes, and client expectations all have a direct impact on sample size decisions.

Textbooks and professional research suppliers treat sample size as a technical decision. They use tables that give the relative confidence that can be placed on the results as the sample size gets larger. The most difficult question to answer is "How much precision is enough?" Statistically, we can easily measure sample precision. However, people, pose a problem, for psychological issues and politics often become intertwined in the decision. In addition, whereas budget and resources limitations may restrain the research effort, technical and emotional factors may inflate research budgets unnecessarily. You need to be sensitive to both the practical and the emotional factors associated with any decision process.

Table 7.4 (Continued)

After the data have been collected and the analysis completed, your next task is to write a final report that will act to disseminate the findings. You must tailor the report to the needs of your audience. Use clear writing. Where possible use present tense, short paragraphs, short sentences, and short words. Avoid vague modifiers, jargon, and buzzwords. Your report should clearly separate research fact from your personal opinion. Here is a guideline for writing an effective report.

Parts	What You Should Accomplish	Details
Purpose of the study	Clearly state the purpose of the study.	
Executive Summary	This orients your reader to the general study findings.	Arrange the information in order of importance.
Methodology	The methodology should include ➤ Sample source ➤ Types of interviews ➤ Number of completed interviews ➤ Nature of respondents ➤ Location of respondents for interviewing ➤ Projectability of the results	This section should give all the necessary information so that the reader can understand the reliability and validity of the study.
Findings (a) Tables	The tables present the numbers.	Condense tables if necessary. When it enhances your reader's understanding of the data use graphic displays.
(b) Analysis	After each table briefly tell your reader the concepts indicated in the table. Use bullet paragraphs to point out key information in the table. Use insightful ways to compare data. If necessary, use data from other parts of the research or prior research. Look for interesting differences among subgroups.	Ask these key questions: ❑ What do the data mean? ❑ What impact do they have? ❑ What have we learned? DO NOT simply repeat obvious information in the table.
Actionability	Take your reader beyond descriptive statistics and provide diagnostic insights.	What do you need to do, given the research findings? What portion of the information can be used to enhance marketing or communication efforts?

SUMMARY

This chapter has addressed the sports manager's need for and acquisition of information. It has provided you with an outline of the market research process and pointed out some of the definitional problems a researcher encounters. You also learned that there are three broad research methodologies: survey research, experimental research, and open-ended explorations. You have gained some hands-on experience by conducting a focus group interview, you have developed a questionnaire, and you have written a research report. If you have done a good job here, you should think about putting this project into your portfolio to show a future employer.

Now you are ready to worry about how you are going to finance your idea. Sports organizations frequently use sponsorship as a major financial tool. In the next chapter I will introduce you to this financial medium.

STRATEGIC PLAN WORKSHEET–CHAPTER 7

What You Should Know about Market Research for Your Event

Your Goal: ....

To provide an overview of the research you have done that contributed to the development of your event

Questions you should answer:

Check when completed

- What research did you do?
- Where and under what conditions was research conducted?
- What were the objectives of your research?
- What research must still be done?
- What did your research tell you about how your product idea should be designed to meet target market needs?
- What do the research results tell you about your
  - ✔ potential participant consumers?
  - ✔ potential sponsors?
- What spin-off products did you discover during your research?
- Have you tested your product idea in the marketplace?
  - ✔ ease of implementation
  - ✔ primary and secondary consumer acceptance
  - ✔ labor instruction or training required
- What major problems did your research uncover?

REFERENCES ....

Bogdan, R., and S. J. Taylor. *Introduction to Qualitative Methods.* New York: John Wiley and Sons, 1975.

Clader, B. J. "Focus Groups and the Nature of Qualitative Marketing Research." *Journal of Marketing Research* 14 (1977): 353–64.

Cook, T. D., and D. T. Campbell. *Quasi-Experimentation: Designs and Analysis Issues for Field Settings.* Chicago: Rand McNally, 1979.

Higginbotham, J. B., and K. K. Cox. *Focus Group Interviews.* Chicago: American Marketing Association, 1979.

McClave, J. T., and P. G. Benson. *Statistics for Business and Economics.* San Francisco: Dellen Publishing Company, 1985.

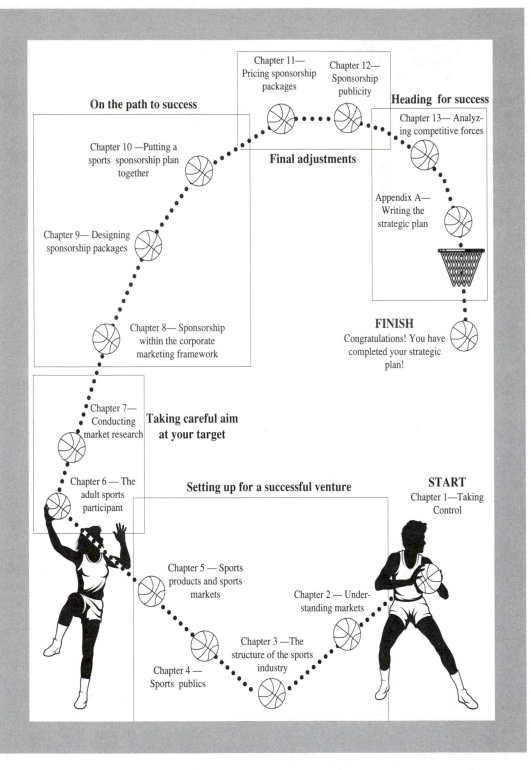

On the path to success

Chapter 11— Pricing sponsorship packages

Chapter 12— Sponsorship publicity

Heading for success

Chapter 13— Analyzing competitive forces

Chapter 10 —Putting a sports sponsorship plan together

Final adjustments

Chapter 9— Designing sponsorship packages

Appendix A— Writing the strategic plan

Chapter 8— Sponsorship within the corporate marketing framework

FINISH

Congratulations! You have completed your strategic plan!

Chapter 7— Conducting market research

Taking careful aim at your target

Chapter 6 — The adult sports participant

START

Chapter 1—Taking Control

Setting up for a successful venture

Chapter 5 — Sports products and sports markets

Chapter 2 — Understanding markets

Chapter 3 —The structure of the sports industry

Chapter 4 — Sports publics

Sponsorship within the Corporate Marketing Framework

•••••••••••••••••••••••••••••••••••••••

> In the factory we make cosmetics. In the store we sell hope.
> — *Charles Revson*
> *President of Revlon, Inc.*

You have invited John Barr, Director, Regional Site Communications of Eastman Kodak Company, to your class to speak about his company's sponsorship philosophy and programs. You arrive early so that you can get a front-row seat. After a few minutes your professor calls the class to order. A hush falls over the room, and your professor introduces Mr. Barr. "Thank you for inviting me," he says.[1] "I have been asked to talk to you about how Kodak uses sponsorship to boost sales. I'm going to do that, but I also want to talk more generally about sponsorship—what it is, how it works, and how Kodak has used it to their advantage." Barr continues: "Business sponsorship is now a major source of funding for many sports events because more and more companies have discovered that sports sponsorship can be a powerful marketing tool. The question is: How can we maximize the effectiveness of sponsorship for both business and sport?

"To be effective, sponsorship of any event must serve the interest of four constituent groups:

- It must serve the business interest of the sponsoring company.
- It must serve the best interests of the event and its participants.
- It must have a positive impact upon the sponsor's direct customers—the dealers and retailers who sell its products.
- It must benefit the consumers who buy those products.

"Sponsorship is not philanthropy. To be effective, it must serve the business interest of the sponsoring company. While this might sound hard-headed, it does, in fact, make good sense both for businesses and event organizers. In today's highly competitive, cost-conscious business environment, companies must see a positive return for their sponsorship dollars. The bottom line is simple: Sponsorship must increase sales. From the point of view of event organizers, that's probably a good thing. After all, which company is more likely to make a sponsorship commitment, a company that anticipates it will increase sales, or one that views sponsorship as "charity" or as simply an exercise in "image polishing"?

ADVANTAGES OF SPONSORSHIP

Why should a company use sponsorship to achieve its business objectives—rather than other types of advertising or sales promotions? There are a number of excellent reasons.

It Creates Identity   A sponsorship creates a link between the identity of the event and the identity of a brand or product. For many consumers, that link translates into a strong quality message. Surveys of American consumers indicate that:

- 33% believe that "official product" designation is awarded to the best products
- 33% would be inclined to buy a product because its maker is a sponsor
- 44% felt that sponsorship raised their opinion of a company
- Further, these surveys indicate that the greatest awareness of the product/sponsorship link is in the prime middle income group. In Kodak's case, this is the target group for the majority of our consumer products.

Increases Sales   By themselves, these general benefits are not enough to justify sponsorship. To gain maximum benefit from a sponsorship, a company must also have well focused and reachable objectives. These will vary from company to company and from event to event. But increasing sales will be first and foremost.

For example, in the case of Kodak Film products, our sponsorship objectives are very specific:

- We want people to buy more film.
- We want them to try types of film they haven't previously used.
- We want them to have the film processed by a Kodak Colorwatch dealer.
- And we want them to act immediately.

In addition to such product-specific objectives, other sponsorship goals might well include:

- Maximizing brand awareness.
- Increasing brand loyalty.
- Establishing new contacts with decision makers in the public and private sectors. Kodak's past sponsorship of the FIFA under-16 Soccer Championships in China, for example, opened doors to key trade officials and helped pave the way for Kodak's entry into the Chinese market.

Promotes Business-to-Business Contacts   Sponsorship can also help promote business-to-business contacts and sales by providing access to other sponsoring organizations. That can be especially important for large, diversified companies like Kodak. Kodak is well known as a photographic company. Not so well known is the fact that we are also a major supplier of products ranging from copiers to blood analyzers . . . from electronic imaging systems to biochemical products . . . from pharmaceuticals to mass memory systems. So one of our sponsoring objectives is to "bundle" participation by multiple Kodak business units. For example, Kodak has been a supporter of the Special Olympics since 1972. The company was a principal sponsor of the recent International Winter Special Olympic Games, in Reno, Nevada.

In addition to providing financial and human resources support to the Games, Kodak's participation involved six Kodak lines of business. Among other products and services, these businesses provided:

- The copier/duplicators used in scoring and keeping statistics
- Films, photo supplies, and on-site technical support for news photographers covering the Games
- Video ID systems for credentialing participants
- Blood analyzers and strep-throat test kits for medical support
- A photo information center for amateur photographers
- 24-hour processing of color prints.

This "bundling" of participation by multiple business units helped maximize the effectiveness of our sponsorship, both for Kodak . . . and for organizers and participants in the Special Olympics. The 6,000 volunteers who supervised the events benefited from the products, services, and financial support Kodak and other sponsors provided. The 1,500 athletes and their families were given an important opportunity to join in sports events that recognized exceptional effort and spirit. And from a business point of view, sponsorship showcased Kodak's capability to other organizations participating in the Games. The Reno Games provided a dramatic illustration of the value of such business-to-business contacts. Kodak sponsorship of the Games helped close over a quarter million dollars in copier sales to Harrah's Casino in Reno. Here's how our sales manager described the impact of our sponsorship:

> As you know, the sell cycle here has been a long, hard road. The people at Harrah's were very impressed with Kodak's commitment both of people and finances to the Special Olympics. It's my feeling that as a result of this sponsorship,

we were able to complete the final transaction. It's nice to see something that was done for a good cause can also give us an exceptionally positive marketing influence!

Clearly, that wouldn't have happened had Kodak's involvement in the Games been limited to a financial contribution alone. What I'm suggesting, in other words, is that to be most effective, sponsorship really has to be a partnership. It has to add value for all participants in the event. Let me give you another example:

Kodak enjoys a valuable sponsorship agreement with New York State's Olympic Authority. Like any good partnership, this long term contract benefits all the parties involved. The mission of the Olympic Authority is to promote New York's Lake Placid Region. Among other goals, the organization seeks to use sports to leverage the vacation value and improve the economy of the region. The photogenic beauty of the Adirondack area, and the fact that over two million tourists who visit the region annually, influenced Kodak's decision to form a partnership with the Authority. A strong Kodak presence in the Lake Placid area is a catalyst for increased brand visibility, broader retail penetration, and increased sales of Kodak products and services.

One key to accomplishing these goals is through promotion of a highly photogenic, Olympic-related sports venue. The Kodak Sports Park is the first permanent freestyle skiing training center of its kind in North America. The 1991 World Freestyle Championships were televised nationally from the park area with a 50,000 attendance. The overall sponsorship of the park, and subsequent freestyle competitions, has positioned Kodak at the center of a rapidly growing sport that is also generating increasing popular appeal.

Another element of our contract is the Kodak-sponsored Olympic Tour. This is a self-guided automobile tour of the Olympic Authority facilities. Sponsorship of the Tour, which provides hundreds of wonderful picture-taking opportunities, is a natural tie-in for Kodak. The partnership has paid off in increased retail sales. In fact, Kodak consumer product sales in the area increased 25% last year.

Constituent Benefits   During the first year of our sponsorship, Kodak's focus was on consumer products. Beginning this year, additional business units are taking a more visible role in the Lake Placid area. Last January, our Edicon group installed a video identification system in the Olympic Center. Professional Photographic Division is establishing press centers at select Lake Placid competitions. It was also because of our sponsorship that Snomax—a snow-inducer produced by one of our subsidiaries—is regularly used to make artificial snow at Gore and Whiteface ski resorts.

As other Kodak business units "come on board," we think the value of this sponsorship to the company will continue to grow. For example, the potential for our business-to-business units to make sales contacts with state officials in Albany is an invaluable benefit.

The other constituents of the sponsorship also benefit:

- Clearly, the sponsorship helps achieve the Olympic Authority's objective of increasing the vacation appeal of the region
- Athletes benefit through enhanced facilities and promotion of their sports
- Kodak dealers and retailers in the Lake Placid area benefit from improved sales
- And visitors to the area benefit from the added value of new facilities and enhanced opportunities to enjoy this unique region.

We're very enthusiastic about the Lake Placid sponsorship. But for prestige, immense popularity and sheer audience, nothing beats the Olympics. The Olympic themes of international good will and the development of high physical and moral qualities provide a natural link to a company like Kodak. Our 1988 global Olympic program buttressed our own commitment to competition, quality and excellence. The challenge was to link those broad, positive themes to Kodak product promotions. The stronger the tie between a sponsor's product and an event, the more effective a sponsorship will be.

A good example of this was the linkage between the Olympics and Kodak's Gold Top batteries. In the States, we developed a theme which used Olympic excitement and Americans' natural impulse to root for the "home team" to communicate the unique qualities of our product. This tied the strong Olympic themes of quality, leadership and excellence directly to a new Kodak product. This theme was further reinforced as Kodak publicized its donation of batteries to all American athletes. This example illustrates several important points about maximizing sponsorship effectiveness:

- First, choose the right event to sponsor on behalf of the company, its customers and its products
- Second, develop a theme that ties the product directly to the event
- And third, ensure you commit sufficient human and financial resources, in addition to the cost of the event, to merchandise it fully.

In the near term, these keys maximize the marketing impact of the sponsorship. Longer term, these keys reinforce the company's image of excellence and strengthen ties with both direct and indirect customers.

Business Customers Most people associate sponsorship with boosting retail sales of specific consumer products. Yet, it's important to again emphasize that many consumer-based corporations also utilize sponsorship as a way to market their products to commercial and industrial customers. At Kodak, for example, we have many separate lines of businesses. Most of them sell, not to the consumer market, but to other businesses and organizations. So clearly, we have an obligation to promote more than just consumer films and cameras. For that reason we consistently look for opportunities to tie our non-consumer products into an event contract. As we've seen, a sponsorship may put a corporation into contact with government officials, other companies, schools, financial and healthcare institutions, and others who represent business-to-business opportunities.

So, event sponsorships can have an additive effect. When effectively merchandised across all product lines, they can contribute to a company's overall corporate visibility while helping to unify its marketing efforts.

Evaluation of Sponsorship Effectiveness

So far, I've been talking about maximizing the effectiveness of a sponsorship. Let me conclude by asking how companies and event organizers can evaluate that effectiveness. Perhaps the best approach is to ask how well the sponsorship served each of its major constituent groups. As we noted earlier, the sponsorship must serve the business interests of the sponsoring company. In evaluating the success of a sponsorship in serving these business interests, there are a number of objective measures:

- Sales are a key indicator. Did they move up during the sponsorship period?
- The success of promotions can be judged from the number of coupons redeemed or rebate responses received.
- On-site sales, attendance, and the amount of money raised by an event can indicate the number of people reached.
- Surveys of attendees or customers can tell us whether we reached certain objectives.

In addition to such objective measures, there are a number of subjective, but very important ways to judge the effectiveness of a sponsorship:

- Did all pertinent areas of a company support the sponsorship?
- Did it open new doors that resulted in new contacts, new contracts, or stronger business relations with customers?
- Did the sponsoring company achieve a higher profile, increase brand awareness, or increase market share?

If the answer to most of these questions is yes, the sponsorship was successful from the company's point of view. But companies are only one constituent of an effective sponsorship. Just as important are the organizers of the event and its participants. Here, the simplest measure of success, obviously, is financial. After all, most sponsorships are awarded on a financial basis. But as the examples I've cited show, effective sponsorship often involves more than simply raising revenues. For example:

- Did sponsorship promote interest in the event?
- Did it increase media attention, attendance or public awareness?
- Did sponsorship help meet the overall objectives of the event organizers?

Often these objectives reach beyond the success of a specific event to include broader goals, such as promoting tourism, in the case of New York's Olympic Authority, or changing public perceptions about the mentally or physically disabled, as in the case of the Special Olympics. Sponsorship should also have a positive impact upon the sponsor's direct customers— the dealers and retailers who sell its products. For example:

- Did it increase product movement and store traffic for dealers and retailers?
- Did it increase overall demand for the product, creating new retail opportunities—as our Olympic Authority sponsorship has in the Lake Placid area?
- Did sponsorship produce a long-term increase in retail demand, or was it a "one-shot" surge?

Finally, sponsorship must add value for the consumers who buy the sponsor's products. At the most basic level, this may be as simple as a special offer or rebate, tied to the event. But that's only one way sponsorship may add value. Companies might also ask:

- Did it create new opportunities for consumers to benefit from the product?
- Did the sponsored event or activity provide a direct benefit for consumers? Our Olympic Tour, for example, provides visitors to the Adirondack area with a unique service.
- Did the promotion add value by informing consumers about a new or worthwhile event such as freestyle skiing or the Special Olympics?

As questions like these show, maximizing the effectiveness of a sponsorship program requires much more than the willingness to sign a check. It requires carefully thought out objectives, intense effort, and a close working partnership between corporate sponsors and event organizers.

Is sponsorship worth the effort? In the case of sports events, such as the Olympics, the answer from Kodak is a definite, yes. Sponsorship of quality sports events has long been a tradition at Kodak. It's a tradition that combines the human drama and achievement of sport with the equally challenging demands of leadership in today's highly competitive global markets. The Olympic motto— "Faster, higher, stronger"—could describe our own determination to continue to be a world leader in quality, excellence and competitive strength in the markets we serve. Kodak's support for sports reflects a natural partnership. It's a partnership we're proud of, one which will continue to benefit both the company and the events we sponsor."

Here, John Barr gives you some idea as to how one specific company thinks about its sponsorship program. But ask ten Chief Executive Officers (CEOs) from other companies about how sponsorship fits within their marketing framework, and you will likely get ten different responses. To use the proverbial analogy, the answer depends a whole lot on what part of the elephant the blind person is touching. How do you even begin to conceive an elephant when all you feel is a trunk, a leg, a tail, or an ear?

Let's analyze some examples that will illustrate the problem we have.

- When Tang associated itself with the Mother's Against Drunk Driving (MADD), its purpose was to enhance its image beyond a breakfast drink and become a symbol of righteousness. In the words of Dan Schrieber, developer of the Tang MADD sponsorship campaign, "Righteousness is worth a whole lot more than plain old vitamin C any day of the week."[2] How does image enhancement fit within the marketing framework?

• The Rice Growers of California, a group of small rice farmers, ventured into sports for better *public awareness*. How does this fit into the marketing framework?

• Cadillac uses sponsorship to *reach out and touch* its markets directly. What is happening here?

• Coke bought the rights to be the exclusive soft drink of the 1984 Olympic Games, and it was the only soft drink sold in Olympic venues. What use of sponsorship is this?

• What about IBM's association with golf? When IBM becomes the official computer of a PGA stop and sets up hospitality tents on site for potential customers, what use of sponsorship is this?

• Many companies, including RJR Nabisco, maintain a stable of athletes. RJR Nabisco calls them Team Nabisco. In the past the athletes on this team were paid more for occasional public appearances than the average senior vice president: Bill Meredith got $500,000 a year, Frank Gifford $413,000 (plus a New York office and apartment), golfer Ben Crenshaw $400,000, and golfer Fuzzy Zoeller $300,000. The king was Jack Nicklaus, who commanded $1 million a year. According to Ross Johnson, CEO of RJR Nabisco, "jocks" yield big benefits in wooing supermarket people. But the distinction between corporate and personal use of Team Nabisco by Johnson was quite often blurred.

> LPGA pro Judy Dickinson also gave Laurie Johnson (Ross Johnson's wife) golf lessons. Gifford emceed benefits for Johnson's favorite charities like the New York Boys Club. A pair of retired New York Giant fullbacks, Alex Webster and Tucker Frederickson, maintained offices at the Team Nabisco office in Jupiter, Florida; Frederickson ran an investment counseling business from his.
>
> For all the money Johnson doled out for Team Nabisco, some of the athletes weren't easily managed. Nicklaus was notoriously difficult. For one thing, he didn't like playing golf with Johnson's best customers, which was his highest and best use. And he considered himself above the task of working the room solo at some Nabisco function. Although he was making more money than anyone at RJR Nabisco except Johnson and Horrigan, the "Golden Bear" growled at doing more than a half-dozen appearances a year. After several run-ins with subordinates, an arrangement was struck where only Johnson and Horrigan could personally tap Nicklaus's services.
>
> Then there was the O. J. Simpson problem. Simpson, the football star and sometime sports announcer, was being paid $250,000 a year, but was a perennial no-show at Team Nabisco events. So was Don Mattingly of the New York Yankees, who also pulled down a quarter million. (Bryan Burrough and John Helyar, *Barbarians at the Gate* [New York: Harper & Row, 1990], p. 96)

How does Team Nabisco fit into the RJR Nabisco sponsorship framework? By now you probably see the point. There is no single answer to the question. The problem we have is how to begin drawing the elephant from the description we get from all those independent blind folks? One way to begin tackling the process is to examine the parts as closely as possible and then piece them together into a conceptual model that captures all the ways corporations use sponsorship.

SPONSORSHIP AS A UNIQUE MEDIUM

Sponsorship has distinctively different qualities from other communication mix elements such as advertising, public relations (PR), personal selling, and sales promotion. Events allow a company an intimate relationship with its consumers. We can assume that people attend events because they want to; therefore, because they are relaxed and their guard is down, they are in a more receptive mood to receive product messages. Sponsorship integrates the energy, excitement, and emotion of the event with a consumer's experience with the product or company sales rep. Since most events reach a narrow audience, they have been less attractive to mass marketers. In this case events are generally used to complement traditional marketing efforts. For marketers who want to reach a highly segmented target, however, events can be an ideal vehicle.

Sponsorship, then, has special properties not available with traditional communication mediums. Because of its intimacy and segmentation qualities, marketers are trying to use sponsorship to counteract problems they face in reaching their consumers in today's cluttered marketplace. Instead of forcing customers to come face to face with a product in a showroom or supermarket, sponsorship allows a marketer to take the product directly to the consumer. Sponsorship is a way to interact with consumers on an emotional level.

Of all the elements in the marketing mix, sponsorship is the only one that exposes people to a product in an environment encompassing their lifestyles. A television commercial interrupts a consumer's enjoyment of a favorite program. Sponsorship, however, does not generally intrude in such an obvious manner. And as we saw in the Ross Johnson case, sponsorship can enhance a consumer's enjoyment of a favorite pastime by allowing the consumer access to professional athletes. It is lifestyle compatibility at its best.

What Type of Medium Is It?

Let's examine the sponsorship medium further. Depending upon corporate objectives, the sponsorship medium has two functions: It amplifies a message and it aims the message.

Amplify a Message   Sometimes the function is to amplify the message. By amplify we mean that sponsorship can enhance the visibility of the message so that it is more noticeable to the desired target. Take the Rice Growers Association as an example. This is a group of small rice farmers who have joined forces so that they can be more competitive in the marketplace. Since the Rice Growers are in competition with a very large company, Uncle Ben's, they needed to find ways to shout their message louder than their competitors. They decided to sponsor bicycle racing as one approach to accomplish this.[3] Fratelli Ice Cream uses sponsorship for similar reasons: They found the constant clutter of traditional media drowned their messages. Sponsorship allowed them to separate their voice from the crowd.[4] In both these instances the marketing director assumes that the company will be more noticeable if it associates with the favorite pursuits of potential consumers in an uncluttered environment. It is in this manner that sponsorship enhances or, as we say, amplifies the message.

Aim the Message   You can also think of sponsorship as a scope on a rifle. A scope permits a more accurate aim. Marketers frequently use sponsorship to minimize the inefficiencies of the communication process. It allows them to zero in on a "captured" target group. The target is captured in the sense that potential consumers are in one place for some common purpose. This makes them easier communication targets, with the sponsorship platform the targeting apparatus. Cadillac is a good example. The upscale car segment is one of the fastest-growing and most fiercely competitive arenas of the automobile industry. Never before has innovative targeting been so important in this particular market. It is now necessary to go beyond advertising to reach out to consumer markets directly. Events accomplish this for Cadillac, and they will become even more important as the marketers of this particular car position it for the 1990s.[5]

How the Medium Works

If sponsorship performs an amplifying and aiming function, what business strategies are accomplished? The answer is threefold: communicating, targeting, and differentiating. Let us now examine how these three relate to the effective commercial use of sponsorship.

> **POINT 1: Most** corporations that use sponsorship are not *marketing* in the accepted definition of marketing. They are communicating, and sports are the communication medium.

To understand this statement we must briefly review the marketing concept. To many people, the word *marketing* usually means advertising. In the sports world it often means sales promotion efforts such as "bat days." However, advertising and sales promotion are only a small part of the total marketing process, which in fact encompasses four interacting activities:

- identifying the needs of consumers
- conceptualizing those needs into something the consumer wants

- communicating the conceptualization of those needs to the consumer
- distributing the product

Or, in the words of Theodore Levitt, "marketing starts with trying to understand what people want and value, looking at their choices and resources (like money, time, etc.) available to them, and then designing products, delivery systems, sales programs, communications, price and a lot of other things appropriate to what you've found out about those people."[6] By the time most companies decide to link up with sports, the product (which may also be a service or idea) is already available. The problem the manager faces at this point is how to effectively communicate via the communication mix tools, namely, advertising, personal selling, publicity, and sales promotion. It may simply be the case that the CEO wants to give exposure for the company or to express goodwill among many important groups. Aside from the consumer, these groups might include employees, distributors, retailers, and legislative groups.

Marketers are seeking new and more effective communication strategies because of the clutter now inherent within traditional media. In order to sell products business managers must be able to tell consumers about their products. In the early 1980s this became an increasingly difficult task as corporate marketers found themselves battling in a world of information clutter. With advertising the most pervasive element of the communication mix, total ad spending in the United States reached $123 billion, or almost $500 for every man, woman, and child. Of that, $40 billion went toward advertising in national consumer media, including magazines; newspapers; outdoor, network, spot, syndicated, and cable TV; and network and spot radio. Another $83 billion was spent on unmeasured media such as direct mail, promotions, cooperative programs (joint ventures between manufacturer and retailers), couponing, catalogs, and *sponsorship*.

Going hand in hand with the clutter is rising advertising costs and audience fragmentation, which dilutes the advertising effectiveness of the traditional mass media, particularly television. Cable has had an especially large impact on fragmentation of television audiences. It now costs more to reach television audiences. Add to this the problems caused by videocassettes and commercial zapping, and you can perhaps see how devastating this has all been for companies trying to sell a product or service. Marketers have looked to sponsorship to overcome some of these problems.

One stroke of genius designed to appeal to corporate communication needs is offered by Championship Auto Racing Team (CART). The entire sport of auto racing organizes around the notion of providing relatively inexpensive television time. Although the relationship between sponsors and the media has been stormy at times (see the next exhibit), many sports organizations such as CART have increased the value of the product they offer to corporate marketers by actively fostering television coverage of their events. In 1987 CART began putting together its own TV shows, purchasing network time to remove the uncertainly of television decision makers. Close to 200 companies use CART to supplement their communication needs and have helped make CART's series of Indy-style racing the richest in motor sports history.

Sponsors and the Media

The first corporate sponsor on the PGA TOUR was the Hershey Chocolate Company in 1933 . The Hershey Open was supposed to promote the company's resort/golf course, but what Hershey really wanted to do was sell chocolate bars and syrup. By staging the Hershey Open at the Hershey Country Club in Hershey, Pennsylvania, newspapers had to use the name Hershey somewhere when they were reporting on the tournament.

Twenty years later, newspapers and television decided that the name of a corporation or the brand of a product would not be used. Newspapers and television, for example, called the Buick Open "the Flint Open," since the tournament was held in Flint, Michigan. Such decisions to use or not use corporate names were not clean cut, however. In sponsoring the Miami Open, the Miami Chamber of Commerce was not necessarily selling golf so much as promoting tourism and the virtues of Miami as a place to live and prosper. But newspapers did use the Miami Open. Apparently, in the minds of newspaper publishers and television executives there was a difference between the Miami Chamber of Commerce and Buick in terms of who could get free advertising and who could not.

The problem with corporate name use in event names stemmed from the disc jockey payola scandals of the 1950s where payoffs were made to get a record played and to get it mentioned in editorials. At the same time, television producers were cutting their production costs by displaying brand-name products in their shows. The audience saw the products—the products got the exposure, and the company paid for it. Congress eventually passed laws to curtail the practice. A product used on a television program had to be legitimately within the context of the script. At the end of the program any use of the product for a "promotional consideration" had to be acknowledged.

This all affected the PGA TOUR where corporate sponsors wanted newspaper and television exposure but couldn't get it: Throughout the 1950s and 1960s the chambers of commerce were the dominant Tour sponsors, although a few corporate sponsors remained involved— Labatt, Carling's, Miller High Life, and Blue Ribbon Opens; the Lucky International (also beer); the Convair—San Diego Open; the Buick Open; the Kemper Open; the Monsanto and National Airlines Opens; the Avco Classic; the Pepsi Invitational; and the Kaiser International.

Getting corporate names in the newspapers was a hit-or-miss operation. It depended on a publisher's or editor's whim. One way, although not guaranteed, was to have a connection with a city or resort hotel or a title that could not be shortened. The Kemper Insurance Company was one of the first to learn this trick. Because their tournament had to be called something, it was run as the Kemper Open. The Andy Williams—Shearson-Lehman Brothers San Diego Open could not pass the editor's blue pencil.

In the 1970s the Associated Press (AP), the country's biggest news wire service, changed its policy of not using corporate names because of professional football. The organization felt that a professional team, such as the Chicago Bears, was effectively a commercial entity. To be consistent with earlier AP policy, the team would have to be listed as the Bears Team That Plays Out of Chicago. So the AP started using corporate names. However, with the prolific increase of corporate involvement in sports, the AP was once again forced to rethink its policy. When the Sugar Bowl college football game became the USF&G Sugar Bowl during the 1980s, it simply became the Sugar Bowl in AP line stories.

Around 1977 television networks developed a policy that forced corporate sponsors to consider purchasing advertising time. If a corporate sponsor purchased enough advertising either for the telecast of its tournament or on the network as a whole, its events would be mentioned on air by their official names. Here again the Kemper Insurance Company was in the lead, being the first to make this type of deal, with the networks.

The loosening of print media and television network policy restricting the mention of corporate names helped bring an extensive corporate presence to the PGA TOUR. And this, in turn, had quite a lot to do with the exponential growth of the circuit in the 1980s.

Adapted from Al Barkow, *The History of the PGA TOUR* (New York: Doubleday, 1989), pp. 191–194. Copyright © 1989 by PGA Tour, Inc. Used by permission of Doubleday, a division of Bantam Doubleday Dell Publishing Group, Inc.

POINT 2: In the modern era of market segmentation, sponsorship becomes an effective method for targeting clusters of consumers.

During the 1960s, firms set about mass marketing a stream of new products through the media. By the 1980s it became clear that the mass market no longer existed, at least in its pure form. Today's marketplace is one of segments, and this creates many problems, including fragmented budgets, higher selling costs, and dilution of effort.

Although market segmentation remains an inexact science, it has become so essential to developing marketing strategies that marketers pay an inordinate amount of attention to locating clusters of consumers who are the most likely to want certain types of products. Sports are a natural clustering mechanism in that the characteristics of specific sports consumers appear to be similar. The U.S. National Senior Olympics attracts Southwestern Bell Publishing and TWA, who want to reach adults over fifty-five years of age. Tractor pulls and rodeos are blue-collar consumer sports. Marketers believe these spectators are brand-loyal purchasers of jeans, cigarettes, beer, and pickup trucks. For this reason Ford and Budweiser justify spending more than $2 million on sponsorship packages associated with rodeos and tractor pulls.

POINT 3: Sponsorship allows a marketer to gain a competitive edge through the process of *image enhancement* or, *value adding*, which subsequently helps differentiate the company, its products, or its brands from others in the marketplace.

Besides communicating and targeting there is yet a third dimension to selling a product, namely, product differentiation. To gain an edge on competitors, marketers attempt to differentiate their products from those of competitors by creating a special image. Thus, point 3 captures this notion of value adding or image enhancement. When people buy a product, whether it is drink, jeans, cars, or beer, they are buying the perception they have of the product. Imaging gives a brand a unique and memorable attribute so that it becomes different from, and more desirable than, competing brands. While there are many reasons contributing to the difficulty marketers have differentiating their products, four dominate: villain products, competitive edge, product maturity, and power realignment.

Villain Products   Cigarette and alcohol companies use image enhancement to counteract negative images. Both products are sold as illusions—moments filled with fantasies. In reality cigarettes and alcohol can cause serious health problems—clearly not a desirable image. So, sports are used for the image association of health and well-being. Sports, with the associated connotation of youth, activity, and health benefit, even today, from tobacco and beer money.

Competitive Edge   Sports are useful to companies wishing to change their image in order to remain competitive. The intent of the Bausch & Lomb alignment with the U.S. Archery Team, for example, is to capture the image associated with a sport requiring superlative eye-hand coordination. This allows this company to separate its products from the many other eye care products available. Subaru uses the U.S. Ski Team to differentiate the snow-and-ice-handling capabilities of its four-wheel drive compact passenger car from competitors' models that have similar capabilities. K-Mart Corporation's use of professional golf was to help upgrade its stodgy, blue-collar image. K-Mart found the lower end of the department store segment was becoming increasingly competitive, and it wanted a more upscale image. The tie-in with golf, an upscale sport, helped reposition K-Mart so it appealed to a higher economic sector of the population.

Product Maturity   A large number of products are entering the maturation phase of their life cycle. Without some other differentiation strategy, price becomes the dominant consumer buying incentive. An athletic platform or events-oriented marketing plan can provide a product differentiation that can help keep a brand out of price wars.

Power Realignment   There has been a shift in power from manufacturer to distributor. The manufacturer must now spend both time and money enhancing distribution channel relationships. The hospitality opportunities at sporting events like golf tournaments, Wimbledon, and the like, are valuable tools for making friends with a retailer.

THE CONCEPTUAL MODEL

So far we have described sponsorship as a medium that helps amplify and aim a message. We have also discussed the communication, targeting, and differentiating capacity of this medium. It is now time to attempt to develop a conceptual model that will help us understand how these components fit together with corporate goals and objectives.

To capture the spectrum and scope of corporate goals and objectives for sponsorship, a conceptual model has to encompass three dimensions (Figure 8.1).

Dimension 1

The first dimension relates to what particular unit of the company is the target for action. This may include the company, a product, or a brand.

- **The Company**. Sometimes, the entire company is the target. Cannon, for example, claims spectacular improvement of its public profile with its three-year, £3.2 million sponsorship of an English soccer league.[7]
- **The Product**. Other times a line of products might be the target. International Business Machines (IBM) already has a well-known corporate image. Its involvement in sponsorship is to demonstrate the capabilities of its line of computer products to IBM business customers.[8]
- **The Brand**. In some cases, a specific brand will be the target. Quaker Oats International, for example, sponsored the Italian entry to the Whitbread Round-the-World Race with its Gatorade brand.

Dimension 2

The second dimension, which intertwines with the first, relates to the goal a company has for its targeted unit. A goal can be either strategic or tactical. A strategic goal indirectly affects sales and include such objectives as

- enhancing visibility/awareness
- enhancing image/ repositioning image
- combating negative publicity
- developing distribution channels
- reaching new market segments
- combating competitors
- gaining recognition in a market dominated by larger companies
- developing a bonding between consumer, distributor, and/or employees
- bypassing legal constraints

A tactical goal has a more direct and measurable impact. In this age of reduced marketing communication budgets, a common tactical usage of sports sponsorship is to stretch the communication dollar. Corporate sponsors feel that the pub-

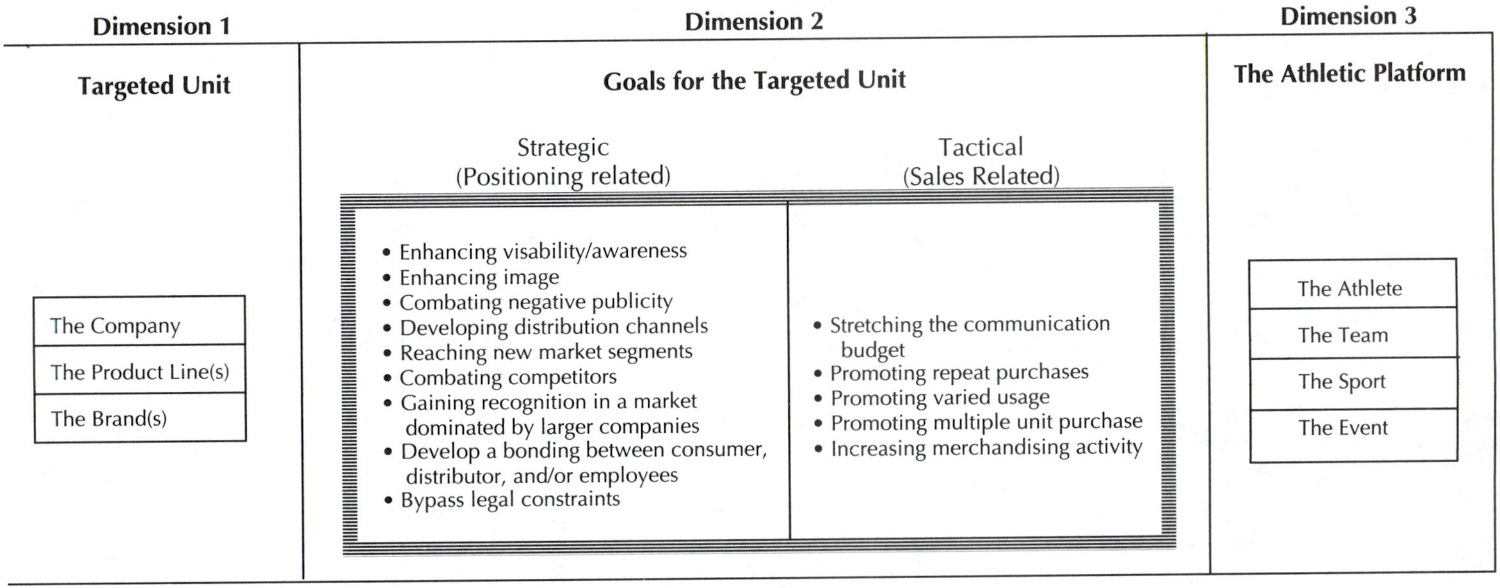

Figure 8.1   The Three Dimensions of Sponsorships

licity and wide exposure afforded by sponsorship is a cost-effective method of getting a company name in the media. Preliminary research indicates that corporate sponsors feel the most important part of the communication mix that sponsorship offers is public relations/publicity (mentioned by 96 percent of the respondents). The next is advertising (mentioned by 82 percent of the respondents), followed by sales promotion (46 percent) and personal selling (32 percent).[9] Other tactical objectives include

- stretching the communication budget
- promoting repeat purchases
- promoting varied usage
- promoting multiple product purchase
- increasing merchandising activity

Both strategic and tactical goals aim ultimately to improve profits. We might logically assume, for example, that a strategic goal such as developing a bond between the consumers and distributors or between the distributors and employees ultimately improves company profits. Similarly, we might expect that giving a product more exposure will result in improved sales. However, the influence of these types of strategic goals cannot easily be measured.

The impact of tactical goals, on the other hand, is more readily measured. It is easy to assess the effectiveness of an on-site sales promotion or to measure an increase in store traffic that has resulted from a competition tied to the sponsorship.

Dimension 3

The third dimension relates to the athletic platform, which has four components: the athlete, the event or competition, the sport, and the team. Depending upon corporate goals, some of these elements are more desirable than others. Some companies refuse to associate with individual athletes because of the danger of drug use and other illegal or embarrassing behavior by athletes. Associating with a team carries similar inherent dangers. Although aligning with events or sports is certainly a safer strategy, there are problems here as well. Many corporate sponsors, for instance, believe that men's professional tennis is poorly organized and fraught with questionable ethics.[10] The publicity surrounding the racially exclusionary membership policy of the Shoal Creek Country Club made corporations leery about paying to have their names associated with the PGA Championship scheduled for that course.[11] However, despite the positive and negative aspects of these athletic platform elements it is possible to use any one of them to accomplish the goal of the targeted unit.

EXAMPLES OF STRATEGIC AND TACTICAL USES OF SPONSORSHIP

We will take a brief look, now, at some actual examples of strategic and tactical uses of sponsorship. As you read through these examples, you will notice that many companies have more than one goal for their targeted unit and it is sometimes difficult to separate them.

Strategic Uses of Sponsorship

Enhancing Visibility/Awareness One of the dominant uses of sponsorship is to improve corporate and/or brand awareness. There is a wide range of targets for awareness campaigns. These targets include the media, politicians, financial institutions, the company workforce, the general public, and shareholders. Centinela Hospital Medical Center in Inglewood, California, for example, was a sponsor of the 1984 summer Olympic Games. It is also the official hospital of the PGA, the senior PGA, and the LPGA (Ladies Professional Golf Association), its prime purpose being to increase name recognition and highlight special programs.[12]

One goal of an awareness campaign is to obtain media exposure. Some corporations will, therefore, state the visibility/awareness goal in tactical terms; in other words, their stated goal is to stretch their communication budget. Others, particularly those manufacturing products largely restricted from access to the electronic media, want to bypass legal constraints. Thus, these companies will couch their awareness goals in slightly different terms. It is important that you determine the real motivation for enhancing visibility and increasing awareness because this will determine exactly what type of sponsorship package will interest the company. For instance, a company's liaison with you may indicate that media exposure is a prime objective; in practical terms, this generally means the company is looking to obtain product awareness within the marketplace. If you can find out why the company is having difficulty obtaining market awareness with traditional advertising, then you will be closer to designing a sponsorship package more directly suited to the company.

Enhancing Image Companies with image objectives want to counter adverse publicity, project the company as a caring organization involved with its community, and suggest a particular corporate image with a particular market segment. Examples here include the following:

1. The American Express sponsorship of the Statue of Liberty and Coca-Cola's involvement in the Hands Across America project. One way a company can demonstrate good citizenship is by giving back to the community.
2. When Anheuser-Busch introduced its Bud Light brand in 1981, marketers feared beer drinkers would view it as a brew for wimps. In contrast, they wanted Bud Light to have a healthy, low-calorie image. As a result, Anheuser decided to sponsor the Ironman Triathlon in Hawaii.[13]

Sponsorship is a useful repositioning tool for changing market attitudes. M & M/Mars used its Official Olympic snack food status to reposition its candy as a snack food. The whole emphasis was to move away from its image as an indulgent treat to that of a nutritious snack.[14] Mars also sponsors the London Marathon to reinforce its energy platform. The belief here is that events can give a brand personality. Timberland, a manufacturer of rugged outdoor footwear, sponsored the Alaskan Iditarod simply for the purpose of associating its brand with the harsh Alaskan conditions.

Developing Distribution Channels Many corporations are looking for ways to foster closer ties with their distributors. Volvo is a case in point here. Sponsorship presents the opportunity to involve distributors more fully in promotional campaigns. It provides the opportunity to use guest hospitality facilities to reward key distributors and to forge closer trade alliances. Nabisco, for example, sponsors approximately eighty Grand Prix (tennis) tournaments both in the United States and abroad. Nabisco used the French Open to court a major French grocery chain that had previously rejected Nabisco products. The lavish entertainment facilities provided Nabisco with the opportunity to socialize with key decision makers and make inroads with this critical distribution channel.[15]

Reaching New Market Segments *Golf Illustrated*'s (GI) Short Game Spectacular is a strategy designed to reach new subscribers. The Spectacular begins in the spring and runs through December in a format that encompasses several day-long festivals in target markets for golfers of all ages and skill levels: the festivals culminate in a national event. One purpose of the Spectacular is to bring the magazine to the attention of a broad audience of amateur golfers. Another goal is to reach potential advertisers by showing them that GI is serious about being a force in the golf business.[16]

Combating Competitors RayBan sunglasses, a division of Bausch & Lomb, became an official sponsor of the America's Cup to counteract an effort by the French producer of Vuarnet sunglasses to capture a niche in the American sunglasses market. RayBan's goal was to increase its visibility among yachties and yachting's international sporting crowd. At Newport in Rhode Island, site of the America's Cup races, RayBan sponsored a ferry boat—known as the RayBan launches—to ferry sightseers out to the spectator vantage points. The company also placed signage at the event and distributed a newsletter about the yacht races and other Newport activities.[17]

Gaining Recognition in a Market Dominated by Larger Companies Fuji Photo Film, U.S.A., used sponsorship to gain recognition in the U.S. market dominated by Eastman Kodak. Fuji became the official supplier of the 1984 Los Angeles Olympics. Being in the company of United Airlines, Coca-Cola, and IBM did a lot to enhance the image of Fuji as a major worldwide company. According to Fuji, the 1984 Games increased the number of distribution channels for Fuji products. Fuji marketers believe that the tie-in with the Olympics allowed them to accomplish in two or three years what would have taken twice as long to achieve through conventional advertising.[18]

Developing a Bonding between Consumers, Distributors, and/or Employees As the official bank of the 1984 Olympics, First Interstate Bank of California was asked to host a party for incoming dignitaries. The intent was to boost the morale of its employees, some of whom even took part in the events.[19] Some high-powered corporate entertainment can occur during sponsored events. A hospitality tent at the U.S. Open Golf Championships costs upwards of $75,000. However, companies contend it's worth the cost to impress clients, for relaxed time at the golf course is an intimate way to get to know clients and develop a business relationship.[20]

Bypassing Legal Constraints This is a more oblique use of sponsorship. It is especially valuable to cigarette companies forbidden by law to advertise their products directly on television. Since the early 1960s the cigarette industry not only has been denied access to television but is considered one of the world's greatest demons. This has forced the industry to be extremely creative in gaining access to TV. All elements of the athletic platform have been used—from Virginia Slims and women's tennis to Martina Navratilova wearing the Kim cigarette logo on her shirt during the 1982 Wimbledon women's finals.[21]

Tactical Uses of Sponsorship

Stretching the Communication Budget Domino's entered CART to gain a presence on network TV. Ten years ago Domino's was unable to afford a national media campaign, and CART offered them affordable national coverage.[22]

Promoting Repeat Purchases Until recently companies hardly ever defined sponsorship objectives in terms of sales. Although sales or market share may be the overall "hoped for" objective, sponsorship usually has strategic, and not tactical, objectives. Hertz, for example, arranged for free admission privileges at selected sports clubs across the country; all an individual had to do was present a Hertz car rental agreement and he or she was treated as a regular member at one of the participating clubs.[23]

Increasing Merchandising Activity An exception to the strategic rather than tactical objectives is the sponsorship of beverage companies. The Coca-Cola company signed an agreement to become the "Official Soft Drink" for the 1984 Winter and Summer Olympic Games. The objective of this promotion was to increase sales, shares, and profits and to project the image in the minds of consumers that Coca-Cola is number 1. Coca-Cola ran a "Win a dream trip to the Olympics" sweepstakes in which consumers had to spell the word *Olympics* from bottle caps.[24]

COMPANY ANALYSIS

With a clear view of how sponsorship fits within a corporate marketing mix, you are now ready to undertake an analysis of potential corporate sponsors for your athletic platform component. The first decision is the selection of your target companies, that is, those companies that you feel can benefit from your sponsorship opportunities.

The difference between the target company analysis approach and the hit-or-miss approach is the difference between using a rifle and a shotgun. In the first instance you can aim at your target; in the second you simply hope you can get close enough to score some points. The more precisely you identify the sponsorship needs of a company and aim your sponsorship package to them, the more successful you will be. The key mistake to avoid is to assume that all companies will want, need, and use a sponsorship package in the same way. Also, don't overlook companies that are not presently using sponsorship. These companies can sometimes be important new target markets for sponsorship packages. However, nonsponsoring companies will likely require a great deal of servicing, since they will have very little knowledge of how sponsorship can potentially fit their needs.

Use the Target Company Analysis Worksheet as a guide to the type of information you should collect about potential sponsors. You should never, *never* approach a company about a sponsorship package without first undertaking this analysis.

SUMMARY

This chapter began by presenting an insider's views on the role of sponsorship within the corporate marketing mix. From the corporate standpoint a sponsorship must include four ingredients: It must serve the business interests of the company, it must serve the interests of the event and its participants, it must have a positive impact on the sponsor's dealers and retailers, and it must benefit the company's consumers. It is the attainment of these four ingredients that sets the tone for a successful sponsorship.

Then we specified the differences between sponsorship and other communication mix elements such as advertising, PR, personal selling, and sales promotion. We found that sponsorship both amplifies and aims the corporate message to a very special targeted group of consumers. A conceptual model graphically illustrated how a company uses sponsorship to its advantage. The conceptual model encompassed three dimensions to fully explain the scope of corporate sponsorship objectives. These dimensions included the targeted unit (company, product line, brand), the goals for the targeted unit (strategic or tactical), and the athletic platform (the athlete, team, sport, and event). The remainder of the chapter showed you how these three dimensions intertwined with each other, and many sponsorship possibilities became evident.

To obtain some first-hand experiences in gathering the type of data you need to fully understand corporate sponsorship, select a local business, interview the manager or owner, and discuss your findings with your fellow students. Once you have done this, you are ready to design a sponsorship package. You will learn how to do this in the next chapter.

STRATEGIC PLAN WORKSHEET–CHAPTER 8

Target Company Analysis

Your primary consumers are _____

Based on your primary consumers you feel that the following companies will benefit from your sponsorship opportunities: _____

_____

	Company Name
Location	
Local	
Regional	
National	
International	
Company Background	
History	
Ownership	
Types of consumers	
Products/services	
Number of employees	
Major suppliers	
Current trends	
Major competitors	
Sponsorship Buying Habits	
Events of interest to the company	
Targeted unit	
Goals for targeted unit	
Athletic platform component most frequently used	
Kinds of packages purchased	
Frequency of purchase	
Volume of purchase	
Timing of purchases in relation to business cycle	
How sponsorship is funded	
Accessibility to the decision maker	
Special needs	
Does company work with an agent (who, relationship)?	
Have they ever quit as sponsors (if so, why)?	

STRATEGIC PLAN WORKSHEET

(Continued)

Questions to Answer

Does the company appear to need or want your sponsorship opportunity? _____

Does the company have the ability to give you what you need from it?_____

Is the company able and willing to spend money to purchase your sponsorship opportunity? _____

If so, would the company give a positive or negative image to your organization?

What is your strategy for approaching this company?_____

_____

_____

REFERENCES

1. This speech was provided to the author by John Barr, Director, Regional & Site Communications, Eastman Kodak Company.
2. Reported in Hanley Norins, *Traveling Creative Workshop*, made available by Young and Rubicam, 230 Park Avenue South, New York, NY 10003-1566.
3. Jack Kenward, Director of Communications, Rice Growers Assn. of California. Reported in *Special Event Reports*, February 8, 1988, p. 7.
4. John Morse, founder of Fratelli's Ice Cream. Reported in *Special Events Reports*, July 24, 1989, p. 4.
5. Sheri Perelli, Director of PR, Cadillac Motor Car Division. Reported in *Special Events Reports*, November 21, 1988, pp. 4–5.
6. Reported in R. Bagozzi, *Principles of Marketing Management* (Chicago: Science Research Associates, 1986), p. 31.
7. Frank Taylor and Arthur Young, "Commentary," *Accountancy*, June 1988, p. 27.
8. Donna M. Lynn, "If the Shoe Fits," *Public Relations Journal*, February 1987, pp. 16–20.
9. R. Abratt and P. S. Grobler, "Evaluation of Sport Sponsorship," *International Journal of Advertising*, 8 (1989): 357.
10. Joe Jares, "Leaving Tennis to ATP Has Been a Pretty Big Mistake," *LA Daily News*, August 2, 1990.
11. Randall Rothenberg, "Sponsors Now Cautious about Their Image after Furor over Shoal Creek," *New York Times*, August 10, 1990, p. B9.
12. *Special Event Reports*, August 10, 1987, p. 6.
13. "Nothing Sells like Sports," *Business Week*, August 31, 1987, pp. 48–50.
14. Bill Robinson, *Best Sales Promotions* Lincolnwood, Ill.: NTC Business Books, 1989.
15. Roger Lowenstein and Hal Lancaster, "Nation's Businesses Are Scrambling to Sponsor the Nation's Pastime," *Wall Street Journal*, June 25, 1986, p. 33.
16. Lynn, "If the Shoe Fits," pp. 16–20.
17. Ibid.
18. Yaron Steinbach, "Selling through Arts, Sports," *Journal of Commerce*, August 14, 1986, p. 1.
19. Lad Kuzela, "Olympic Boomerang," *Industry Week*, August 6, 1984, p. 21.
20. "Nothing Sells like Sports," *Business Week*, August 31, 1987, pp. 48–50.
21. Eric Clark, *The Want Makers* (New York: Viking Penguin, 1989), p. 253.
22. Presented in a lecture on "Corporate Sponsorship" to University of Michigan students by Anna Schmidt Heatlie, the former director of sponsorship, for Domino's Pizza, Sept. 1989.
23. Robinson, *Best Sales Promotions*, p. 269.
24. Ibid.

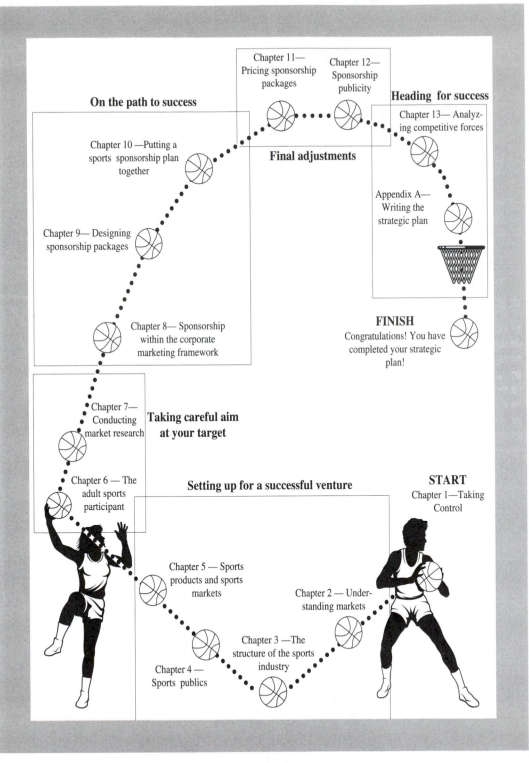

Designing Sponsorship Packages

....

> Everyone lives by selling something.
> —*Robert Louis Stevenson*
> *(1850–1894)*

You are sitting nervously on a couch in the reception room of a large soft-drink distributor waiting to pitch your sporting event to the vice-president of communications. You have come prepared with a neatly bound, carefully researched, four-page written document. It contains details about the event, including spectator and participant size and demographics. It demonstrates why your event is potentially more effective than other events the company is presently sponsoring. Your document also lists the exposure opportunities for the company's products and demonstrates how your event can benefit the company in a cost-effective way. What you have in your hand is a *sponsorship proposal*.

It wasn't that long ago when the acts associated with sponsoring a sport were fairly rudimentary and did not require a written document of any great substance. For a small fee, the sponsor's name would appear on T-shirts, on banners, or in the event program. As the popularity of sports sponsorship has grown, though, its framework and the solicitation process have become increasingly elaborate. As we saw in Chapter 8, from the company's perspective sponsorship programs embrace many levels of structural complexity. It is no less complex from your viewpoint. Understanding how you should structure a modern sponsorship package will help demystify the process and help you devise impressive sponsorship proposals of your own. If you use an agent, it will allow you to judge the quality of his or her work.

Before we begin, take a few minutes to think back on the last time you ate at a restaurant. How was the food? How was the service? Did you find dried coffee marks on the side of your cup? Did the person waiting on you smile and make you feel welcome? Write down your experiences on a piece of paper; try to recall the atmosphere, your mood, whether people were smoking around you, if young children were misbehaving, and the menu selection. Now, using your notes to recreate your experience, think about the factors that made the eating experience pleasant or unpleasant. The point here is that your satisfaction in consuming this meal was due to a combination of tangible and intangible factors involving the meal itself and the service you received. Similarly, your product (the sponsorship package), and the services you provide (the extra touches), will be important to the overall sponsorship experience for your client company. You will have to consider both these dimensions as you design your sponsorship package.

THE TYPICAL SPORTS SPONSORSHIP PACKAGE

Describing the typical sports sponsorship package is not a straightforward process. In Chapter 8 we discussed the three dimensions that affect its structure, spectrum, and character. These were the targeted unit, the goal for the targeted unit, and the athletic platform. We saw how the mixing and matching of these three dimensions can result in many different sponsorship needs. But this information alone is insufficient. You must also understand what has value to a sponsor. You begin this understanding process by taking an audit of your athletic platform, where you note the following:

- The athletic platform component you want to offer
- The characteristics of your primary consumers
- Your athletic platform image
- The market size of your participants
- The market size of your spectators
- The market size of television spectators

The data you collect by conducting this audit will provide you with a summary of your tangible and intangible assets. Figure 9.1 provides you with an example of such an audit completed for a college recreational three-on-three basketball tournament. As demonstrated in Figure 9.1, first position your athletic platform component in the center of the chart. Then analyze its primary consumers, geographical scope, and market niche. Describe the current staff's ability, the image of your athletic platform, and other intangible factors that may influence how companies will evaluate your athletic platform. Each year you run your event, you should gather additional data to give you more insight about your product.

Once you have completed an audit, you are ready to write a summary statement about who you are. Keep this summary statement short and to the point. A one-sentence or two-sentence response to the following will suffice:

Athletic Platform Component
Participants

Characteristics of Primary Consumers	Athletic Platform Image	Market Size of Participants	Market Size of Onsite Spectators	Market Size of Television Spectators
College students (predominantly males) who are recreational basketball players Athletic males Beer drinkers High consumers of snack and fast food Potential upscale consumers of the future Overrepresentation of Afro-American students Highly competitive Tend to be solid supporters of the varsity basketball team.	No known problems with image in terms of participants. However, our scant research indicates that local companies do not believe sponsoring such an event increases traffic in their stores. Some have had some bad experiences with similar events that might affect the ability of this one to attract sponsors.	Approximately 2,000 entrants expected this year. Anticipated expansion to 4,000 students in five years.	Number of spectators is not expected to be significant until the event matures in five years.	Event will be videotaped and used as a publicity tool. The videotape will be shown in three high-traffic areas on campus a. immediately after the event so participants can recapture their experience b. as a publicity tool for next year's event to encourage registration. Estimated student exposure expected to be approximately 15,000 students.

Major Weaknesses	Solution
We don't have sufficient information about participant characteristics to help us position this event with sponsors. For example, is there anything distinctive about the consumption patterns of this group that would make them an attractive company target?	Conduct an intensive consumer study of recreational basketball players on campus.
Very male dominated. Could be viewed as a sexist event leading to possible protests by women.	Find out why the event does not attract women.
Event is run by inexperienced sports management students. Each year there is a new management team; this is leading to problems in obtaining sponsorship, since there is no long-term sponsorship strategy. Could be viewed as unorganized, unreliable, and mismanaged.	Need to set up a committee to see if we can solve this problem.
Market expansion limited by facilities.	Begin looking for creative ways to develop playing space.

Figure 9.1   An Athletic Platform Audit of a Recreational Three-on-Three Basketball Tournament

- Describe your organization.
- What is your event?
- What impact do you have on the local economy?
- What is the purpose of your event?
- How will you affect local businesses?
- How will you involve the community—that is, local businesses, cultural groups, and local residents?
- Will your event heighten public awareness about physical activity, your sport, the plight of a certain social group?
- How does your event allow sponsors to reach out and touch their consumers?
- Is your event based on another similar successful event?
- Why is your event unique?
- What is one significant advantage you offer a sponsor who ties into your event?

Table 9.1 provides you with a summary statement for an indoor windsurfing competition. When your summary statement satisfies you by capturing the essence of your event, you are ready to begin work on your sponsorship categories.

SPONSORSHIP CATEGORIES

There are four categories of sponsorship: *exclusive* sponsorship, *primary* sponsorship, *subsidiary* sponsorship, and *official supplier*. Various events may have different names for these categories. Tennis, for example, employs the term *presenting sponsor* for a *subsidiary* sponsorship and *title sponsor* for a *primary* sponsorship. Despite the label variation, every sponsorship type will fit into an exclusive, primary, or subsidiary sponsor or official supplier category. Keep in mind that there is no unique, established list of rights for each of the categories. These sponsorship categories have no legal meaning other than what you and your sponsor agree to. There is, however, a general pattern that distinguishes the four sponsorship categories from each other. We will discuss these first and then come back to ways you can customize the sponsorship categories to suit your own needs and those of your potential sponsor. To help you see the difference between each sponsorship category, a summary is presented in Figure 9.2 on page 188.

Exclusive Sponsorship

An exclusive sponsor is the only sponsor associated with the athletic platform component.[1] Advantages of an exclusive sponsorship are threefold. First, an exclusive sponsor can generally negotiate its name within the event title, or the team name, or it can attach its name to trophies. Second, the sponsor has sole use of the platform component for promotional purposes. This makes it possible for the company to maximize advertising and other communication, targeting and differentiating opportunities without concern for the needs of other sponsors. Third, the prestige associated with being an exclusive sponsor may add value to

Table 9.1   Summary Statement for an Indoor Windsurfing Event

---

Describe your organization. Sports Entrepreneur–Business Student Club.

What is your event? An indoor windsurfing event.

What impact do you have on the local economy? Affects the sports management department by raising funds for student career excursions. Potential impact on local windsurfing dealers through additional sales of windsurfing equipment to new consumers.

What is the purpose of your event? Promote and provide exposure for windsurfing as a recreational option among adults (predominantly under thirty-five years of age).

How will you involve the community, that is, local business, cultural groups, and local residents? Invite local recreational windsurfers to participate in the amateur division. Opportunity for people interested in windsurfing to get free lessons, see demonstrations, exposure to top professionals in the sport. Opportunity for local windsurfing dealers to display equipment on-site, to hand out flyers about clinics, etc.

Will your event heighten public awareness about your sport? Will expose local residents to an upscale and unique recreational sport.

How does your event allow sponsors to reach out and touch their consumers? On-site sampling, windsurfing industry exposures to a new group of potential consumers. Allows sponsors access to an upscale group of young adults.

Is your event based on another similar successful event? Based on the successful French Super Fundoor Event.

Why is your event unique? This event will generate considerable interest because it is totally different from other events occurring on campus or in the local area. Will attract windsurfers from at least a fifty-mile radius — possibly farther.

List some advantages for sponsors who tie in to your event? Extensive publicity and press coverage expected because of uniqueness of the event. Will allow a foreign company like Bic or Swatch access to an American consumer market. Also likely to be an attractive event for other windsurfing equipment manufacturers that are desperately trying to expand their markets. Approximately 10,000 spectators anticipated, TV and newspaper coverage. May also attract some national coverage.

---

the sponsor's products. Tennis fans, for instance, might feel more positive toward a company that is supporting *their* sport. The hope is that this will make them more likely consumers of the sponsor's products.

The main disadvantage of this kind of sponsorship relates to the fact that an exclusive sponsor is the only source of funding for the platform component. If unexpected costs occur, you must rely on your exclusive sponsor to increase its financial commitment. If your event flops, the team or athlete loses consistently, or your sport has widespread drug abuse, an exclusive sponsor stands to lose substantial sums of money and may also suffer serious damage to its image. For this reason you can expect an exclusive sponsor to demand a major say in how you manage and organize your event.

Sponsorship Category	Commitment	Brief Description
Exclusive sponsor	Sole financial commitment.	Sole use of the athletic platform for promotional purposes. May even own the event. Usually has a major say in the organization and management of the event.
Primary sponsor	Major financial commitment but shares the athletic platform with one or more companies that are providing a smaller financial commitment.	Has the best opportunity to maximize exposure opportunities with minimal effort. Can have a major say in how the event is organized and managed.
Subsidiary sponsor	These are the companies that are providing the smaller financial commitment behind a primary sponsor in the form of cash, product, or service.	Generally has exclusivity of sponsorship within a product category. The product and service is frequently essential to the event — gymnastic equipment for a gymnastics meet, timing devices for marathons, etc.
Official supplier	On the same level as a subsidiary sponsor but the products are not crucial to the competition. Depending upon the financial return to the company, the price of an official supplier category can be substantial.	Generally have exclusivity of sponsorship within a product category. Any product category can be an official supplier, including snack foods, soft drinks, pizza, sunscreen, etc.

Figure 9.2   Summary Analysis of Sponsorship Categories

Primary Sponsorship

The sheer operational cost of most athletic platform components has almost made the exclusive sponsorship category extinct. Most events today demand that several sponsors share the event expenses. When there are multiple sponsors, it is sometimes advantageous to structure the sponsorship packages so that corporations can enter at various financial levels. Primary sponsorship packages are generally at the upper end of the financial commitment scale. In return, a primary sponsorship category tries to ensure that these sponsors have the opportunity to maximize their exposure with minimal effort.

For all practical purposes, however, a primary sponsor has exclusivity even when there are many other sponsors. A primary sponsor can generally negotiate its name within the event title, and its name is usually mentioned in a newspaper write-up or a TV news item in conjunction with the event. This gives a primary sponsor the image of exclusivity. Spectators and participants may even begin identifying the team or event by the primary sponsor's name or product. One advantage the primary sponsor has over an exclusive sponsor is that it shares the financial risk of the event with several other sponsors. A disadvantage to the event occurs when a primary sponsor withdraws from the sponsorship program, since this causes considerable disruption to the financial stability of the event. The more you can integrate a primary sponsor with your event, the more difficult it is for it to terminate the association with you.

Subsidiary Sponsorship

Subsidiary sponsorship is a second level of sponsorship involving several companies that are divided into product categories. Thus a company may be the only tire company, the only oil company, or the only timing device company. The price of such a sponsorship can range from a few hundred dollars to several thousand and can be in the form of cash, products, or services. On the positive side, subsidiary sponsors usually have exclusivity of sponsorship within their own product category; thus, with some creative planning and hard work a subsidiary sponsor can achieve the same promotional capacity as a primary sponsor—but for substantially less money. Since there is minimal risk in being a subsidiary sponsor, a company inexperienced in sponsorship can test the waters before extending the risk into primary sponsorship.

Subsidiary sponsors are sometimes difficult to retain because they can generally withdraw from a sponsorship program without serious disruptions to their marketing program. There may be many reasons a subsidiary sponsor will drop out. An athletic platform component often becomes cluttered with too many subsidiary sponsors, reducing the impact of the sponsorship for specific companies. Certain types of well-known platform components—the big event or famous athletes—may become too expensive to fit the advertising or promotional budget of smaller companies. Sometimes, a subsidiary sponsor has difficulty obtaining media exposure. It requires considerable knowledge about how to leverage a subsidiary sponsorship and many companies do not have this knowledge.

Official Supplier

The official supplier is a special case of subsidiary sponsorship. Like subsidiary sponsors, official suppliers frequently have exclusivity in their product category. However, subsidiary sponsorships and official suppliers differ in one important respect: A subsidiary sponsor's products are frequently crucial to the competition, whereas an official supplier's products, more often than not, have little obvious connection. The official supplier of soft drinks or of a credit card, for example, is not essential to the survival of any platform component. There can be an official supplier of almost anything. Alcohol and cigarettes are sometimes unwelcome product categories, but even these products sponsor many platform components—ironically, sometimes with the title of official supplier.

To be the official supplier of a unique international event can be important for the image of an international company with a worldwide marketing strategy. However, there are many ways for a company to become involved with these unique events, and this may dilute the sponsorship category. Top athletes competing in the Olympic Games, for example, will have primary and subsidiary sponsors of their own. These sponsors often obtain more promotional value from the Olympic Games than official suppliers of the Olympic Games themselves. Witness the number of runners wearing the familiar NIKE swish. NIKE is not an official supplier of the Olympic Games. It is, however, a primary or subsidiary sponsor of a sizable number of athletes, and this is the reason you see this brand of shoe dominating the footwear of athletes.

There is no adequate way of estimating the actual value of the promotional exposure offered the various levels of sponsorship. Regardless of their financial commitment, all sponsors at any level can inform anyone who will listen that they are affiliated with the event, team, athlete, or sport. If the team or athlete wins, all the sponsors can use this to their advantage. It's just a little easier for primary and exclusive sponsors to leverage this exposure. On the negative side, the clutter caused by too many small sponsors can dilute the impact of any sponsorship category. Sponsors must also worry about potential incompatibility with other sponsors. Some may try to negotiate veto power over the type of company permitted to become a sponsor of the event.

Summarize Your Opportunities

In this phase of the sponsorship package design you begin to summarize the opportunities you offer sponsors. Figure 9.3 provides an opportunity summary for the windsurfing event we discussed earlier. This is the *event opportunity formula*. It requires that you think about the types of sponsorship programs you are going to offer, what categories of businesses will benefit, what benefits your event will offer sponsors, and the types of services you are willing to provide. You do not need details at this point, just brief notes to stimulate your thinking. Once you have done this, you are ready to customize your sponsorship packages so that they appeal to the needs of the sponsors you have in mind.

Figure 9.3   Opportunity Summary Chart for A Windsurfing Event

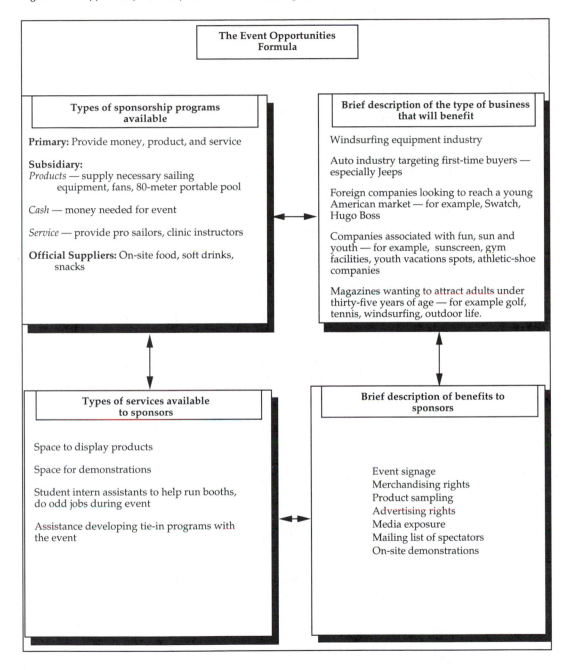

CUSTOMIZING SPONSORSHIP PACKAGES ....

Here are some of the things you should consider as you customize your sponsorship packages:[2]

Official Status
What is the sponsorship category?
Are there veto rights with this category—that is, can a sponsor dictate who else can be a sponsor?

Sponsorship Fee
What is the fee?
How and when does a sponsor pay the fee?
Is the fee refundable for any reason?

Title rights
Will the sponsor's name appear in the title?
How will you name the trophies?
Who will present the trophy or prizes?

Television exposure
Who owns and controls TV rights?
Does the sponsor have rights of first refusal on television advertising spots?
Is there a ratings guarantee? Will there be a rebate if ratings fall below this guarantee?
Can the sponsor use TV video footage in its regular advertising?
Does the sponsor need to obtain permission prior to using video clips for commercial reasons?
Who is responsible for negotiating television time?

Public relations and media exposure
Will key athletes mention the sponsor's name when the press interviews them?
Will media releases include the sponsor's name?
Who is responsible for media releases?
Can the sponsor develop its own media marketing campaign?

Logo use
Under what conditions can the sponsor use athletic platform logos or trademarks?
Who owns special logos?
Can the sponsor use the logo to promote its own image and products?
Does the sponsor have merchandising rights—that is, can it make and sell souvenir items?

Signage
How many banners, athlete patches, placards, arena boards, or flags can the sponsor use? What size?
Where can a sponsor place banners, and what can appear on them?

Who is responsible for making and paying for the signage?
Who is responsible for placing the signage on-site?

Advertising rights

In what manner can the sponsor use the platform component for advertising purposes?
Will the sponsor's name be on stationary or in the program?
Can the sponsor use event photographs for product promotion and general media advertising?
Who gives permission to use the photographs in advertising?
Are there limitations on the use of photographs?

Athlete use

Will athletes make personal appearances on behalf of the sponsor?
Will key athletes or coaches attend pre- or post competition parties?
Will athletes wear the sponsor's name during competition?

Hospitality rights

Does the sponsor have access to a hospitality tent?
Where can the sponsor place the tent?
Does the sponsor get free tickets for tie-in contests, to give to key clients, or for other use?

Point-of-sale promotion

Can the sponsor sell products on-site? What type—cigarettes, alcohol?
Who gets the profit from on-site sales?
Can the sponsor run on-site or off-site promotions associated with the sponsorship?
Can the sponsor team up with other companies to form cooperative promotions?

Direct-mail lists

Will mailing lists of ticket holders or athletes be made available to the sponsor?
What from of promotions can the sponsor undertake with these mailing lists?

Product sampling

Will there be a product display and sampling station?
What type of products can a sponsor display? Will you accept cigarettes and beer?

Legal liabilities

Who is responsible for injuries to spectators, participants, or officials?
What if it rains or there are TV problems? Who pays existing expenses?

Future options

How many years does the sponsorship last?
Does the sponsor have renewal options?
How many years does the option last?
How do you determine the sponsorhip fee in the future?

Questions You Should Ask About Your Sponsorship Package

Whatever athletic platform component you use, there are some basic questions you should attempt to answer.

What is its purpose?

Does it solve or address an opportunity for your targeted company?

How does the sponsorship package achieve its purpose?

What are its unique features (cost, design, quality, capabilities)?

Is the package labor intensive?

Will you subcontract some of the sponsorship package activities?

Does your survival depend on getting a certain type of company to buy your package?

How can you adjust your package to meet the changing needs of a client company?

Are you violating sanctioning body rules and regulations?

What liabilities are there associated with your package?

Are there insurance requirements?

If more than one sponsorship package is being offered, are there clear distinctions between them?

How do your sponsorship packages compare to similar packages offered by competitors?

What are some special requirements of each package?

What are the related services you will provide?

How will these services enhance the profitability of the sponsorship package?

Preparing the Package

Once you have decided what you can offer the various categories of potential sponsors, have completed the research on company sponsorship needs, and have filled out the necessary worksheets, the next step is putting the package together and writing a proposal. When you ask for advice about sponsorship proposals from experienced sports managers, you will get a mixture of opinions. The content of a proposal depends upon the company, the situation, and the athletic platform component. You must know the needs of the prospective company before you even begin to design your package and write your proposal. Here are five commonly asked questions and some general answers.

Q: How detailed should I make my proposal?

A: It depends on the size and type of event. If you have researched your company, you will know quite a bit about how detailed you should be. Some company sponsorship decision makers want considerable details in the initial proposal. They want details on the sponsorship package and its benefits, as well as a breakdown of cost. Others just want a concise letter and perhaps a brochure of the event. If possible, collect and study other successful proposals from similar events.

Q: Should I include press and video clips?

A: Again, this depends upon whom you want to reach. Larger events, such as the Kentucky Derby, use a video to demonstrate the kind of exposure sponsors receive. It is an effective way to illustrate signage, promotional opportunities, and what the hospitality areas look like. The Special Olympics uses video to capture the essence to its event. Several NGBs also have videos that capture their identity. Generally, though, videos appear to be unnecessary unless you have a large event that will attract regional or national exposure. Small-scale events will not need a video. If you do decide to go the video route, hire professionals to do it. An amateur affair will not present a very good image.

Some events include press clips to prove to sponsors that the athletic platform will attract media attention. It is usually more meaningful to present media attention in terms of gross impressions or target audience reach. Sometimes sports managers will calculate the advertising value of the media exposure.

Q: How should I present sponsorship cost?

A: You should know in advance the level of sponsorship that interests a company. You do not want to go to a company with a subsidiary sponsorship package design when that company is usually a primary sponsor. A large event like the America's Cup has three levels of sponsorship, each with a specific set of benefits and a specific price, whereas smaller events will generally have a more flexible price structure. Some companies will want details on how you arrived at your price, and in this case you will list the benefits and the price you are charging. Most sponsorship packages, however, simply list all the benefits and the total cost.

Experienced sponsorship packaging agents avoid quoting a price. You are better off if you offer benefits and then try to customize a sponsorship package that will fit a company's sponsorship budget. Whatever you do, make sure you present the budget professionally. This will give company decision makers a good feeling about your capabilities and your athletic platform.

Q: Are there key success factors in obtaining a sponsor?

A: Do your homework—

- Know your targeted company and know what you have to offer.
- Don't take rejection personally. After five to ten rejections many neophytes will feel the situation is hopeless. You should know that finding sponsors is a lengthy, time-consuming task.

- Show an interest in the sponsor's business and a willingness to help the sponsor accomplish desired objectives.
- Allow yourself ample time to find a sponsor.
- Follow up on your proposals.

Q: Do companies have specific forms I should complete?

A: Some do. These companies require specific information about an athletic platform and its sponsorship opportunities. Coors Brewing Company, Inc., for example, provides its own proposal format that designates the information this company needs before it can evaluate the sponsorship for its promotional purposes.

Selling Your Proposal

Attitude is everything! You will need perseverance, drive, a whole lot of optimism, a thick skin, and a little bit of luck.

The best way to obtain a real-life view of the process of getting a sponsor is through the experience and advice of those involved in doing so. For this purpose you should read the following case study. Here you will see the experiences of an amateur athlete, Andrew Goldman, who was a 1988 sailing (Flying Dutchman class) Olympian. He decided to pursue a spot on the 1992 Olympic sailing team, but he needed a corporate sponsor to help support him financially.

CASE STUDY | Pursuing Corporate Sponsors

> **The Athlete:** *Andrew Goldman*
> **The Sport:** *Sailing*
> **Brief Overview:** *Andrew Goldman, a 1988 Flying Dutchman Olympian and 1992 campaigner, spent over a year chasing corporate sponsorship before he found two companies to fund his Olympic program. Here is his story and advice for others.*

Just after the 1988 Olympics, I decided to take a year off from sailing and consider my plans for the future. I envisioned graduating from school, getting a job, owning a dog—I even pondered marriage. Quickly coming to my senses, I remembered the magic of walking into the Olympic stadium for the Opening Ceremonies, the thrill of the racing, and the worldwide attention. It's all too much to walk away from. I realized my decision was made.

With no financial resources, funding another campaign held slightly less romance than sailing in one. An idea struck me: why not get a corporate sponsor? It sounded easy enough—just make a few calls, send a few letters, and let's go sailing! Then, after 13 months of learning the promotion business, I called my partner J. B. Braum to cry on his shoulder. Fortunately, he reassured me, "If it were easy, it wouldn't be worth doing." In the 14th month I finally closed a deal with a sponsor. When John Kraus, president of Genesee Management, a division of Wilmorite, said, "We're in," I felt that race-winning adrenal rush. But I also realized how much I learned in my race to get a sponsor.

Let's consider the whole idea of raising money. When trying for the Olympics, practicing and time on the water win gold medals. Money may equate with time, but, despite the gold standard, it doesn't equal gold. Look at the old East German team, for example. They built their own boats and raced with sails that may as well have been cotton, yet they nonetheless managed to win regattas. For sure, they could have done better if they had more money, but they made it quite clear that even a lack of cash is a surmountable problem. Undeniably, though, cash allows a certain degree of freedom. A corporate sponsor can ensure a working budget to help with the bills. A corporate sponsor, however, doesn't (usually) mean unlimited funds. Olympic campaigns are small time promotions with limited exposure, so you can be sure that your campaign's budget will exceed its promotional value to any company.

This brings us to the first rule of corporate fund-raising: *The amount of money that you ask a corporation for depends on the exposure and publicity that you can offer, not on your budget.* For a sponsor, your Olympic campaign is a promotional tool. A company may buy the opportunities you offer, if you can meet their needs (i.e. reach the right people), and if you offer a competitive price. Hence, it is your job to put together a package that shows how many people will be exposed to your promotion, who these people are, and how much it will cost to reach them.

Think of your sales pitch in terms of a typical analogy: There is steak, and there is sizzle. The steak embodies the sponsor's tangible benefits: the number of positive exposures made by getting the corporate name in front of the public. The sizzle remains forever intangible, but it makes the steak a whole lot more appetizing. The deal has sizzle when you sell the emotion of the Olympics; the unabashed quest for perfection. Both steak and sizzle are critical in gaining a corporate sponsor.

Many sailors don't understand that every dollar a company spends on advertising and promotion is carefully quantified with a number of exposures, and the quality of the exposure is assessed. A strong advertising and PR campaign will reach the maximum number of well-targeted individuals—people who have the resources and inclination to buy the company's product or service.

There is a relationship between exposure and sponsorship worth. In order to maximize sponsorship value you must also maximize the promotion's exposure. Because Olympic sailing campaigns typically don't gather much exposure, they tend to have minimal promotional value. Consequently, you have to find ways to put your Olympic campaign in the public's eye.

This requires some creative thought. Magazines, newspapers, television, and events are the easiest ways to gain exposure, so consider doing a trade-out with a publication or television station. This would involve exchanging sponsorship of your campaign for product (in this case, advertising) rather than cash. Trading goods often costs a company less than giving cash. This makes it easier for them to join your team. If you can put together one of these media deals, then you will increase your chances of getting a cash sponsor, because the guaranteed exposure in your sponsor's medium means you can offer your other sponsors more exposure too. Think along these lines to increase the number of people who will see what you are doing.

Our deal with Wilmorite, an East Coast mall developer, works along these lines. We sold our sponsorship as a "cool, race-car-type attraction" for their malls. The deal entails setting the boat up in the malls, providing an exciting action video, and mingling with the crowd. This all adds excitement to their product, but it also increases our exposure. We have a similar arrangement with Gieves & Hawkes, an upscale British clothier. They are coming out with a new yachting line called Gieves & Hawkes Marine, and we are putting together new product promotions in stores like Bloomingdales and Triplers.

Our arrangement with Gieves & Hawkes also illustrates another important aspect of sponsorship: the necessity of making sure the people exposed to your campaign fit into the target market of the corporation. For Gieves & Hawkes, we have modeled our image to match theirs, so that we can better promote their product. For an upscale clothier, an exposure that doesn't reach someone interested in wearing the highest quality and best-looking clothes has little value to them. An exposure in Marblehead harbor is valuable, while exposure in a dinghy park offers limited benefits.

In your proposal you must develop a promotional plan that will reach the company's target market. Look at the company's advertising campaign, and try to figure out what kind of people the advertising targets. In your campaign schedule, do you ever come into proximity with these people? If the company's target market will not see your campaign, then there probably isn't a good match between your promotion and their marketing strategy.

If you see a match, put together a proposal offering logical benefits to the sponsor (see the next Exhibit). Keep in mind that you have to prove that you can gain exposure to well-qualified potential consumers. The people evaluating your proposal are inherently more skeptical than you; they need to be convinced that you have something unique and exciting to offer.

Once you have proven your promotional merits, it's time to move into the sizzle. Sell the excitement of trying out for the Olympics. A

A Sailor's Benefit to a Corporate Sponsor

Title sponsor of the Braum/Goldman 1992 Olympic Campaign

- All regattas will be entered as the X racing
- All exposure will be aimed towards X

Signage

[The benefits in this category depend on both the class and the regatta. The signage below pertains to the FD class in regattas that allow advertising. Your class may have different rules regarding advertising. Make sure you understand what you can and cannot do before sending out any proposals.]
The FD Class allows:

- Sponsor graphics on the back 3/4 of boat
- Logos 1/3 length of hull on each side of boat
- 5' x 6' logo and graphics on spinnaker
- 4' x 4" logo on boom

The following signage should be possible in most classes:

- 5' x 6' logo on *practice* spinnaker
- 5' x 6' logo on *practice* main
- Boat covers can have logo graphics
- Trailer can have logo and graphics
- Team vehicle can have logo and graphics

Two promotional appearances at point of purchase

- Team members will be available for two appearances at point of purchase
- Boat will be brought on site and rigged
- Team "action" video will be available for display
- Distribution of any direct marketing programs

One advertising appearance per year

Two personal appearances after the 1992 Olympics

(Company must understand that you may or may not be Olympians.)

Opportunity to design custom benefits

well-presented sales pitch will make the corporation feel like an integral part of the team; every time you are on the race course, they are there with you. J. B. and I no longer call ourselves the Braum/Goldman Olympic Campaign; we're now the Gieves & Hawkes Racing Team presented by Wilmorite. We want each member of Wilmorite and Gieves & Hawkes to share the emotion and experience involved in attaining an Olympic gold medal. This may sound ridiculous, but just remember that we are talking about the Olympics. How many Olympians do you know?

In terms of mechanics (cooking the steak), your proposal should ideally be sent to someone with whom you have a connection. However, if you think you have a good match, don't be afraid to send it cold. Find the name of the company's PR director in the *Standard & Poor's Book of Standard Advertisers* (available in most libraries) and address the cover letter and proposal to him or her. When sending cold proposals, I like to hit a group of competing companies rather than a single one. Sending multiple proposals requires extra work, but it increases the chance that you will reach someone who takes interest in your promotion. *Standard & Poor's* lists all advertisers by category. This makes it easy to pull out a whole group of related companies. Even though the companies share some characteristics, you must still learn about each one's marketing strategy. Once again, look at their advertising; both the content and placement will offer insights. (It's important to keep in mind that, if you are a member of the U.S. Sailing Team, you will have to be careful about approaching companies that compete with the companies already sponsoring the team as a whole.)

About a week after you send the proposals, start making follow-up calls. Don't be surprised when it's hard to reach people. Just keep at it with the same vigor with which you attack the race course after a third-row start. One more tip: Be friendly to whoever answers the phone. Many times, assistants will push your proposals on to their boss's desk, or file them you-know-where. As a rule, always get the assistant's name, and do your best to establish a rapport with them. Without help from Pam, Sally, and Richard, I don't think I would have closed any of these deals.

Through this whole process, keep J. B.'s words in mind: "If it were easy, it wouldn't be worth doing." For all of us trying to claim one of the 10 Barcelona spots, remember that this is one of those experiences of a lifetime. But never forget how exciting it is for all your supporters, friends, and family. Robert Gieve, vice-chairman of Gieves & Hawkes, said, "All of us at Gieves & Hawkes from Savill Row to New York City take pride in our team and share the excitement of the quest for excellence." This makes J. B. and me feel good about what we are doing; we're sharing one of life's great experiences with thousands of others.

Source: Andrew Goldman, *Sailing World*, June 1991, pp. 14-16. Reprinted with the permission of *Sailing World* and the author.

SUMMARY ....

This chapter discussed how to design a sponsorship package. There are several steps to the process. First you conduct an audit of your athletic platform. Next you write a summary statement about who you are. Following this you will decide whether you are going to offer an exclusive sponsorship or some combination of primary and subsidiary sponsorship. You are then in a position to summarize the opportunities you offer a sponsor so that you can more readily customize sponsorship packages that will meet the needs of specific companies. Finally, you are ready to write your proposal and begin solicitation of your targeted companies.

STRATEGIC PLAN WORKSHEET–CHAPTER 9

What you should know about designing sponsorship packages

Your goal ....

To design a sponsorship package for potential sponsors and write a sponsorship proposal

Check when completed

- What does our present athletic platform situation look like (Worksheet 9.1)?
- Who are we and what opportunities do we offer sponsors (Worksheet 9.2)?
- What does a summary chart of our opportunities look like (Worksheet 9.3)?
- What should we offer sponsors in our packages (Worksheet 9.4)?
- What is our general event exposure profile (Worksheet 9.5)?
- Write a sponsorship proposal (Worksheet 9.6). Note: This format is only a guide. You should recognize this to meet your specific needs.

WORKSHEET 9.1

Athletic Platform Descriptive Organizer

Athletic Platform Component

Characteristics of Primary Consumers	Athletic Platform Image	Market Size of Participants	Market Size of On-Site Spectators	Market Size of Television Spectators

Major Weaknesses		Solution

WORKSHEET 9.2

Who Are You?

Describe your organization.

What is your event?

What impact do you have on the local economy?

What is the purpose of your event?

How will you affect local businesses?

How will you involve the community, that is, local business, cultural groups, local residents?

Will your event heighten public awareness about physical activity, your sport, the plight of a certain social group?

How does your event allow sponsors to reach out and touch their consumers?

Is your event based on another similar successful event?

Why is your event unique?

What is one significant advantage for a sponsor who ties in to your event?

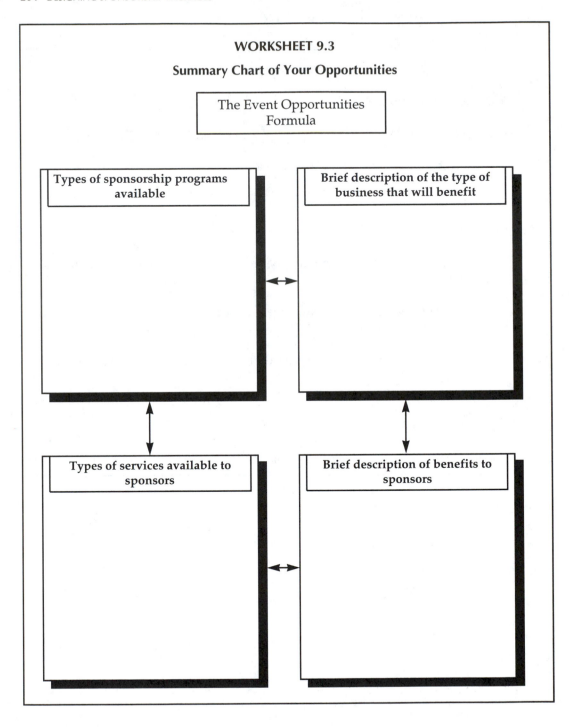

WORKSHEET 9.3

Summary Chart of Your Opportunities

The Event Opportunities
Formula

Types of sponsorship programs
available

Brief description of the type of
business that will benefit

Types of services available to
sponsors

Brief description of benefits to
sponsors

WORKSHEET 9.4

Sponsorship Package Checklist

1. **Sponsorship Class**	Exclusive Sponsor	Primary Sponsor	Subsidiary Sponsor	Official Supplier
Official status				
Fee				

2. Communication, Targeting, and Differentiating Opportunities

Television rights				
Public relations/ media exposure				
Logo use				
Event signage				
Advertising rights				
Merchandising rights				
Hospitality rights				
Use of athletes				

3. Product Promotion Opportunities

Point-of-sale promotions				
Direct-mail lists				
Product Sampling				

4. Other

Future options				
Special Requirements				
Services				

WORKSHEET 9.5

General Event Exposure Profile

Describe who your event will reach.

  Participants

  Spectators

  Others

How will you let people know about your event?

  Publicity

  Brochures or flyers

  Coupons

  Newsletters

  Classified advertising

  Personal networks

  Advertising in newspapers

  Other

How much exposure do you anticipate getting?

Is the media likely to be attracted to your event?

What other extra effort will you use to get exposure for your event?

WORKSHEET 9.6

Proposal Format

A ▒▒▒▒▒ year, $ ▒▒▒▒▒ program with ▒▒▒▒▒▒▒▒▒▒▒ [*your sport*], of ▒▒▒▒▒▒▒▒▒▒▒▒▒▒▒▒▒▒▒▒▒▒▒ [*location*], for a program pertaining to the ▒▒▒▒▒▒▒▒▒▒▒ [*event*]. The event will be held ▒▒▒▒▒▒ [*date*] at ▒▒▒▒▒▒▒▒▒▒▒▒ [*place*] starting ▒▒▒▒▒▒ and concluding ▒▒▒▒▒ .

Rationale

The ▒▒▒▒▒▒▒▒▒▒▒▒▒▒▒ [*event name*] is an ideal communication, targeting, or differentiating tool because of the following areas:

1. _____
2. _____
3. _____
4. _____
5. _____
6. _____
7. _____
8. _____

The demographics of the event are

Participants

- _____ Age range.
- _____ % men and _____ % women
- _____ % 17 and under
- _____ % 18–20
- _____ % 21–24
- _____ % 25–29
- _____ % 30–34
- _____ % 35–49
- _____ % 50 and older

Spectators

- _____ Age range.
- _____ % men and _____ % women
- _____ % 17 and under
- _____ % 18–20
- _____ % 21–24
- _____ % 25–29
- _____ % 30–34
- _____ % 35–49
- _____ % 50 and older

Affluence

- Annual income in excess of $_____
- Spends an average of $ _____ on sporting events/trips during the season
- Purchases new sporting equipment annually $_____

WORKSHEET 9.6

(Continued)

College educated

- _____% have attended graduate school
- Over_____ % have college degrees or are currently attending college

Occupation

- _____% are professional
- _____% are managers/administrators
- _____% are craftsmen/foremen
- _____% are students/educators

_____ [*your sport's name*] represents that it's not a seller of competing products of the potential sponsor

How it works

1. _____
2. _____
3. _____

What your sponsor receives

1. Sponsorship name:_____
2. The following components, produced by _____ [*your event*] would carry the sponsor's name and logo in a prominent position:

A. _____
B. _____
C. _____
D. _____
E. _____
F. _____
G. _____
H. _____

Additional activities would include

A. _____
B. _____
C. _____

WORKSHEET 9.6

(Continued)

Costs:

1. A $_____contract with the first right of renewal for the next year.
2. The contract will contain a clause stating that the costs for the next year and succeeding years should not exceed _____% of the previous year's costs.
3. The sponsor will pay for and provide the artwork for all signage and merchandising items. The event will pay for the construction and installation of all signage/banners along with producing all merchandising items.

Insurance

1. Risk (s): _____
2. Present coverage _____
3. Other insurance items to be considered: _____

Other

Your proposal should also answer the following questions:

- Is the program unique?
- Will the program affect a large group of spectators locally, regionally, and/or nationally?
- Will the program provide an opportunity for dominance by the sponsor?
- What spin-offs and outreach opportunities will the program provide?
- Can the program serve as a vehicle for a major consumer promotion and/or additional advertising (electronic and print)?
- Will the event offer continuity?
- Is the event cost effective and executionally feasible?

Source: This proposal format is based on the Coors Brewing Company, Inc., proposal. Used with permission, the Coors Brewing Company, Inc.

REFERENCES ....

1. For more information on sponsorship see BAGEHOT, R. and G. NUTTALL. *Sponsorship, Endorsement & Merchandising* (London: Waterloo Publishers, 1990) and S. SLEIGHT. *Sponsorship: What It Is and How to Use it* (Berkshire: McGraw-Hill, 1989).

2. For an excellent guide to sponsorship legal issues see M.H. REED, *IEG Legal Guide to Sponsorship* (Chicago: International Events Group, 1989).

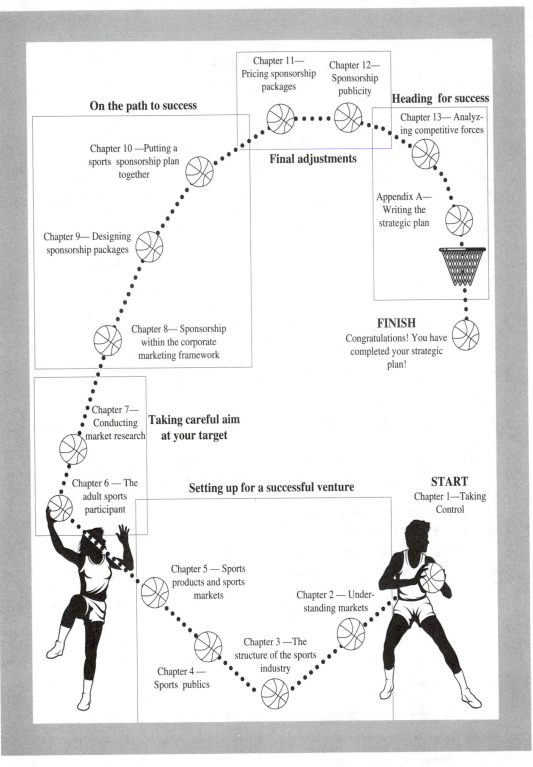

Chapter 11—
Pricing sponsorship
packages

Chapter 12—
Sponsorship
publicity

On the path to success

Heading for success

Chapter 13— Analyz-
ing competitive forces

Chapter 10 —Putting a
sports sponsorship plan
together

Final adjustments

Appendix A—
Writing the
strategic plan

Chapter 9— Designing
sponsorship packages

Chapter 8— Sponsorship
within the corporate
marketing framework

FINISH
Congratulations! You have
completed your strategic
plan!

Chapter 7—
Conducting
market research

**Taking careful aim
at your target**

Chapter 6 — The
adult sports
participant

START
Chapter 1—Taking
Control

Setting up for a successful venture

Chapter 5 — Sports
products and sports
markets

Chapter 2 — Under-
standing markets

Chapter 3 —The
structure of the sports
industry

Chapter 4 —
Sports publics

CHAPTER TEN

Putting a Sports Sponsorship Plan Together

• •

> Execution can become content, it can be just as important as
> what you say. . . . The facts are not enough . . . don't forget that.
> Shakespeare used some pretty hackneyed plots, yet his
> message came through with great execution.
> — *William Bernbach*
> *(1911–1982)*

You have researched potential sponsoring companies, located a few possibilities and persuaded the managers to listen to opportunities you can offer them. Now what? Well, unless you are dealing with a company experienced in the use of sports to further its commercial goals, you may find it necessary to adopt the role of a sponsorship consultant. Therefore you must know how to outline a suitable sponsorship program. This is a time-consuming task; but in the long term, a company with a sponsorship program that works to its commercial advantage will be with you for many years.

As you now know, sponsorship is a complex medium. Compared with advertising, it is an unfamiliar tool to many corporate managers, who will not know how to use it properly. Your job in the role of consultant is to ensure that your sponsor becomes an integral part of your athletic platform and avoids typical mistakes.

This chapter discusses the sponsorship design process outlined in Figure 10.1. To keep the chart simple, the scheme shows a linear arrangement of the steps involved. Decisions at each step interact with each other. Figure 10.1 does not depict these interactions, since it would make the chart far too complicated. The result of these interactions, though, means that the mental gymnastics required to sort out how a decision made at one step affects the outcome of another step can be formidable. The challenge is to constantly think ahead: If I do this,

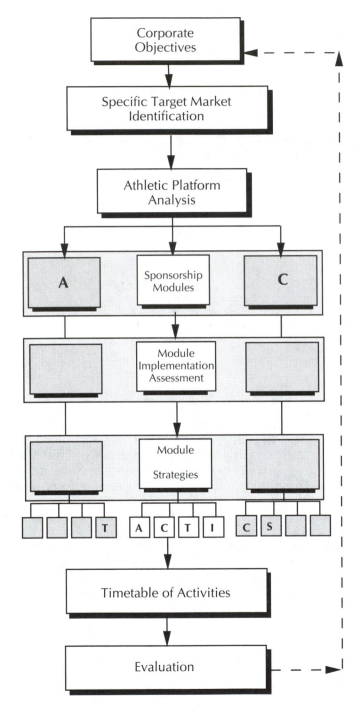

Corporate Objectives
▸ A statement specifying the targeted unit and the goals for the targeted unit

Specific Target Market Identification
▸ A number of specified targets for the communication message

Athletic Platform Analysis
▸ An analysis of what type of athletic platform will enable the company to accomplish the goal of its targeted unit

A   Sponsorship Modules   C
▸ A number of broadly conceived methods of using the athletic platform. These modules are organized into a unified sponsorship package specifically aimed at attaining the goals of the targeted unit

Module Implementation Assessment
▸ An analysis of all the factors potentially preventing maximum use of the sponsorship package to accomplish the goals of the targeted unit

Module Strategies
▸ A number of very specific decisions on what target market strategies to implement via each module of the sponsorship package

T A C T I C S
▸ A listing of specific activities required for sponsorship target market strategy implementation

Timetable of Activities
▸ Actual month-by-month outline of when the activities are to be done, how they are to be done, and who does them

Evaluation
▸ An assessment as to whether or not the modules accomplished their objectives

Figure 10.1   The Mechanics of the Sports Sponsorship Plan

this will happen, which in turn will have this impact. So, while we will discuss the sponsorship plan as if it is a linear process, the real world is never as basic as it appears in a model. The interactions can cause many unforeseen problems.

Before we continue with the sponsorship plan here are a few simple rules you should always keep in mind. First, a stable and proven athletic platform is important to sponsors. This is why it is much easier to obtain sponsors for an established event than for a recently developed one. Second, get your sponsor involved in the planning process. They should feel that they have a vested interest in your organization and that the sponsorship plan belongs to them. Third, educate company personal about your sport and how to use it for commercial purposes. Teach them how to use the media — both print and electronic — to their advantage (more about this in Chapter 12). The more knowledgeable they become about your athletic platform and how they can maximize sponsorship opportunities, the longer your relationship will last. Finally, find ways to tie the knot between the company and your athletic platform tighter so that it becomes more difficult to sever the relationship. If some of the proceeds of your event go to charity and the sponsor's name is attached to those proceeds, when the company withdraws from the sponsorship it also withdraws from the charity. The chance of adverse publicity for the company is, therefore, compounded, and so managers will think twice before dropping out of the sponsorship.

SPORTS SPONSORSHIP—A BRIEF OVERVIEW

Chapter 8 discussed sponsorship and its relationship to the marketing mix. There, we discovered that the key feature about sponsorship is that it is a unique communication medium through which we maneuver a message. The sponsorship medium may be designed for many purposes. Sometimes we want to amplify the message. By amplify we mean that we use sports to increase the visibility of the message.

We can also think of sponsorship as a scope on a rifle. A scope permits a more accurate aim. Marketers frequently use sports to minimize the inefficiencies of the communication process. They can zero in on a "captured" target group. We think of the target as captured in the sense that potential consumers are usually in one place for some common purpose. This makes them easier communication targets, and sponsorship is the targeting apparatus.

Figure 10.2 shows the mechanics of the message transfer process through the medium of sponsorship. When trying to send out a message about their company, products, or brands, marketers have two major problems to solve: First, they must make sure the target of their message is listening; second, they want to ensure that their message says what they intend it to say. Many factors interfere with the process. The steps in sending a message to a receiver look like this. Marketers send out a message, manipulating it through the medium of sponsorship. Noise—such as other competitors who are also using the same sport—distractions during the competition or event, or many other factors may disturb the message transfer. The target interprets the message, and it is at this point that it could be a garbled approximation of the original. To find out if the message is re-

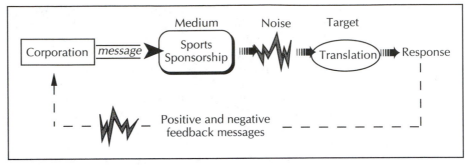

Figure 10.2 The Transfer of a Message through the Sports Sponsorship Medium

(Adapted from Don E. Shultz and Dennis G. Martin, *Strategic Advertising Campaigns* (Chicago: Crain Books, 1979), p. 6.)

ceived by the target in the intended format, it is imperative to have some form of feedback. Is it positive or negative? Does the target like or dislike the product, the company, or the brand more or less?

ASSEMBLING THE SPORTS SPONSORSHIP MEDIUM

The sponsorship planning process deals directly with how we assemble the sponsorship medium so that we deliver the desired message to the correct target. The assembly process is not unlike building a patio in your backyard. Imagine that you have eight slabs of stone of various shapes and sizes lying in your backyard. You decide to use them for an outdoor patio. There are many ways you can assemble these slabs to form a patio. The final structure depends on many factors. First, it probably will depend on the purpose of the patio. It will also depend on the nature of the ground on which you are building the patio, and it will depend on your creativity. In Figure 10.3, for example, patio variation A allows for an outdoor eating area and a place for you to study. Variation B surrounds a mound of rocks and a parking area. Variation C provides a walkway through many rose-bushes planted around the yard. In each case you use the same stones—you just alter the design to fit your needs and the environment.

Similarly, there are many ways to assemble the sports sponsorship medium while using the same basic components. Like the patio, a sponsorship medium has several slabs, which we call modules. It is possible to rearrange these modules in many ways depending upon corporate commercial needs. The sponsorship planning process you are about to study here helps direct the assembly of the sponsorship modules. We will discuss the sponsorship design process in the same order that it is outlined in Figure 10.1.

Determining Sponsorship Objectives

Even today a company may embark on a sports sponsorship program simply because the CEO happens to enjoy a particular sport. Golf has received a sizable

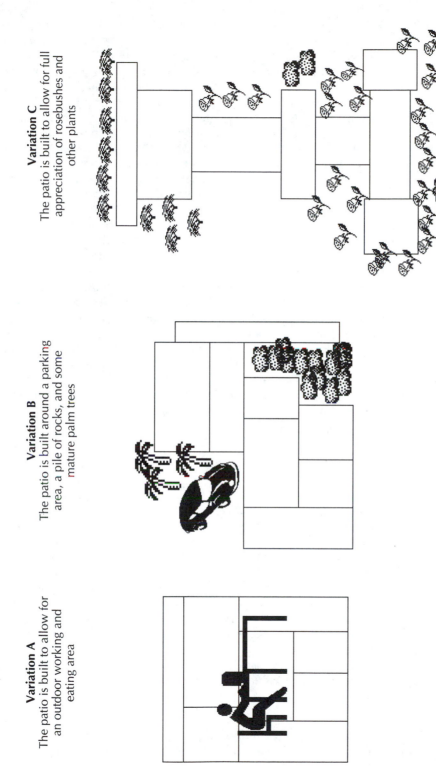

Variation A
The patio is built to allow for an outdoor working and eating area

Variation B
The patio is built around a parking area, a pile of rocks, and some mature palm trees

Variation C
The patio is built to allow for full appreciation of rosebushes and other plants

Figure 10.3 Variations in the Use of the Same Slab Stones to Build a Patio

chunk of corporate sponsorship dollars under this condition. Another common reason you find corporations involved in sponsorship is because a sport marketing agent has convinced a corporate marketing director to purchase the rights to an athletic platform owned by the agent. The marketing director is then left wondering how to use that particular athletic platform for corporate commercial gain. In both these situations you will generally find that a corporation has moved into the sports sponsorship arena without giving any thought as to how sponsorship relates to corporate commercial objectives. As a result, one basic rule for a sponsorship consultant to follow is *not to assume that corporate marketers have thought much about their sponsorship goals and how they mesh with company marketing needs.* You must help the corporate manager define and explain its sponsorship program in terms of corporate objectives and provide the guidance needed to build a sponsorship model, that will help meet those objectives. By dedicating time to the task of building a sponsorship model, you can help the company manager tailor-make a sponsorship program that will work.

As a rule, then, a sponsorship model has two basic characteristics: It focuses on meeting corporate commercial needs, and it has a series of strategies directly aimed at fulfilling those needs. So the first task is to decide what the corporate objectives are and how sponsorship can contribute to achieving them. To assess this, you will need to study the entire corporate marketing communications program. Such an examination can ensure that the sponsorship medium complements other communication mediums—TV, radio, newspapers, magazines, outdoor billboards, and so on. In this regard, it is sometimes useful to write the following question on a piece of paper and place it in full view of those involved in the sponsorship process.

How does this sponsorship idea help accomplish corporate commercial objectives?

It will quickly become obvious that to answer this question adequately you will need a thorough knowledge of the commercial benefits of a whole range of sports so that you can determine your particular niche. You will also need to understand the societal impact of each sport, how each can be used as a communication, targeting, and differentiating medium, and an ample portion of gut feeling, educated judgment, and creativity. That single perfect match between corporate needs and a specific athletic platform hardly ever exists. But many suitable, albeit imperfect, alternatives will always be available. From the corporate point of view the trick is to select the best available and affordable option, whereas from the sports manager's perspective the task is to adapt what he or she has available so that it is the best match possible.

There are four phases to ensuring the match between corporate needs and sponsorship is as close as possible: You must define the unit that is the target of the sponsorship campaign, define its goals, specify the publics, and provide other details.

1.   Start by defining which unit of the company is the target of the sponsorship campaign. Is the target the entire company, a product, or a single brand

(see Figure 10.4)? Also, indicate whether the target is primary, secondary, and so on.

	Primary Target	**Secondary Target**	**Target if possible**	**Not a Target**
Company				
Product				
Brand				

Figure 10.4   Identifying the Targeted Unit

2.   Decide on the goals for the targeted unit. Table 10.1 lists the typical goals.

Table 10.1   Typical Goals for the Targeted Unit

Strategic (Positional related)	Tactical (Sales related)
• enhance visibility/awareness • enhance image • combat negative publicity • develop distribution channels • reach new market segments • combat competitors • gain recognition in a market dominated by larger companies • develop a bond between consumer, distributor, and/or employees • bypass legal constraints	• promote repeat purchases • stretch the communication budget • promote varied usage • promote multiple-unit purchase • increase merchandising activity

3.   In broad terms specify the desired public you are trying to reach:

• Potential consumers?—specify age, education, income, and so on.

• Media?

• Employees?

• Distribution channels?

• Other?

4.   Specify the other details:

• number of people you want to reach

• the time of year you want to reach them

- frequency of message exposure
- length of sponsorship association
- desired impact
- desired image

After the corporate marker has been guided through these four phases, everyone involved should have clearly identified the sponsorship objectives. For example, you might outline objectives as follows:

> We want our product to be the primary target of our sponsorship campaign. We want to penetrate more distribution outlets for our products in the East. To accomplish this we need to develop better relationship with potential eastern distributors so they will carry our products. We want these distributors to view us as a reliable, friendly company that is interested in their financial well-being.

At this point you should fully assess how the sponsorship goals fit with other activities the company is doing, or would like to do. You are now ready for the next phase of the plan—the athletic platform analysis.

Athletic Platform Analysis

The next question is probably the most difficult and time consuming to answer. It is as follows:

> Which component, or combination of components of the athletic platform—the athlete, the team, the event or the sport—lends itself best to accomplishing corporate objectives?

In other words evaluate your athletic platform components for specific business development opportunities. Many questions will arise during this process. Here are some of the more common:

- What aspect of the athletic platform will be of most interest to the company's consumers who are the target of the sponsorship program?
- What are the opportunities for image enhancement?
- What about advertising? Consumers who are not receptive to a corporate ad campaign may be more receptive to one focused on a sponsorship campaign.
- PR is usually important to most corporations, and you must consciously incorporate a PR program into the sponsorship package. What elements have potential for media interest? (See Chapter 12 for details on marketing sports information to the media.)
- How about merchandising and sales promotion? Can you tie the sponsorship directly to sales? Can you produce merchandise that will help sharpen communication and broaden the scope of the sponsorship? Can you help your sponsors design cross-promotion opportunities (see the next exhibit)?

- Hospitality is another useful tool. Can you use any aspect of the athletic platform as a vehicle to talk to key prospects on a one-to-one basis?

When you select an athletic platform component, you are choosing that component you think will deliver a specific target audience. Delivery, however, is nothing more than potential. There is never any guarantee that you will reach the population an athletic platform component has to offer. The goal of a sponsorship planner is to increase the probability that it does.

Some issues influencing athletic platform selection:

- What is the budget? This will determine the type of athletic platform component the company can afford to purchase. When assessing budget, factor in twice the athletic platform purchase rights for target market module strategies. (You'll see why you need to do this shortly.)

Establishing Cross-Promotion Opportunities for Your Sponsors

Cross-promotions are cooperative arrangements among several sponsors so that they can maximize their sponsorship tie-in with the event. It is an excellent way for new sponsors to maximize their investment in an event, especially when they are operating on a limited budget. It helps give new and minor sponsors immediate credibility if you can link them with existing sponsors. Cross-promotions also provide any old sponsors you might have with new opportunities. Here's some strategies you might use as you help encourage cross-promotions among your sponsors.

- Hold meetings for sponsors so that they can meet each other and introduce them to the idea of running cross-promotions.
- Be persistent in actively helping sponsors put plans together that will benefit them. Encourage sponsors to team up for coupon offers. For example, the purchase of one sponsor's products earns buyers a discount coupon toward the purchase of the other.
- The sponsors could distribute booklets with product discounts or rebate offers, including a reduction on the ticket price to your event.
- The sponsors could jointly run TV and newspaper ads promoting your event and their products. In this way they can get the impact of larger newspaper ads for one-third the price.
- Establish a task force to help sponsors get PR and media visibility for their promotional tie-ins with your event.
- Develop a themed, scratch-card game that is based on your sponsors' products.
- Develop contests where sponsors' products are used as prizes.

- What is the desired geographic scope? Is it international, national, regional, or local? This, too, will influence the type of athletic platform the sponsor will want to purchase. Generally, a wider geographic scope means a more expensive athletic platform.
- What component of the athletic platform is most suitable for meeting corporate objectives? Figure 10.5 provides you with at least twelve options.

The Sponsorship Modules

So far we have simply assessed the number of stone slabs we have available to us. We have also taken note of their shape and size. The next step is to decide exactly how you will use the athletic platform. In essence, this is the stage where you rearrange the patio stones (modules) to meet company needs. Sponsorship modules are broadly conceived methods of designing the athletic platform. Such modules include the following:

Sponsorship class
- exclusive sponsor
- primary sponsor
- subsidiary sponsor
- official supplier

Communication, targeting, and differentiating opportunities
- television rights
- public relations campaigns
- logo use
- event signage
- advertising rights
- merchandising rights
- hospitality rights
- use of athletes

Product promotion opportunities
- point-of-sale promotions
- direct-mail lists
- product sampling opportunities

	Professional	Collegiate	Recreational
Sport			
Event			
Athlete			
Competition			

Figure 10.5   The Twelve Components of the Athletic Platform

It is not possible to explain precisely what specific modules will suit the diverse needs a corporation may have. It is a matter of assembling the modules in such a manner that their final structure fulfills corporate needs, while also adapting to the environment and to the particular consumer the company desire to reach.

Module Implementation Assessment

This aspect of the sponsorship planning process assesses all those factors potentially preventing maximum use of the athletic platform. In essence, you are analyzing your ground before laying your patio stones. Sports sponsorship implementation assessment has three parts: competitive analysis, athletic platform problem analysis, and sponsorship history analysis.

Competitive Analysis. It is tempting to set up a sponsorship program without first considering the sponsorship strategies used by competitors. A company's sponsorship strategy must take into account what competitors are doing. Should the company fight it out with competitors in the athletic platforms they use, or explore other athletic platform components? Part of the answer depends on the sponsorship program budget compared with competitors. Another consideration is whether the company's targets are the same as its competitors'. If the targets are different, then you can use different athletic platforms. If the targets are identical, then you may have no choice but to use the same or similar athletic platforms. Finally, it is worth examining how effectively competitors are using their sponsorship. Are there indications that they are inexperienced in the sports sponsorship arena? If so, even though your sponsor may have a smaller budget, it may successfully use the same athletic platform as competitors by being more creative and effective. Thus the basic competitive analysis should provide the following information: What do competitors sponsor? How? When? Dollars spent? What impact does this have on your corporate sponsor?

Athletic Platform Problem Analysis. Never take problems associated with the athletic platform lightly. They could indirectly affect the company. Search for such problems as drugs, violence, association with other potentially poor image products (tobacco, alcohol), poor organizational management, over-commercialization, poor media coverage, association with a previous sponsor, and poor athletic performance or low competitive ranking. Decide what effect each problem has and how you can correct it.

Sponsorship History Analysis. As you analyze sponsorship history over the past three to five years, look for any potential barriers that will inhibit a new sponsor's use of the athletic platform. You might analyze (a) the type of companies that have been a sponsor in the past; (b) the type of sponsorship package they had; (c) why they are no longer a sponsor; (d) who the sponsors are now; (e) the compatibility of present sponsors with each other and with the company you are now helping.

Module Strategies

A strategy sets down the basic logic, but not the specific details, of how you intend to use the athletic platform modules. Whenever there are many ways to accomplish a goal, there is the need for a strategy. Sports sponsorship provides many different opportunities to use an athletic platform module, and inevitably it becomes a challenge to know what course of action will be optimal. A strategy statement provides guidelines about the target market that will be served and the ways in which the athletic platform module will be used to reach that market.

Usually there are many target markets; these might include the media, spectators, TV, employees, participants, and so on. Therefore you will need module strategies geared toward reaching these diverse groups. You will also need image association strategies. After all, part of what you purchase from the athletic platform is the right to associate with its image.

The module strategy phase sometimes becomes a "best-match" process. Most sports will not offer all the modules you might need to reach your designated targets effectively. It will therefore be necessary to match the target markets with the modules that are available. In doing this, you will find it helpful to take a blank sheet of paper and list the target markets on the right hand side of the page. Next, list the available module strategies on the left-hand side. Finally, match the target markets with the most effective module strategy.

For example:

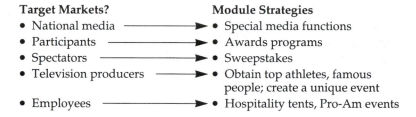

Target Markets?	Module Strategies
• National media ⟶	• Special media functions
• Participants ⟶	• Awards programs
• Spectators ⟶	• Sweepstakes
• Television producers ⟶	• Obtain top athletes, famous people; create a unique event
• Employees ⟶	• Hospitality tents, Pro-Am events

Figure 10.6 presents an example of a module strategy. The aim of this module is to develop a list of potential Volvo buyers. The strategies for obtaining this list include a tennis tournament and a golf tournament. The target markets include Volvo owners, direct prospects, parents of children, indirect prospects.

Module Tactics

Having a strategy does not guarantee success; and although there are many ways to carry out a strategy, even the most well thought out strategies will go astray without a precise listing of the activities needed to implement each strategy. In the case of Figure 10.6, module tactics would include all the activities required to generate a list of names from golf and tennis participants and get these individuals to visit to the Volvo car dealer's showroom. Module tactics, then, are the decisions you make about what you must do to execute a module strategy.

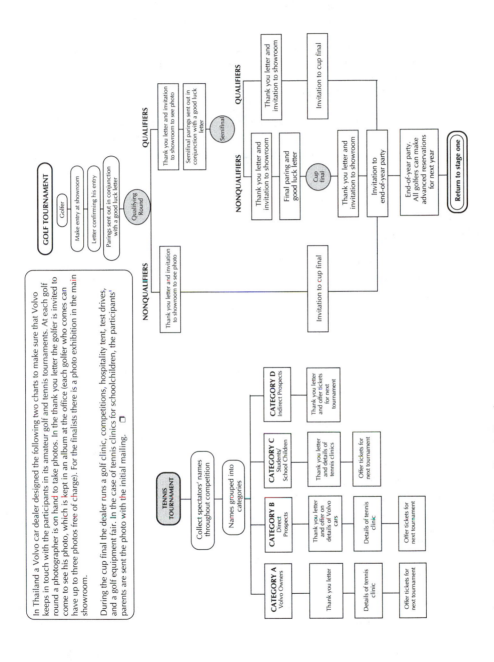

In Thailand a Volvo car dealer designed the following two charts to make sure that Volvo keeps in touch with the participants in its amateur golf and tennis tournaments. At each golf round a photographer is on hand to take photos. In the thank you letter the golfer is invited to come to see his photo, which is kept in an album at the office (each golfer who comes can have up to three photos free of charge). For the finalists there is a photo exhibition in the main showroom.

During the cup final the dealer runs a golf clinic, competitions, hospitality tent, test drives, and a golf equipment fair. In the case of tennis clinics for schoolchildren, the participants' parents are sent the photo with the initial mailing.

GOLF TOURNAMENT

- Golfer
- Make entry at showroom
- Letter confirming his entry
- Parings sent out in conjunction with a good luck letter

Qualifying Round

NONQUALIFIERS

- Thank you letter and invitation to showroom to see photo
- Invitation to cup final

QUALIFIERS

- Thank you letter and invitation to showroom to see photo
- Semifinal parings sent out in conjunction with a good luck letter

Semifinal

NONQUALIFIERS

- Thank you letter and invitation to showroom
- Final paring and good luck letter

Cup final

- Thank you letter and invitation to showroom
- Invitation to end-of-year party
- End-of-year party. All golfers can make advanced reservations for next year

QUALIFIERS

- Thank you letter and invitation to showroom
- Invitation to cup final

Return to stage one

TENNIS TOURNAMENT

- Collect spectators' names throughout competition
- Names grouped into categories

CATEGORY A Volvo Owners
- Thank you letter
- Details of tennis clinic
- Offer tickets for next tournament

CATEGORY B Direct Prospects
- Thank you letter and offer on details of Volvo cars
- Details of tennis clinic
- Offer tickets for next tournament

CATEGORY C Students/School Children
- Thank you letter and details of tennis clinics
- Offer tickets for next tournament

CATEGORY D Indirect Prospects
- Thank you letter and offer tickets for next tournament

Figure 10.6 The Thai Way to Keep in Touch

(Adapted from Volvo in Sports, Event Management Corporation, Twon House, Neerveldstraat 105, B-1200 Brussels, Belgium.)

A **sponsorship module** answers the question, What is the sponsorship goal?

Volvo's Answer: Generate a list of potential Volvo buyers.

The **module strategy** answers the question, What are our methods of accomplishing our goal?

Volvo's Answer: A golf and tennis tournament

The **module tactic** answers the question, How do we tie the module strategy to our business?

Volvo's Answer: Via letters, invitations, photos, and so on.

In other words, in the module tactic phase you deal specifically with details of how to tie the sponsorship module into the business objectives of the company.

List all activities of the target module strategies in detail. Take, for example, an event module designed to generate a list of contacts for Volvo dealers. The tactics required to implement this module involve activities needed to generate that list.

Timetable of Activities

The next step, setting a timetable of activities, merely places the module activities on a schedule showing the completion time for each and who is responsible for the tasks. In this step you should list all months covered by the sponsorship as well as the activities that occur during each month.

Evaluation

The final question you will face in the sponsorship design process is

How are you going to evaluate the return on the sponsorship investment?

Critical evaluation is an alien concept in most sponsorship plans mainly because we know very little about what constitutes a suitable evaluation tool. But there is now a trend toward making sponsorship program directors more accountable for sponsorship investment. As the price of sponsorship escalates, marketers are more consciously scrutinizing the productivity of their sponsorship dollars. In other words, there is a move toward sponsorship *value management*. This means that sponsors are beginning to demand better strategies for assessing how sponsorship is adding value to the company, its product, or its brands.

The fundamental problem in evaluating sponsorship programs is showing that the sponsorship medium you have assembled works better than more traditional methods of advertising, promotions, or PR. Under what conditions does sponsorship work better than these mediums? What does sponsorship do for the company that advertising or sales promotion can't also do—perhaps cheaper? These are not easy issues to tackle, but they are issues that will surely arise if you deal with a sponsor long enough. It therefore pays to have some notion of what your sponsorship programs can and cannot do, and how successfully they are doing it.

Measuring the effects of sponsorship is problematic for at least two reasons. First, a company is usually using other marketing communication tools besides sponsorship. This makes it difficult to isolate the sponsorship element and measure its effect. Second, a competitor's activity, fluctuating economic conditions, and other external factors introduce uncontrollable variables into the equation. The impact these external variables have on the sponsorship program may be positive or negative, and it is difficult to isolate these kinds of interactions.

Occasionally you will find sponsors abandoning research and simply proceeding with an intuitive feeling. Testing adds to the cost, and sponsors will sometimes feel it is not worth the expense. But research is important for other reasons besides helping sponsors evaluate their sponsorship programs. Sports managers can use it as a sales tool when trying to attract additional sponsors. Research findings are particularly important to advertising and public relations agencies as they assess sponsorship effectiveness compared with communication program alternatives their clients might consider using. It can show cities and towns an event's value to local businesses and residents. Finally, broadcast companies can use research to sell advertising when they broadcast your event. In short, good information is always an asset.

Assuming you adopt the philosophy of always evaluating a sponsorship program, if not for your sponsor's purpose then at least for your own, what kinds of things do you measure? Here is a sample of the kind of knowledge commonly sought.

Image. If image is a goal, then you need to somehow assess how the sponsorship package has helped the company's image. You might want to gather data on customer attitudes, knowledge, and preferences about the company's product compared with competitors before and after the sponsorship program. A company may evaluate results by determining the degree to which consumers associate it with the sponsored activity and whether that activity altered corporate or brand image.

Media Exposure. Perhaps media exposure is the sponsorship objective. If so, measuring the duration of the broadcast coverage, as well as column inches of print coverage, is a widely used evaluation strategy. However, the level of exposure merely indicates the extent of publicity resulting from the sponsorship, and this, on its own, does not evaluate the effectiveness of that exposure. Some of the more sophisticated sponsors attempt to improve media exposure measures by taking the type of coverage into account. A name in headline or photo, for example, might be given a higher value than company mention in the body of the story. They will then use some, usually arbitrary, formula to place a value on the total media exposure as a result of that sponsorship. Again, the effect of the sponsorship on the consumer is hardly ever measured—but it should be.

Communication Effectiveness. This is simply an evaluation of the message effect on the consumer. You might assess a sponsorship program in terms of any of the following:

- Image of sponsored activities
- Awareness of who sponsors them
- Awareness and knowledge of sponsoring companies
- Image of those companies
- Source of awareness, types of contact, and quality of contact with sponsoring companies
- Awareness of activities sponsored by the company

Hospitality. When the prime objective of a sponsorship program is to provide hospitality to distributors, employees, trade contacts, or decision makers, monitoring the effects the hospitality program has on these publics can provide direct feedback on whether or not the program has had the desired effect.

Sales. Sales tie-ins are becoming a common feature of sponsorship programs for certain types of companies. Methods for measuring the effect of sponsorship on sales include:

1. Comparing sales during a period (perhaps two to three months) surrounding the sponsorship to the same period in the prior years
2. Measuring sales in the immediate event area against other areas not affected by the sponsorship program
3. Tracking sales by tying them directly in to the sponsorship, for example, by offering ticket discounts with proof of purchase

Event-site Exposure. You can estimate event-site exposure in terms of number of exposure vehicles present at the event site, the length of the event, and the attendance figures. Event-site banners, program advertising, and public address announcements during the event all contribute to a sponsor's exposure. You might want to develop a formula that will account for all these event-site exposure opportunities.

....

| CASE STUDY | VISA International and Its Olympic Sponsorship

In 1988 VISA International became a worldwide sponsor of both the Summer and Winter Olympic Games. As you read through this case study, see if you can identify the various phases of the sponsorship design process that we have covered in this chapter.

VISA's Objectives for Its Olympic Sponsorship

Increase market share and sales volume
Enhance image in travel and entertainment market

VISA's Purchase of Sponsorship Rights from the USOC

By purchasing sponsorship rights, VISA was trying to prevent avenues for its competitors—American Express, Discover, and so on—from ambushing its Olympic sponsorship. For example, if American Express became sponsor of the USOC, this company could easily fool the public into thinking it was also an Olympic sponsor.

VISA's Sponsorship of National Teams around the World

VISA selected sports with high media exposure in various countries where it could maximize its Olympic sponsorship bond and keep out competitors. It sponsored 120 different national teams world wide.

VISA's Use of Olympic Symbols

VISA had exclusive use of the Olympic rings and informed VISA Bank members that this was the preferred logo use, although the company also had purchased rights to the logos of the Calgary and Seoul Olympic Games. VISA used the Olympic logos to create Olympic-themed cards, special-edition ATM decals for merchants, Olympic pin give-aways, posters, and merchandise premium offers, and to generally enhance the image of VISA. Olympic-themed card promotions were used to set the bankcard program apart from competitors.

VISA's Reason for Using Olympic Symbols

The Olympic symbols stand for dedication, quality, and excellence. VISA hoped that the public image of the Olympics would become associated with the VISA card. This could give the VISA group a competitive advantage in the marketplace.

VISA's Fund-Raising Activities for the U.S. Olympic Team

Among the VISA Bank merchants fund raising was the one most common promotional activity used. Merchants could use the following fund-raising activities:

- "Pull for the Team" donation-per-transaction program
- Cardholder-direct donations via USOC provided statement inserts
- Donations to USOC from annual cardholder fee on Olympic VISA cards
- Per-transaction matching donations
- Fund raising from sales of Olympic premium merchandise items
- Other member-direct donations

Over half (53 percent) of the members engaged in VISA's "Pull for the Team" donation-per-transaction promotion, with 50 percent using inserts in statements and 20 percent employing messages in VISA cardholder statements. Thirty-two percent promoted cardholder-direct donations by way of the USOC-provided statement inserts, and 12 percent donated all or part of their annual cardholder fees obtained from Olympic VISA cards to the USOC.

VISA's Reason for Fund Raising

The company wanted to tie in with the national pride and support that Americans feel for their Olympic team and consequently increase card usage.

VISA's Rights to the U.S. Ski Team

One of the 120 national teams to which VISA purchased rights was the U.S. Ski Team in 1988, the most highly nationally televised team in the United States. This established a direct association with a highly publicized team, giving VISA the exposure it wanted on television, magazines, and radio. Everywhere the U.S. Ski Team competed, whether in the United States or around the world, VISA was there displaying banners and maximizing its high-profile association with skiing and the Olympic Games.

VISA's Public Awareness Activities

- VISA-arranged ("Win the Winter Games") sweepstakes.
- Ex-Olympic athletes used for speeches or demonstrations in employee events, public exhibitions, and advertising.
- USOC public service announcements to local television stations.
- Participation in Olympic reunions for fund raising.
- Olympic Games radio contests.
- Ski-lift promotions at local ski spots.
- Fifty Special Olympians selected to be VISA's hosts at the Winter Games. News releases were sent to the hometown newspapers of these Special Olympians.

VISA's Sponsorship Guide

VISA published the VISA Olympic Sponsorship Manual, which was designed to guide VISA Bank merchants on how to use the Olympic sponsorship.

VISA also supported its Olympic sponsorship with regular bulletins and kits illustrating the VISA programs and an extensive communications effort.

Evaluation (As reported by VISA International representatives at the Olympic Sponsorship Presentation Annual Meeting, May 1988)

Results cannot be measured simply in smiles and letters of thanks when we've made a multi-million dollar investment in sponsorship fees and promotion. We're looking at 3 pieces of basic research, our regular, semi-annual attitude and awareness tracking study, a special Olympic Gallup study that analyzes all sponsors' awareness levels, and our own Member satisfaction study, a sort of report card on our effectiveness. First, let's address our primary assignment—creating awareness of our sponsorship. During the six months leading up to and just following the Olympics, we raised the level of VISA sponsorship awareness by 50%, while all others in our category fell accordingly. Compared to others, VISA outperformed some bigger, first time sponsors. These included IBM, Federal Express, and United. We realized about the same level of awareness as GE, and as expected trailed the big 3 long-time sponsors: Coke, Kodak, and ABC.

Generally, the study also found that consumers are considerably more likely to use a sponsor's product—3 out of 5 said so. More specifically this finding was duplicated among credit card holders, as this analysis from our tracking study underscores. Again, 3 out of 5 were likely to use a sponsor's card more often. Our regular tracking study showed VISA with the highest levels and greatest advantage over competition as best overall card that we've ever achieved.

So, on the first two measures—awareness of sponsorship and attitude toward our products—we feel we have achieved our objectives. From a behavioral standpoint, we looked at our two primary audiences—members and consumers.

Members showed their interest in two ways; first in the fact that 365 members, representing 54% of VISA volume, made a conscious decision to participate actively in issuing cards or in using athletes, to name just two activities that were available.

All members also participated automatically, in fund raising and in generally sharing in the image enhancement of the sponsorship. We surveyed both participants and non-participants among our members and found that packaged promotions like the Olympics, appealed to participants and non-participants alike with over 90% concluding that it is a desirable thing to do. Both respondent groups agreed overwhelmingly that VISA's perceptions was strengthened as a worldwide card, and that its image was strengthened overall by the sponsorship while a clear majority of participants thought the sponsorship also helped their institution's image and increased VISA volume. Those members that chose not to participate did so because they had other plans, or felt costs exceeded benefit since they couldn't use the sponsorship to differentiate themselves. We were pleased that no participants cited lack of awareness as a reason for non-participation.

Finally, we looked at consumer behavior where during the fund-raising promotion in the second half of '87, sales were approximately 18%, a full 50% ahead of forecast, not entirely due to the Olympic sponsorship, but certainly influenced by it. Our assessment at this point is that sponsorship has been a positive experience here in the U.S. and that the investment is returning dividends in image and business gains.

We will continue over the Summer to track experience, as will the other regions, preparatory to receiving a proposal from ISL for the sponsorship of the '92 Games. We expect, at this point, to follow a timetable according to the outline here, working up to the key Board meetings and input in September, with ideally a decision in February '89. If favorable, official signing could follow at our Annual Meeting in May, appropriately in France the site of the Winter Games in '92.

In the meantime, planning for the Summer Games, four full months away, goes on. The Five Star Program is still available to Members who want to maximize their benefit. Fund raising for the USOC for the Summer Games is in full swing.

Documentation regarding the VISA International Olympic Sponsorship program was provided to the author by Eleanor Jones, Director of Marketing, VISA U.S.A., Inc.

SUMMARY

This chapter showed you how to help a company design an effective sponsorship program. The steps involved are quite straightforward, but they are frequently overlooked. This often leads to an ineffective sponsorship program for the company. The steps to the sponsorship design process include the following:

1. Make a statement defining corporate objectives.
2. Identify the target markets for the sponsorship program.
3. Analyze your athletic platform for components that will help the company accomplish its objectives.
4. Plan the sponsorship modules that will attain the goals of the company.
5. Analyze all the factors that are likely to prevent the company from maximizing its use of the sponsorship.
6. Determine module implementation strategies.
7. List the specific activities required to implement the modules.
8. Develop a timetable of activities.
9. Design a sponsorship evaluation program.

The next problem you face is how to decide what price you should place on your sponsorship package. We will cover this in the next chapter.

STRATEGIC PLAN WORKSHEET–CHAPTER 10

**How you can help a company develop an effective
sponsorship plan**

Your Goal ....

To design a sponsorship plan for your sponsor
Things to do

- Conduct a sponsorship package audit (Worksheet 10.1)
- Develop a sport sponsorship plan (Worksheet 10.2)

WORKSHEET 10.1

Sponsorship Package Audit

Describe the athletic platform the company has purchased (for example, for Visa, the athletic platform was the Olympic Games).

List the major way a competitor can ambush the company's sponsorship.

List all major exposure opportunities that a competitor could use to ambush your company's sponsorship.

List all the ways your company can use the athletic platform logo to its advantage.

Is there a way your company can raise funds for your organization that will also enhance its sales?

List all the ways your company can let the public know that it is your sponsor.

Could you or your sponsoring company benefit from a sponsorship manual?

WORKSHEET 10.2

The Sports Sponsorship Plan for Company _____

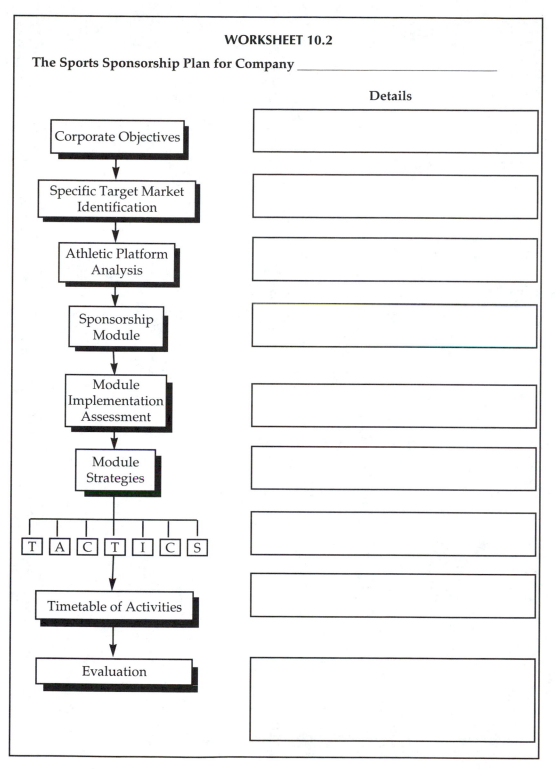

Details

- Corporate Objectives
- Specific Target Market Identification
- Athletic Platform Analysis
- Sponsorship Module
- Module Implementation Assessment
- Module Strategies

T | A | C | T | I | C | S

- Timetable of Activities
- Evaluation

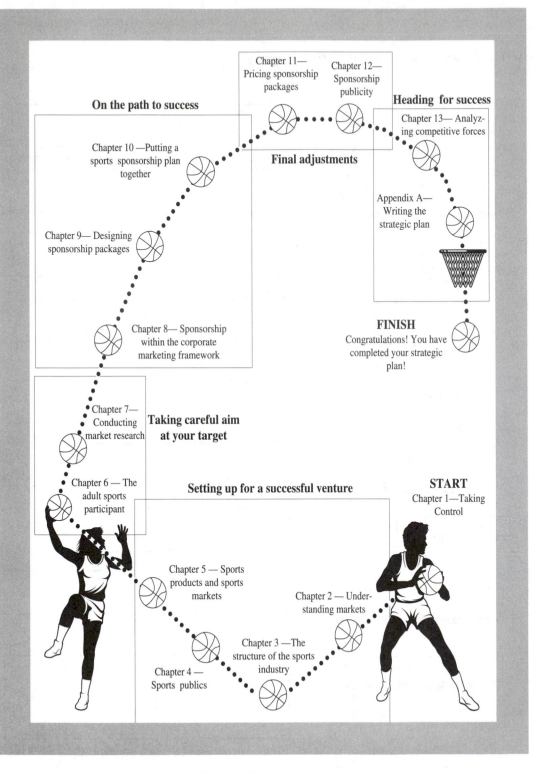

CHAPTER ELEVEN

Pricing Sponsorship Packages

· ·

> At Rome, all things can be had at a price.
> —*Juvenal (A.D.60?–140)*

Price is what your target company pays to receive the benefits of your sponsorship package. It includes money, service, and products. Many factors determine price and this chapter shows you just how frustrating it can be to set a price for a sponsorship package.

Placing Value on an Event

We will assume here that you have followed the steps outlined in Chapters 8–10 and your corporate sponsor has selected the athletic platform that best reaches its desired markets. From the corporate point of view the goal at this stage is to obtain the most favorable sponsorship fee possible. The sports organizer, on the other hand, is seeking to ensure that he or she prices the event at its optimum market value. The question for both parties is, What is an athletic platform worth? Clearly, there is no single answer. The value of an athletic platform varies from sport to sport depending upon corporate sponsorship objectives. Sports that are national in scope are attractive to large companies wanting to reach mass audiences. These types of athletic platforms may cost $100,000 to well over $10 to $15 million. Smaller sports like rowing and kayaking have not only a different consumer scope but also a different personality and therefore attract companies that want to target specific consumers or who have symbolic objectives. These athletic platforms generally cost $50,000 or less.

As you can see in Figure 11.1, sponsorship package price depends, to some extent, upon the alternatives offered. Ultimately, of course, an athletic platform is worth what somebody is willing to pay. The cost of sponsorship may fluctuate widely according to supply and demand, as is the case with the Olympics, the Super Bowl, the America's Cup, and the World Cup (soccer). Sponsorship packages associated with small regional events tend to remain constant in cost, although these, too, will fluctuate depending on certain conditions, which we will discuss shortly.

Estimating sponsorship value, and thus its cost to the sponsor, requires as much judgment as it does hard data. It depends, to a large degree, on the experience of the individual responsible for planning the sponsorship program (we will call this individual the sponsorship planner), the individual purchasing the sponsorship program (sponsorship buyer) and the individual or organization selling the property (the sponsorship seller). Note that the terms *sponsorship planner*, *sponsorship buyer*, and *sponsorship seller* are uncommon terminology in the sponsorship industry. The intent is simply to depict the tasks being accomplished. Note, too, that at this phase of the industry's development, the sponsorship planner and buyer could be the same individual. The sponsorship seller may be a sports marketing agency, the event director (or an event staff member), a television producer (such as Ted Turner for the Goodwill Games), or even a title sponsor who is selling cosponsorship opportunities.

The Basic Factors in Estimating Value

As we have already discovered, the value of a sponsorship package is so athletic platform and corporate objective dependent that its value will differ from company to company and from athletic platform to athletic platform. The outcome, though, is that it must deliver the designated target markets at the lowest possible cost with a minimum amount of waste. Like advertising, the criteria for determining how well the package can accomplish its mission relate to reach, frequency, and impact: What proportion of the target market is exposed to the sponsored athletic platform? Is the frequency of exposure sufficient? Does it have the desired impact? If you can do this at a cost better than other communication mix alternatives available to the company, then you are well on the way to justifying sponsorship as an effective communication strategy. There are several ways sponsorship planners can help ensure that they obtain current athletic platform costs. Let's take a look now at the factors that you need to consider as you assess the value of an athletic platform.

THE MARKETPLACE

It is important to maintain up-to-date records of how the marketplace affects athletic platform price. For example, the price of small local events tends to relate to event production cost and not to inherent value. As these costs increase, event organizers will attempt to pass them on to sponsors. Generally, local-event costs have tended to grow at a relatively modest annual rate compared with larger, national events.

Conversely, large-event costs, particularly those with national and international audiences, are influenced not so much by the value of the event as by the law of supply and demand. You can monitor the marketplace by remaining in regular contact with the event directors and sports organizers. If this is not possible, it might be beneficial to secure the services of a sports marketing agency to fulfill this role. During the course of numerous sponsorship buyer–seller transactions, a sports marketing professional has likely acquired a familiarity with what is occurring in the marketplace. Such familiarity can assist the sponsorship planner in forecasting sponsorship price changes.

SPONSORSHIP CATEGORY

There is considerable diversity of category within the broad realm of sponsorship. Assume, for example, that you are considering buying the sponsorship rights to the tennis tournament in Figure 11.1. Three sponsorship categories are associate sponsor, official sponsor, and Very Important Person (VIP) sponsor. The chart identifies the benefits offered for each category. The task here is to identify the inherent value of audience delivery, media publicity, sales opportunities, and consumer lifestyle association.

Audience Delivery. What is the audience delivery? How targeted is it, how pure is it, and how large is it? According to the information provided by the particular tournament on which the chart in Figure 11.1 is based, national cable television coverage will provide access to a total of 22.975 million subscribers. Note that this is not the number of people who will watch the tournament — it is simply the number of subscribers. Note, too, that not all categories have the same opportunity to reach the television audience. Other factors to consider in estimating the value of audience are these:

- Are the primary consumers likely to be interested in the company's product or service?
- Can the company effectively use the hospitality opportunities this event will provide?
- Will the signage and identification rights provide the company with adequate exposure?

Media Publicity. If media publicity is one of the company's objectives, a sponsorship planner will need to determine how easy it will be to develop a media publicity campaign around this event. How much will this media publicity effort cost the event and the company? Who will implement the media publicity program? Dealing with the media is a very special assignment, for many corporations are extremely sensitive about how the media portrays their corporate image. You cannot afford to make even one mistake.

❑ Designation as a [*category*] Sponsor of the tournament on a
product-exclusive basis ------------------------------------
❑ Right to use such designations in all advertising and promotions --------
❑ One 3' x 9' banner throughout the event -----------------------
❑ Sponsor's name listed as a supporting sponsor in print advertising -------
❑ Listing as follows on the tournament information brochure, of which
125,000 are printed and distributed: -----------------------

❑ Sponsor listing on flyers and press releases ---------------------
❑ Four-seat boxes for all tournament sessions ----------------------
❑ Passes to the Courtside Club offering a VIP lounge area --------------
❑ Reserved tickets for all tournament sessions ---------------------
❑ Invitations to the Kick-Off Cocktail Party ----------------------
❑ VIP parking passes for all tournament sessions ---------------------
❑ Playing positions in the Tournament Pro-Am ---------------------
❑ One full-page advertisement in the Official Souvenir Program ----------
❑ Public address announcements regarding sponsor's affiliation, made
throughout the event -----------------------------------
❑ Special corporate listing in the Official Souvenir Program -------------
❑ Corporate identification on each box --------------------------
❑ Right to set up a booth on site for a promotional display -------------
❑ Invitations to the tournament Press Conference and Draw -------------
❑ Corporate session designation to include the following: --------------

  ▶ Designation of a tournament session as "sponsor's session"
  ▶ Right to conduct a promotion in conjunction with this affiliation
  ▶ One additional banner (3' x 9') in the stadium area during Sponsor's
    Session (Sponsor to supply banner)
  ▶ Right to host a reception for sponsor's guests in an on-site VIP
    hospitality area (catering fees additional)
  ▶ 100 reserved tickets for Sponsor's Session
  ▶ Right to make a presentation on Center Court during Sponsor's Session

❑ Right to conduct promotions (with possible media tie-ins) prior to and
during the event.
❑ Sponsor name/logo or message to appear periodically on electronic
scoreboard located on Center Court ---------------------------
❑ One (1) :30 television commercial sport to be aired during the finals'
telecast (sponsor to supply tape) ----------------------------
❑ Exclusive use of deluxe Sponsor Suite overlooking the stadium.
Sponsor Suite accommodates 8–12 guests and features a bar setup,
dining area, terrace seating, and a fully enclosed lounge. ------------

Sponsorship Fee: ---

Figure 11.1   Example of a Tennis Tournament's Sponsorship Opportunities

ASSOCIATE SPONSOR	OFFICIAL SPONSOR	VIP SPONSOR
✔	✔	✔
✔	✔	✔
In stadium	In concession/entrance	
✔	✔	✔
◗ Sponsor's name listed on title page of brochure ◗ Sponsor's name listed within brochure ◗ Sponsor's logo listed on mailing flap	◗ Listed within tournament information brochure	
✔		
Four	Two	Two
Sixteen	Eight	Eight
Twenty-four	Ten	Ten
Sixteen	Eight	Eight
Four	Two	Two
Two	One	One
Full-color	Full-color	Black and White
✔	✔	✔
✔	✔	✔
✔	✔	✔
✔	✔	✔
✔		
✔	✔	
✔	✔	
✔		
✔	Enclosed sponsor table overlooking center court. (Full lunch and dinner available)	
$27,500	$12,500	$8,500

Sales Opportunities. Can the company use point-of-sale opportunities, direct-mail lists, product-sampling opportunities, cross-promotions with other sponsors, merchandising opportunities, and the promotional tie-ins? If so, how much will each of these cost? Does the company need the athletic platform to run these promotions? Will the sponsorship association improve the company's sales promotion efforts?

Consumer Lifestyle Association. Is the sport an important aspect of the company's target market lifestyle? If so, how much is it worth to a company to show it cares about their consumers' passion? Can you use the image of the sport to the company's advantage? Does the fact that the title sponsor of an event sells cigarettes or alcohol have any potential adverse affect on your image (see the following exhibit)?

OTHER ASPECTS[1]

In pricing sponsorship packages, the successful sports manager must consider a number of aspects other than sponsorship category. Let's consider each aspect in turn.

Magnet Companies. Certain types of companies act as magnets or hooks you can use to attract certain kinds of companies as co-sponsors. If you sign a supermarket chain, for example, it often increases the likelihood of selling co-sponsorship to the packaged-goods companies. If one of your targeted companies is in the position of being a magnet for co-sponsors, you may find it trying to negotiate for expanded benefits or a reduced sponsorship fee.

Leveraging Ability. Some companies are in a better position than others to leverage their sponsorship. Thus, you may decide to price the same sponsorship package differently depending upon the potential leveraging capabilities of the solicited sponsor. A food or soft-drink company, for example, can sell its product on site, whereas a sporting-goods store may only be able to distribute discount coupons. It is clear which business has the advantage. The question is, Should they both pay the same fee? It is worth the effort to make some assessment of a company's ability to leverage the sponsorship compared with the leveraging ability of other cosponsors. There may be room for some negotiation of sponsorship fees.

Competitive Climate. You may also factor into the price the nature of the competitive climate in a potential sponsor's industry. For example, if the same event interests a large number of corporate competitors, this may inflate the price for the sponsorship packages. Since most sponsorship packages are product exclusive, it is usually to an event director's advantage to set up competition among rival companies. Coke and Pepsi, for example, are bitter rivals. If Coke is a sponsor, it is highly unlikely that Pepsi will also be a sponsor, and vice-versa. In

The Danger of Associating with Villain Products

Gerry Smith (CEO of the Women's Tennis Tour Association, WTTA) was acutely aware of the role Virginia Slims had played in making the women's tour a reality. He was just as aware, however, that their presence as the title sponsor at most major women's events in the U.S. made getting women's tennis on television almost impossible. In 1988 the WTTA hired Advantage International to find a new tour sponsor. With more and more pressure being brought to bear by antismoking groups, they felt it was time for a change. Advantage came back with a $6 million offer from Proctor & Gamble.

But Slims wasn't ready to bow out. The company had almost twenty years invested in women's tennis and, through hard work, excellent marketing, and a great public relations staff, had made itself synonymous with the women's game. Philip Morris, the parent company for Slims, came back with a compromise. It would find another company to take over title sponsorship, but Virginia Slims would retain the computer, the U.S. tournaments, and the championships. During the month prior to the WTTA board and player meetings at Wimbledon that year, the women's locker room was a war zone. The Advantage people would grab players, take them in a corner, and tell them why the P&G deal made sense; the Slims people would take up residence in another corner , reminding players about all they had done for the game. In the end, loyalty won out over logic. The older players such as Evert, Navratilova, and Shriver, who had grown up with Slims as the major backer of the game, decided to throw their support to Slims. The P&G offer was turned down.

Kraft General Foods (KGF) succeeded Virginia Slims as the primary sponsor of the women's tour worldwide. KGF was, like Virginia Slims, a subsidiary of the Philip Morris Tobacco Company. It was a choice that left Gerry Smith with some serious headaches—especially with TV. Said Smith:"Right now there is a lack of exposure. Right now we have thirteen U.S. tournaments with the Virginia Slims name on them. Television has banned cigarette advertising. That means that at all those tournaments, no Philip Morris company can buy TV advertising—their lawyers have told them that if they did they would probably get in trouble with the government, because it would be seen as a backdoor way of advertising for Virginia Slims on television."

Adapted from John Feinstein, *Hard Courts: Real Life on the Professional Tennis Tours* (New York: Villard Books, 1991), pp. 106–7.

some cases, a sponsor may decide to pay more than the event is worth just to keep competitors out. In this case, where there is a high degree of rivalry in a product category, a sponsorship seller may be able to inflate the price.

Promotional Spending. The amount of money a company allocates to promote the event may work to a sponsor's advantage. The thinking here is that the more money a sponsor places behind its participation, the more visibility, credibility, ticket sales, and other benefits an event is likely to achieve. Minor sports organizers have been slow to recognize the value of corporate promotional spending. The marketing efforts of Volvo, for example, possibly increased adult recreational tennis league participation. Astute organizers of struggling minor sports may decide to permit free use of their properties in return for corporate marketing expertise and promotional assistance in increasing membership or event promotion. The established events, however, do not concern themselves with corporate event-themed promotions. Promoters of these events believe it is to the sponsor's advantage to use tie-in promotions and other communication mix elements.

SPONSORSHIP PRICING

Sponsorship packages are in a constant state of flux. The environment changes, managers are not always cooperative, advertising agencies will argue against the medium in favor of more traditional communication strategies, distributors will not always see sales value in the medium, athletic platform managers will price companies out of the event, and so on. You will, nonetheless, at some point in your career have to price a sponsorship package. Each sports manager must make pricing decisions that are right for his or her sport or event. There are three general ways to approach sponsorship pricing that at least gives you some control. The first is the cost-plus method, the second the competitive market method, and the third the relative-value method. You will probably finish up using a combination of these three strategies.

Cost-Plus Strategy

When using the cost-plus strategy, you calculate what it costs you to offer a sponsorship package and then you add a predetermined percentage for profit. The chart in Figure 11.2 will help guide you in the cost-plus strategy process. Let's assume your event offers hospitality on site and the other selected benefits listed in Figure 11.2. You would first determine your real cost of providing the benefits listed, then decide what you are going to charge sponsors. Cost-plus tries to ensure a profit to the sports organization, but it tends to neglect the needs of the targeted company. This is a risky method to use if potential sponsors do not perceive you as a desirable athletic platform.

Competitive Market Strategy

At the other extreme are sponsorship pricing strategies based on what managers think the market will bear given the competitive environment. It involves careful research on available sponsorship package opportunities. Competitive market

Hospitality Benefits	Your Cost	Cost to Sponsor
30 VIP Dinners	$	$
30 VIP Pins	$	$
30 VIP Parking	$	$
20 VIP Lunches	$	$

On-Site Benefits		
20 VIP priority seats	$	$
3 Banners	$	$
Display booth	$	$
Sponsor announcements	$	$

Other Benefits		
Color photo of event	$	$
Ad in program	$	$
Exclusivity	$	$
T-shirts for employees	$	$
Labor (time)	$ ———	$ ———
Totals	$ ———	$ ———
Profit		$ ———

Figure 11.2   The Cost-Plus Strategy of Pricing a Sponsorship Package

pricing is usually determined by what the sports organization has to offer and what is offered by other sports organizations. A competitor may also include other methods the company uses to meet its communication mix needs, such as advertising and sales promotion. Reviewing your position within the marketplace requires that you complete the environmental analysis chart in Figure 11.3. For each factor, rank what you offer versus your competitors (1 being the best opportunity for the company and 3 being the worst). Take, for example, the following competitive analysis done for you in Figure 11.3. In this case, compared with your competitors you are at an overall disadvantage. You do have the best consumer match, a fairly good sales promotion opportunity, and good psychological association. This strategy can overlook both the needs of potential sponsors and the event, however. The sports manager must take care to cover costs for the sponsor ship packages and to cosider the company needs in the package design.

	Your Event	Competitor 1 Name:	Competitor 2 Name:
Degree of primary consumer match with company's target market	1	2	3
Size of primary consumer base	3	1	2
Potential media publicity	3	1	2
Sales opportunity	2	3	1
Psychological association	2	1	3
Exposure opportunity	3	1	2
Total Points	14	9	13

Once you have completed your environmental analysis, weigh in such factors as the following:

Is the company a magnet company?
What is the competitive climate like for the company?
Is the target company able to leverage its involvement?
How much money is the company willing to spend to promote the event?
What is the company willing to pay for a sponsorship package?

Figure 11.3 Competitive Market Pricing Strategy

You should note that it is rarely a good decision to price your sponsorship packages below your break-even level—unless you feel that the sponsor is inexperienced in sponsorship and needs to try it before committing large sums of money. In the long-term you may believe this company will be a good sponsor for you if you can get it involved at a low level. In this case, you may decide to underprice the sponsorship package for the first year with the agreement that the price will increase in the second year to its true value.

Relative-Value Strategy

Sports managers who want to show a targeted company the relative value of a sponsorship package use the relative-value strategy. For example, if a company was to purchase the sponsorship package outlined in Figure 11.4 at market value,

Hospitality Benefits
54 stage-side seats @ $75 each
50 VIP event passes @ $25 each
50 general event passes @ $10 each
50 VIP party invitations @ $25
40 VIP parking passes @ $20

Total: $7,850

On-Site Benefits
6 banners @ $100 each
20 X 30 foot display booth: $3,600
30-second on-site TV ad: $500
Event title: $10,000

Total: $14,700

Other Benefits
PR effort by festival staff: $500
Ad in brochure: $500
Festival logo rights: $2,500
Promotional exclusivity: $10,000
120 shirts @ $4 each

Total: $13,980

Total Benefits: $36,530

Sponsorship Fee = $16,500

Figure 11.4   The Relative-Value Strategy

the total package would cost $36,530. However, this package is being offered to a sponsor for a fee of $16,500. Whereas this example does not include exposure value, many sports organizations will add this to the value assessment. For example, you might add gallery exposure (50,000 spectators = $15,000 print advertising equivalency) and television exposure (potential 33 million viewers = $125,000 TV commercial value). For this strategy to work successfully, you must have a good knowledge of the market value of what you are offering, as well as its value to the company.

AUDITING SPONSORSHIP CONSULTING COST

When you help a company plan and implement a sponsorship program, how much the sponsor is costing you will ultimately concern you. If you employ five people and each works 100 hours on one specific sponsor's program, then that is a combined effort of 500 hours. If you pay each individual $15 per hour, that equals $7,500 in paid time. This does not include out-of-pocket expenses such as banners, specialized letterhead with sponsor logos, telephone, postage, travel, and sales calls or other general operating costs involved in developing and implementing the project. Clearly, if your sponsor is paying you $10,000 for the whole process, it may not be worth your effort or time.

Most sports managers are relatively unsophisticated when it comes to analyzing how much locating and servicing a sponsor can cost them. However, it is important for you to identify the real cost of each sponsor and to evaluate this against the market value for your services. The outcome of this information is knowledge about what it costs to take on the role of sponsorship design consultant, the more profitable types of sponsors to pursue, and what profits you can reasonably expect for your services. Staffing and setup time for executing sponsorship programs can be difficult to estimate. Time-tracking studies are cumbersome, but worth the effort, especially in the early stages when you are relatively new at sponsorship design. In a time-tracking study employees keep careful records of time spend on each project.

The cost data you obtain should enable you to better calculate the price of your sponsorship packages. You can compare your costs with those charged by agencies specializing in sponsorship design. This will help you build in a reasonable profit margin and still remain competitive. It will also help you compare how much different types of projects cost, how much labor each project takes, and how efficient you are when you compare yourself with other consultant agencies. You will also have real numbers to show you sponsor, since most will be unaware of the labor intensity of sponsorship program design. You may find that you are undercharging a sponsor. In this case you have one of two options: Talk to your sponsor about ways to hold down costs, or charge more for the sponsorship package. One thing you will invariably discover is that the first year of a sponsorship will cost you much more than it will in subsequent years. For this reason alone you should avoid short-term commitments.

You may also find that the costs are greater than the market is willing to bear for your particular athletic platform. If costs exceed what your sponsor is willing to pay, then you need to redesign the project or think of other ways to scale back the cost. Perhaps you can allocate certain tasks to interns or volunteers. A paid employee checking signage placement at an event site, for example, is an inefficient use of your resources. A less-experienced volunteer or intern can accomplish that job just as effectively as paid staff members. You may also look for ways to pass certain tasks along to the company. You may also have staff performing more than one task. Of course, when each staff member is doing multiple jobs, auditing sponsorship costs can be difficult and it will depend upon whether someone is willing to devote time to the auditing task. In the long run, however, you need to understand not only your sponsor's business goals and operations but your own as well in order to contain your costs.

SUMMARY

Placing a value on an event is not an easy task. Many factors, including the marketplace, audience delivery, media publicity, sales opportunities, and consumer lifestyle association affect event value. You were given three approaches to pricing. The first was the cost-plus strategy, a strategy under which you first determine your real cost of providing the benefits and then you decide what you are going to charge sponsors. This strategy ignores the needs of your targeted company and is not recommended if you do not have a well-known athletic platform. The second approach, the competitive market strategy, is based on what you think the market will bear given the competitive environment. Here you review your position within the marketplace compared with your competitors and decide what you believe will be an acceptable price for your targeted companies. This approach also overlooks the needs of the potential sponsor. The final approach discussed was the relative-value strategy, in which you list the benefits for your targeted company and attempt to illustrate what these benefits would cost if the company used traditional advertising. This strategy requires that you have a good knowledge of market value of the benefits you offer and of the value of these benefits to the company.

Finally, we considered the importance of knowing what a sponsorship is really costing you in terms of out-of-pocket expenses and consultation time. One of the most time-consuming tasks will be your efforts to obtain publicity for your event and your sponsors. In the next chapter you will find out how to develop and implement a publicity plan.

STRATEGIC PLAN WORKSHEET–CHAPTER 11

What you should know about pricing sponsorship packages

Your Goal...

To price your sponsorship package.

Things to do ....

- Price your sponsorship package using the cost-plus strategy (Worksheet 11–1)
- Compare your sponsorship opportunities with your competitors (Worksheet 11–2)
- Price your sponsorship package using the relative-value strategy (Worksheet 11.3).
- Evaluate all three worksheets and assess what price you can realistically place on your sponsorship package.

WORKSHEET 11.1

Cost-Plus Pricing Strategy

Benefit Category

	Benefit Description	Your Cost	Cost to Sponsor
LABOR			
TOTALS		$	$
PROFIT		$	

WORKSHEET 11.2

Competitive Market Pricing Strategy

	Your Event	Competitor 1	Competitor 2	Competitor 3	Competitor 4	Competitor 5
Degree of primary consumer match with company's target market						
Size of primary consumer base						
Potential media publicity						
Sales opportunity						
Psychological association						
Exposure opportunity						
Other						
Other						
Other						
Other						
TOTAL POINTS						

Weigh the Following into the Price

Is your target company a magnet company? _____ High   Medium   Low

Is there a major competitor? _____ High   Medium   Low

Is the company able to leverage its involvement? _____ High   Medium   Low

How much money is your target company willing to spend? _____ $_____

How much money is your target company willing to spend to promote the event? _____ $_____

WORKSHEET 11.3

Relative-Value Pricing Strategy

Benefit Category

	Benefit Description	Market Value	
		Total:	
		Total:	
		Total:	
		Total:	
LABOR		Total:	
TOTAL BENEFITS			$
SPONSORSHIP FEE		$	

REFERENCES ....

1. This section was inspired by Hanley Norins, Traveling Creative Workshop, made available to the author by Young and Rubicam, 230 Park Avenue South, New York, New York.

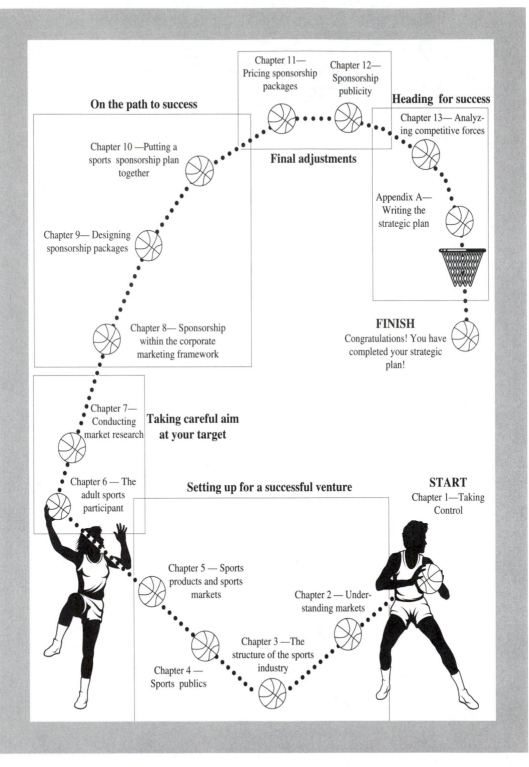

CHAPTER TWELVE

Sponsorship Publicity

••

> I keep six honest serving men (They taught me all I knew);
> Their names are What and Why and When And How and
> Where and Who.
>
> —*Rudyard Kipling*

One objective a company usually has for its sports sponsorship program is to place its name as often as possible in front of the public. You can do this by hanging banners in the stadium so that the company's name or logo is in full view of spectators and television cameras. You can also do it by encouraging the press to publish stories about a corporation's association with the sponsored event. In this chapter we concentrate strictly on how to go about getting the media to publish these kinds of stories.

In its simplest terms sponsorship media publicity is a method of indirectly promoting the company, products, or services in the media by way of a story or an article relating to the sponsorship. The belief is that these "impressions" build name recognition and corporate identity, which ultimately lead to increased sales. The media used for this process are all devices and technologies allowing the company to reach its market. They include magazines, TV, books, newspapers, radio, and wire service. Companies both large and small can participate in the sponsorship media publicity process. It is not just the pastime indulged in by larger corporations with big budgets. Indeed, the sheer number of smaller businesses in the marketplace makes sponsorship media publicity an extremely valuable tool for differentiating one's products or services from those of competitors and for blowing one's horn with more zest and vigor.

In this chapter we discuss how to implement a sponsorship media publicity plan. At the end of this chapter you will find a publicity plan outline that you can use for your own purposes.

Adding Newsworthy Value

In terms of generating news that might attract media attention, a corporation has a basic problem. The company and its products are for the most part boring. An athletic platform, however, has all the components necessary to attract media attention. The linking of a company and its products to a suitable athletic platform makes it possible to shape interesting or newsworthy stories. It is possible to design stories that are either business oriented or sports oriented. For example, the business media finds corporate use of sports and the growth of sponsorship to be interesting business topics. Sports reporters, on the other hand, prefer to report on the event itself; they will report results, occasionally discuss corporate efforts to develop certain sports, and develop other stories related to sports participation. Even establishing a stand for or against some issue affecting sports can bring a company considerable positive press.

How far can we manipulate an athletic platform for corporate publicity purposes? While conventional wisdom suggests that there are probably limits, no one has fully explored what these limits might be. The diversity with which you can exploit the corporate publicity potential of an athletic platform remains an unanswered question.

Understanding the Process

> When the Indianapolis based Synchronized Swimming sold title sponsorship of its national championships to Tambrands Inc. for its Tampax line it found newspapers reluctant to include the sponsor's name. Some editors said they were following their stylebooks. Indeed, earlier in 1987 the Associated Press ruled that corporate names would not be used to identify sporting events unless the events were indistinguishable without them. Others claimed ignorance of the event's proper name. But Betty Watanabe, Synchronized Swimming's executive director, suspects some editors couldn't bring themselves to print the word Tampax. "Having a condom sponsor probably would have brought us more press," she quipped. *Advertising Age*, November 9, 1987, p. S6.

Tampax had assigned two new Master of Business Administration (MBA) graduates to oversee the Synchronized Swimming sponsorship. Besides their problems with the media the most controversial action undertaken by Tambrands was to distribute the tampax product to athletes—even those under the age of menstruation. This did not please many mothers. The Synchronized Swimming Executive Board was equally dismayed. So Tambrands found itself hit from two directions —the press and its potential consumers. Clearly, the classroom did not prepare these two MBA graduates to coordinate, plan, and execute sponsorship programs. Developing and controlling media publicity was an unfamiliar notion for them. The lesson learned at the expense of Tambrands is that sponsorship program development and media publicity planning is not a game for unprepared rookies. It should come as no surprise that Tambrands dropped its synchronized swimming sponsorship in 1987, less than one year after the company purchased it. You can imagine how relieved the mothers, the U.S. Synchronized Swimming Executive Board, and Tambrands were to see the sponsorship association discontinued.

Most corporate sponsors like Tambrands expect exposure from their sponsorship, very few put much time, money—sponsorship media publicity is not free—and energy into getting it. Successful sponsorship media publicity planners must know how to deal with the media; they must fully understand what the media considers news, and they must control how and when the press will use a company's name. In essence, the marketing concept is just as important to formulating sponsorship publicity programs as it is to products and services. This includes identifying needs of editors (research), formulating those needs into a desired story (product development), letting editors know that stories are available (communication), and making the stories easily accessible (distribution).

Unfortunately, media publicity planners seldom consider the marketing concept. Many of those involved in the process are like Alice in Wonderland trying to get somewhere but not sure where.

> "Would you tell me, please, which way I ought to go from here?" "That depends a good deal on where you want to get to," said the Cat. "I don't much care where—" said Alice. "Then it doesn't matter which way you go, " said the Cat. "—So long as I get somewhere," Alice added as an explanation. "Oh, you're sure to do that," said the Cat, "if you only walk long enough."
>
> Lewis Carroll, *Alice in Wonderland*

In the sponsorship media publicity journey, going somewhere by walking long enough will likely get you in a good bit of trouble—wasted resources, wasted effort, and possibly some bad press—and, ultimately, you may discover that somewhere is not really the place you want to be after all.

Getting Where You Want to Go

The basic question sponsorship media publicity planners must ask in order to get where they want to go is, What are the best means of delivering messages through the media about my company, brand, or product through our athletic platform? The sponsorship publicity planning process consists of a series of decisions that provides the best possible answers to this general question. In essence, to avoid ending up somewhere you must ask the questions posed in Figure 12.1. When you have asked all these questions and decided upon the answers, you organize the recommendations and rationale into a document called the sponsorship media publicity plan. This is the blueprint that guides how a sponsor can use the athletic platform for sponsorship media publicity purposes.

Can a carefully planned sponsorship media publicity effort make an automatic success out of a sponsorship? No. But, it can certainly help direct the

What type of media publicity and how much of it does a company want to achieve?

What are the opportunities available via a specific athletic plaform?

What is the plan for stimulating sponsorship media publicity?

Adjust the plan

Is the type and volume of sponsorship media publicity desired being obtained?

Figure 12.1   Model Guiding the Sponsorship Publicity Process

process. It can also help determine the best methods of exploiting the athletic platform and help isolate the most productive strategies to use.

THE SPONSORSHIP MEDIA PUBLICITY PLANNING PROCESS ....

> It sounded like an excellent plan, no doubt, and very neatly and simply arranged: the only difficulty was that she had not the smallest idea how to set about it.
> Lewis Carroll, *Alice in Wonderland*

 In this section we will attempt to lay down a method for going about the media publicity process. The goal is to establish a base from which to develop a plan — simple and neatly arranged—and give some direction as to how to set about it. Keep in mind, though, that a plan is always easier to set out on paper than to implement. In real life there are many difficult decisions to make, especially when it comes to dealing with the media. You will no doubt occasionally wander off into uncharted territory and fall victim to errors. For unlike paid advertising, sponsorship media publicity is unpredictable, and opportunities will never occur at the precise time you need them. As well, you will never have complete control over whether the media will print your stories.

Throughout the sponsorship media publicity planning process you must keep in mind that sponsorship media publicity is merely an intermediate objective. The ultimate purpose is to obtain a desired level of market awareness about the company that will, you hope, lead to sales of products or services. Figure 12.2 presents the steps in this process, which begins by identifying corporate communication objectives. After identifying the objectives, you then examine the answers to the following questions:

- What are the general sponsorship media publicity objectives?
- How many ways can the athletic platform be exploited for media publicity purposes?

- Once the media publicity opportunities have been identified what is the specific purpose of each one?
- What strategies should be used to maximize the opportunities available?
- How should the stories be distributed throughout the media so that the company's target market is effectively reached?
- How much money, time, and effort should be spent on each of the sponsorship media publicity programs?
- How should each program be implemented?
- How should each sponsorship media publicity program be evaluated?
- Did the sponsorship media publicity meet corporate communication objectives?

For our purposes, we will discuss only the process and will not delve into what effect sponsorship media publicity has on people. We will not discuss whether people's attitudes toward a company change, whether there is much or little value in the recall people may have about a corporate association with an athletic platform, or if a sponsorship media publicity message is persuasive. Like the sponsorship field, generally, we have not yet fully researched the sponsorship media publicity field.

Figure 12.2   The Sponsorship Media Publicity Planning Process

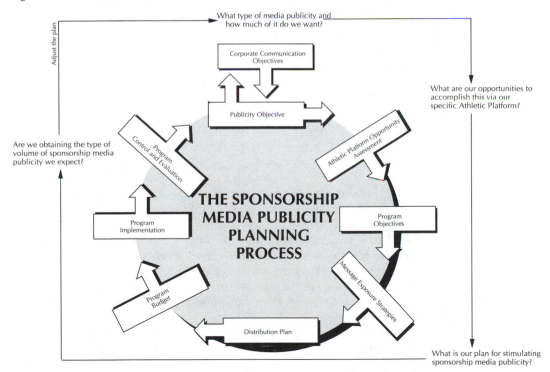

Publicity Objective

Publicity objectives are the goals that a sponsorship media planner believes to be the most important in helping attain corporate communications objectives. Goals might include such things as what targets you want to reach, how many there are, and where you should concentrate your publicity efforts.

Athletic Platform Opportunity Assessment

It certainly is easier to gain media attention when you have a popular athletic platform. However, a better-known athletic platform does not necessarily guarantee media exposure. High-stakes-sponsorship players are likely to find themselves fighting for media attention amidst a pack of exposure-hungry cosponsors. Sponsorship media publicity relies a great deal on a sponsorship planner's ability to understand markets in relation to the athletic platform. It also relies on creativity and packaging skills.

The first step is to establish a clear understanding of the athletic platform. It may be necessary to research the structure of similar sponsorship media publicity programs and how they use the different types of athletic platforms. If you search long enough and think creatively enough, numerous media publicity possibilities will pop up. Media publicity stories may include:

- How sponsors use sports to enhance product sales
- How companies use sports to target consumers
- History of the company's involvement with a sport
- Companies as the "good guys" that are helping a sport survive and grow
- Companies lending their marketing expertise to help a sport better market itself to its participants
- How the company uses its sponsorship to raise money for good causes
- How the company involvement is bringing sports to the recreational participant

Attainable Program Objectives

Once you have explored the media opportunities, you can then outline attainable objectives for each selected component of the athletic platform. Program objectives allow you to assess whether the media plan is worth pursuing. Objectives should also point to a way of evaluating the project and determine if cost will provide adequate exposure to the designated target markets.

There are three levels of an athletic platform: professional, collegiate, and recreational. You can develop media publicity objectives for each of these three levels. For professional sports, for example, you might want to encourage media coverage of the professional event that a company is sponsoring; you might do this by increasing awareness of the event, building local business media contacts, and expanding national media interests. You can reach future consumers by supporting collegiate sports like tennis, track and field, golf, or swimming. To help generate media attention of these low-visibility athletic platform components you may need to add a star athlete as a spokesperson for the collegiate program. Another media attention strategy for a collegiate-level sport is to establish a collegiate computerized ranking system for the sport. Finally, you might decide to encourage the growth of the recreational dimension through the development of leagues or other forms of low-level competition. This will provide a company with local media publicity networks.

Media Exposure Strategy

Journalists want stories that interest their readers, viewers, and listeners. In this respect, two forces affect the sponsorship media publicity process. The first force includes newspapers, magazines, radio, or television editors. These individuals are the gatekeepers who decide if your stories are of interest to their target audiences. The second force involves the sports organizers, consultants, and media advocates who advise the sponsorship media publicity planner on the best way to approach their markets. The goal of media publicity strategy is to use the insights of the second force to find a way through the gates set up by the first force. Figure 12.3 depicts the secret weapons that will help open the gates.

Here are some possible tactics:

- **Facts:** Become a library of facts and statistics about your athletic platform.
- **Corporate Statistics:** Assemble all the information you have about your corporate involvement with the athletic platform, including the following:
- Why they are involved.
- What sponsorship does for their company. Assemble as many facts and figures as possible to back up your statements.
- Why they selected this specific athletic platform. Know your demographics, psychographics, number who watch/participate.

Develop stories around such topics as these:

- How the company achieves sponsorship objectives.
- Interview opportunities for the CEO. Make sure this individual is fully briefed on the athletic platform.
- Concern for your athletic platform and its development.
- How your company is an innovator in the use of sponsorship.
- How your sponsorship helps dealers and distributors.
- The company's sense of responsibility to the community.
- **Videos/Tapes:** Make interesting and unique video and tape clips available for use by TV.
- **Be a Consultant:** Encourage your sports organization to develop their own media publicity program. Show them how to
- deal with the media
- publicize the event
- set up a press room

Figure 12.3   Secret Weapons That Will Open the Sponsorship Media Publicity Gates

- work with public relations agencies
- release information
- **Player Quotes:** Develop an inventory of memorable player/participant quotes.
- **Develop Story Angles:** Search for such story angles as:
- overcoming adversity
- being first—youngest, oldest
- rivalries—among famous players, family members, battle of the sexes
- fantastic accomplishments
- making sacrifices
- out for revenge
- taking great risks
- accomplishing, failing, accomplishing again
- famous moms and dads
- **Photo Files:** Organize a file of interesting photos for magazines and newspapers.

- **Celebrity Spokesperson:** Find a famous athlete to be a spokesperson and promoter of your sponsorship.
- **Sports Promoter:** Help develop one or all the components of your athletic platform—encourage membership, organize visibility campaigns for "future" stars, develop an awareness of the sport.
- **Publicity Materials:** Identify all the publicity materials to help encourage media publicity. Do you need press jackets? Executive photos? Fact sheets? Statistics packets? Posters?

Not all story angles will be suitable for all athletic platforms. But the task is to be ready to seize all media publicity opportunities that are available or that will become available. Develop stories that are interesting, and then manage their distribution through suitable media. Is the story appropriate for the selected media? Are relations with the press fully exploited? Have you developed press advocates?

Press advocates are often overlooked. If you are designing a long-term sponsorship association and media publicity is one of the company's objectives, it may be necessary to spend considerable time developing media advocates throughout the country. "Developing media advocates" means identifying potential writers interested in the athletic platform and targeting them for stories. You should list the areas in the country where the athletic platform is dominant and locate all the media outlets in each area. Then keep track of where media advocates have been developed, the name of their respective newspapers, magazines, television, or radio, and the circulation for each.

Remember, if a company's prime objective is exposure, a critical aspect of a media plan will be to encourage media interest in writing and reporting about the athletic platform. Putting time and money into developing advocates will be essential to the success of media exposure objectives. Sports organizers, especially directors of minor sports with very little media coverage, can learn an important lesson here. If you want the media to cover a sport, you need to spend time identifying and developing advocates.

Distribution Plan

As we have already discussed, a sponsorship media publicity "product" is fundamentally the combination of a corporate name or logo and unique bundles of athletic platform components. This combination is designed to attract media attention. Once the "publicity product" has been packaged, it becomes time to develop a distribution strategy for the stories. Again, a plan of attack is important. Haphazardly distributing stories or news releases to the media usually leads to wasteful spending. Today's marketplace consists of segments of homogeneous groups of people. To appeal to all these different lifestyles, tastes, activities, and interests the communication media itself has become highly differentiated. There are more than 15,000 magazines that cater to every conceivable lifestyle and interest. In a country where there are more than 200 million people, few companies can afford to talk to them all. And not everyone is a prospect for a company's product or service. Although publicity is not being paid for directly, as it is for advertising, considerable indirect cost is involved. Therefore, the more precisely the company's target market is researched and defined, the easier it is to design the necessary story angles and to get them printed. Targeting relevant media is a more economical strategy than the haphazard approach.

Medium, Vehicles, and Reach

The three basic terms to understand as you design a distribution plan are *medium*, *vehicle* and *reach*. **Medium** is used to describe the general carriers such as newspapers, television, radio, or magazines. The **vehicle** is a particular carrier within a medium such as the *New York Times*, *Sports Illustrated*, or CBS. **Reach** is simply the number of people who read, listen to, or watch the vehicle. Planners prefer vehicles that reach an optimum number of prospects. They also prefer vehicles that are cost effective; that is, they reach the highest number of people with minimum waste or nonprospects.

Start by looking for suitable distribution channels among the many media alternatives that target the company's potential consumers. Many comprehensive media directories are available. *Editor and Publisher Yearbook* is one example. This yearbook contains a directory of daily newspapers. It also provides staff members, population, circulation, and trade area statistics. Another helpful reference is the *Gale Directory of Publications*. *Gale* is cross-referenced by region, by frequency of publication and by subject. *The Writer's Market* provides information about magazines, identifying their readers, their editors, and the types of stories they publish.

As you develop your media publicity list keep in mind that reach is not the only criterion. Although weekly newspapers have a smaller reach than do the dailies, you may submit material to these because there is a high probability your material will be used. Understaffing is a common problem among weeklies, and they often have trouble finding adequate material to fill their news holes for each issue.

Access to athletes is another important part of distribution. In speaking before the collegiate coaches, Doug Smith of *USA Today* stressed how important it was for tournament directors, sponsors, and athletes to be aware of the need for press access to athletes. According to Smith, some sports are better at doing this than others. The Women's Tennis Association (WTA), for example, does a much better job than its male counterpart in making the athletes available to the press. This probably relates to the difficulty female athletes generally have in obtaining press coverage, and as a result they make an extra effort to be accessible.

Program Budget

The budget for a sponsorship media publicity effort will vary depending on its complexity and the desired objective. The question is whether or not the objective is worth achieving for the price. For example, are 160 million media impressions worth a total sponsorship budget of $900,000 to a company? The answer to the "is it worth it" question may be no. For instance, John Hancock Mutual Life Insurance Company decided that the Falmouth Road was not worth $60,000.[1] Although the Falmouth race was one of the premier events in the country, John Hancock was not getting the recognition from the race the company thought it needed.

Factors Affecting Budgeting

Many factors will affect a budget. We have just discussed one dominant factor — what you want to do. Besides this, a company's competitors will also be a factor. It is worth investigating what the competition is up to. How much is it spending on its media publicity program? This is especially important if a company's athletic platform has several cosponsors. A competitive analysis may indicate that many sponsors of an athletic platform are all seeking high levels of media publicity. The more sponsors associated with an athletic platform, the harder it is to generate a message that is loud enough to fight through the clutter of sponsors.

The biggest complaint expressed by sponsors is that many are working within a budget so anemic that any worthwhile media publicity program is impossible to accomplish. Persistent whispers will not attract as much attention as one mighty yell. In other words, make sure you fund all publicity projects adequately. It may be better to leave underfunded projects until adequate money is available.

Program Implementation

Program implementation is, in two words, *doing it*. To ensure that you cover all elements of the project, list the activities you want to accomplish and when you want them completed.

Program Evaluation

Although we suspect sponsorship media publicity can have positive effects, no one has yet found a way to draw a direct sales-response curve for them.

Start your evaluation process by taking a general, subjective look at what happened. For example:

- Was the program adequately planned?
- Did everyone understand what was needed?
- Did everyone cooperate?
- How could the results be made more effective?
- Were all pertinent audiences reached?
- Were expected levels of publicity reached before, during, and after the program?
- Were all unforeseen opportunities maximized?
- Did you stay within budget? If not, why?
- Did you plan to measure results?
- Can you use this measurement to improve future programs?

One of the most commonly used measurement tools is exposure. The generic term is *impressions*. If the company's name appears in a newspaper with a circulation of 1 million, that equals 1 million impressions. You can do similar calculations for television broadcasts and magazines and newspaper articles where the corporate name appears. It is helpful to calculate the cost per 1,000 impressions so that you can track sponsorship publicity cost effectiveness on a yearly basis. In this manner, if the cost of the sponsorship increases over the years, it is easy to determine the exact cost of the publicity program each year. A graphic display such as that used in Figure 12.4 can provide you with an immediate picture of the success or failure of a sponsorship media publicity program. It analyzes the program in terms of type of impressions obtained, the total number, and the cost per 1,000 impressions.

Although the number of impressions may be a convenient measurement strategy to use, it can be misleading. The assumption is that those exposed to a media vehicle will also be exposed to the story and to the company name. Clearly, this is easy to disprove. It would be much neater to have data on how many individuals read, viewed, or listened to the story. This kind of information is not generally available. Therefore exposure to the vehicle itself has become the basic measure.

It is also possible to calculate the advertising value of a sponsorship me-

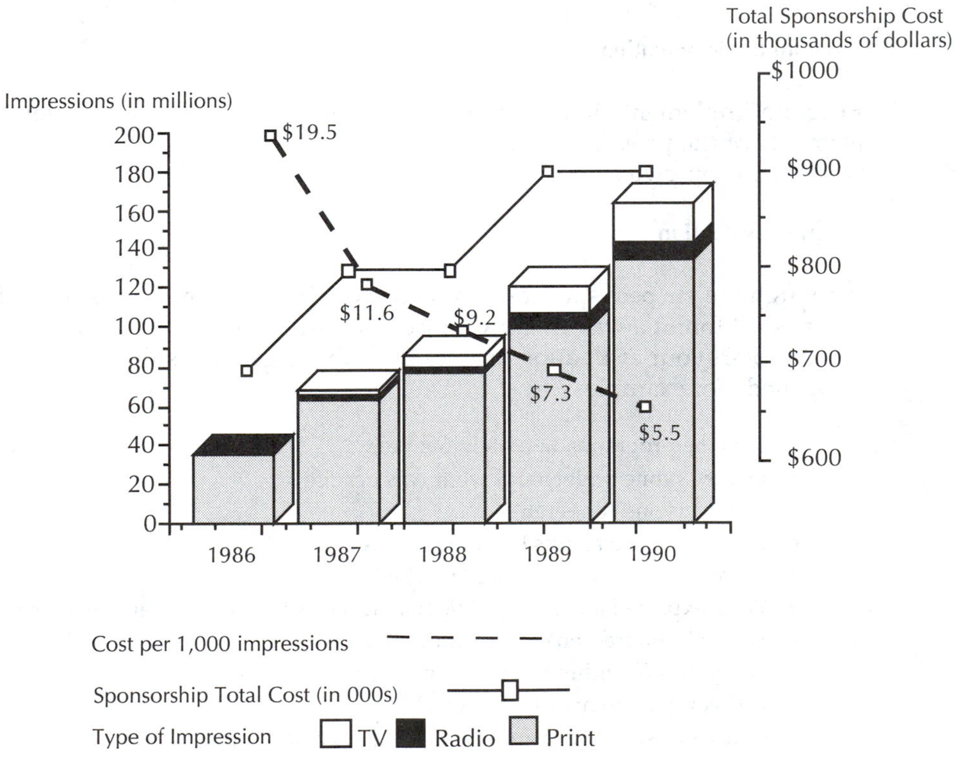

Figure 12.4   Analysis of Type of Media Impressions, the Number, and the Cost per 1,000 Impressions

dia publicity program. Simply measure the size of a picture or article in which the company's name appears, and then calculate a portion (perhaps 30 or 40 percent, or whatever you feel is appropriate) of what it would cost to purchase an advertisement of that size in that publication. You can treat television in a similar manner. Measure the number of seconds a company's banner appears on the screen, estimate what this would have cost if you had actually purchased the time, and calculate a portion of that cost. Of course, exposure is not the only issue. There is the added factor of perception. How does each vehicle affect the perception of an article that it carries? How do people interpret the message? Is it good or bad, and do they even notice the company's name? Answers to these questions are not yet available and clearly require research. Despite the problems, it is reasonable for company CEOs to want some measure of what they get in return for the sponsorship dollar. They want to know such things as the following:

Audience Coverage.   Even if we are at present unable to measure the effect of sponsorship media publicity on product sales, it is a logical assumption that in order to produce results, you must first reach the intended target group. How large an audience did you reach? What were they like? What proportion of the company's target audience do they represent?

Audience Response.   This will require some research. How do members of the audience respond? Do they react favorably or unfavorably to the message? Does it arouse their interest? Does it bore them? Do they understand it?

Communication Impact.   What impact does a sponsorship media publicity message have on its audience? What are the lasting effects?

Process of Influence.   This is a complex issue, but one that we must begin to measure. How does a sponsorship publicity message influence its target audience? How effective is the program in influencing the opinions and behavior of the target audience?

Other Evaluation Methods.   You may also want to develop evaluation tools specific to your Athletic Platform. You should try to assess reach, message conveyed, consumer perception of the message, and value of the article in advertising dollars.

SUMMARY

This chapter showed you how to design and implement a sponsorship media publicity program. In its simplest terms, sponsorship media publicity is a method of indirectly promoting your sponsor in the media by way of a story or article relating to the sponsorship. A media publicity strategy is specific to the company and the athletic platform. The process begins by identifying your sponsor's communication objectives; then you must find as many ways as possible to use your athletic platform for media publicity purposes. If you develop a successful media publicity campaign, the results can be worth thousands of dollars of exposure value to a company. But media publicity is not free. It requires considerable time, effort, and even some money in order to effectively exploit the medium. If you work through the following worksheets, you will begin to realize just how time-consuming it can be.

STRATEGIC PLAN WORKSHEET–CHAPTER 12

What you should know about sponsorship publicity

Your goal ....

To outline your media publicity plan for a corporate sponsor

- ✍ • Describe media goals/objectives (Worksheet 12.1)
- ✍ • Outline strategies (Worksheet 12.2)
- ✍ • Outline your advisory services (Worksheet 12.3)
- ✍ • Outline your distribution ideas (Worksheet 12.4)
- ✍ • Outline your program implementation publicity tasks (Worksheet 12.5)
- ✍ • Describe your program implementation materials (Worksheet 12.6)
- ✍ • Describe your program implementation staff (Worksheet 12.7)
- ✍ • Describe your program implementation timetable (Worksheet 12.8)
- ✍ • Outline your sponsorship media publicity report (Worksheet 12.9)
- ✍ • Outline your program evaluation program (Worksheet 12.10)

The media worksheets were adapted, in part, from the 1990 Volvo Tennis Media Plan, which was made available to the author by William Mergler, VP Corporate Promotions, Volvo North America.

WORKSHEET 12.1

Media Goals/Objectives

Some Ideas

Tie company to the athletic platform	Establish the company as a key sponsor. Strengthen the company's identification with the athletic platform audience. Increase media exposure for local business and distributors by promoting their involvement and financial contributions.	
Increase athletic platform exposure	Increase the number of advance stories, both on and off the sports pages, thereby expanding the scope of each event. Heighten awareness of the sport in regions of the United States where media awareness is low while increasing media contacts in regions where media awareness is high. Increase national awareness of the company-sponsored events by generating media advocates in key market areas.	
Expand publicity network	Establish a comprehensive publicity network utilizing sectional coordinators and public relations personnel. Assist the NGBs to pursue local and national articles about grassroots activities on a year-round basis.	

WORKSHEET 12.2

Strategies

Some Ideas	Your Comments
Brainstorm national publicity targets and story angles.	
Assign staff members to target national media outlets regionally.	
Produce new items for both the press and the public to constantly reinforce the company's predominant position in the sport.	
Pursue speaking engagements for corporate personnel.	
Maintain regular, year-round contact with both local publicity personnel and local media.	
Produce press releases for local distribution, tracking the progress of the local winners throughout the year.	
Develop story angles for arts, food, health, style, and women's pages.	
Provide advance footage of top entries.	
Design photo sessions with athletes to provide unique photos for advance feature placement in local markets.	
Develop relationships with wire services and national radio networks to provide on-site coverage.	
Hold media receptions at each event, to include non-sports journalists.	
Identify dominant media markets.	
Develop athletes' understanding of media relations through the media training seminars.	
Maintain up-to-date biographies on athletes, media guides on the teams, photo file and videotapes pertaining to the sport.	
Promote recreational programs by distributing quarterly press releases to update the national media on the status of the greassroots aspect of the sport.	
Distribute highlighted press clippings to executive directors, presidents, coordinators, and public relations volunteers to illustrate the value of publicity activities.	
Distribute releases to local business and sports editors in areas containing strong distributor support.	
Distribute overview of public relations operations, including sample press releases to sectional coordinators and PR volunteers.	
Conduct meetings with the NGB public relations staff to encourage more active participation in year-round publicity activities.	
Identify dormant media markets by analyzing media coverage in each section and assisting appropriate coordinators with press release distribution and media advocate contact.	

WORKSHEET 12.3

Advisory Services

A company should be an integral part of media operations. The staff can help generate new ideas for event publicity.

Some Ideas	Your Comments
• Assist in updating event media lists and target new and potential advocates. • Write and edit press releases. • Assist in producing press jackets and informational materials. • Organize advance media tours, interviews, and press conferences. • Assist in directing on-site media operations, distributing results, and securing on-site interviews with company executives. • Organize media functions during events. • Coordinate post-event reports, including compilation of clippings and recommendations.	

WORKSHEET 12.4

Distribution—Media Target Lists

Possible Media Targets		Targeted Media	Target Date	Type of Story
Advertising Age	Inside Sports			
AdWeek	Los Angeles Magazines			
Associated Press	Los Angeles Times			
Atlanta Business Journal	Marketing & Media Decisions			
Atlanta Constitution	Memphis Business Journal			
Atlanta Magazine	Modern Maturity			
Automative News	Nation's Business			
Auto Week	Money			
Barron's	New York Times			
Boston Globe	Newsday			
Business Month	New York Post			
Business Week	Reader's Digest			
Chicago Times Magazine	San Francisco Focus			
Christian Science Monitor	Sporting News			
CEO Magazine	Sports Illustrated			
Changing Times	Sports Travel			
Connecticut Monthly	Southern Living			
Cosmopolitan	Sport			
Crain's Chicago Business	Student Life			
Dossier	UPI			
Financial World	USA Today			
Forbes	Wall Street Journal			
GQ	Washington Business Journal			
Harvard Business Review	Washington Post Magazine			
Heartcorps	Washington Post			
Industry Week	Washingtonian			
In-Flight Magazines				

WORKSHEET 12.5

Publicity Tasks

Some Ideas	Your Comments
• Advance Publicity Produce media plan at least four months prior to event. Distribute press releases according to plan; schedule weekly, beginning two months before event. Schedule phone interviews for players, sponsors; distribute business/sports pitch letters and program kits. Hold media tours/press conference for players, sponsors within six weeks of event. Develop specific story angles for on-going feature use and releases once media plan is completed. Produce and distribute player black-and-white action/head shot composites for releases. Prepare operational checklists for local press officers. Schedule informal luncheons and meetings for sponsors and tournament officials at varying times prior to event. Organize a list of media discounts and distribute to the media, including hotel and airfare, in addition to receptions and other functions on site.	
• On-Site Publicity Target daily publications for daily faxing of notes and results. Coordinate player interviews for local media and phone interviews for regional and national press. Provide tournament backdrop for post-match press conferences. Schedule business and sports media interviews for company personnel. Distribute daily videotape match highlights to local, regional, and national television stations and networks. Host media receptions at each site. Determine player story angles upon completion of daily schedule and feed to stations that day.	
• Post-Event Publicity Track and record clippings coverage and send highlights to events. Distribute wrap-up photos to national and regional sports publications, general interest, and business magazines. Prepare tournament reports with emphasis on recommendations for following year.	

WORKSHEET 12.6

Materials

Some Ideas	Your Comments
A. Printed Materials Cube pads targeted to media advocates and representatives for the professional, collegiate, and recreational programs. Posters. **B. Photography** Established files on player, hospitality, promotion, and facility subjects. A file of participants in action, trophy, and team photos for use in producing materials and servicing the media. Videotape highlights. **C. Press Kits** **Overall Program Kits** The company in sports CEO bio CEO photos Demographics of target audience Corporate sales data Sports marketing article reprints Awards brochures Athlete spokesperson bio and photo Data about the sponsorship **Event Kits** Ticket brochure Sponsor profile Charity release (if applicable) Tournament program Composite player release Event fact sheet TV release (if applicable) Special presentation release (if applicable) Past-event winners Player fact sheet Current rankings **Media Gift Bags**	

WORKSHEET 12.7

Staff

Ideas	Your Comments
Who will do these tasks? • Supervise the overall media program. • Pitch the program to national media. • Coordinate national publicity efforts of the media staff and for creating new concepts and ideas. • National sports and business media placement. • Supervise the liaison with the NGB. • Manage the press room and advance media for events. • Oversee tracking of national media efforts and impression numbers for the various programs. • Coordinate media reporting efforts. • Count and calculate value of press clippings. • Produce press kits. **Official photographer** • Supply photos of top players. • Work with media staff to place photos. • Supply photos of corporate functions. **Videotape** • Provide videotapes to local and national television outlets.	

WORKSHEET 12.8

Timetable

	Overall Sponsorship Program List what is to be accomplished.	Specific Sponsored Program List what is to be accomplished.
January		
February		
March		
May		
June		

Note: You should develop your own copy of this worksheet that includes the relevant months.

275

WORKSHEET 12.9

Sponsorship Media Publicity Report

Name of the Event:

Dates:

Prize Money:

Winners:

Attendance:

New Attendance Change (%):   Attendance Previous Year:

Local Media Representative/Affiliation

Duties   ❏ Write/distribute releases
              ❏ Organize advance press conference
              ❏ Organize media activities
              ❏ Direct on-site operation
              ❏ Arrange one-on-one interviews
              ❏ Produce press kits
              ❏ Chart clippings

Other:

# of Staff On-Site

# of Media On-Site

List Key Media On-Site

Materials Distributed: ❏ Press kits
                              ❏ Media guides
                              ❏ Credentials
                              ❏ Player information
                              ❏ Sponsor information
                              ❏ Event fact sheet
                              ❏ Player photos

Other:

Major Placements:

WORKSHEET 12.9

Sponsorship Media Publicity Report–Page 2

Special Media Promotions:

Performance Rating

	Poor	Below Average	Average	Good	Excellent	
Advance Publicity	1	2	3	4	5	N/A
On-Site Publicity	1	2	3	4	5	N/A
Post-Event Publicity	1	2	3	4	5	N/A
Press Conference	1	2	3	4	5	N/A
Media Reception	1	2	3	4	5	N/A
Corporate Publicity	1	2	3	4	5	N/A
Special Promotions	1	2	3	4	5	N/A

Comments:

Recommendations:

Other:

List Major Media Placements:

WORKSHEET 12.10

Program Evaluation

Name of Media Vehicle _____

	Degree of match	How does this help us accomplish corporate communication objectives?
Demographics of company target market		
Demographics of media vehicle		
Reach of media vehicle (prospects only)		
Message conveyed in article		
Consumer perception of message (research will be necessary)		
Value of article in advertising dollars (cost of buying space the size of the article in that publication) × a portion of the advertising value (e.g., 30 percent)	$	
General evaluation notes		

REFERENCES...

1. *Special Events Reports,* October 24, 1988, p. 5.

This chapter was influenced by the following authors:

Beals, M. *Expose Yourself: Using the Power of Public Relations to Promote Your Business and Yourself,* Chronicle Books: San Francisco, 1990.

Goldman, J. *Public Relations in the Marketing Mix.* Lincolnwood, Ill.: NTC Business Books, 1984.

Pinskey, R. *The Zen of Hype: An Insider's Guide to the Publicity Game.* Ontario: Citadel Press, 1991.

Goff, C. F., ed. *The Publicity Process.* Ames: Iowa State University, 1989

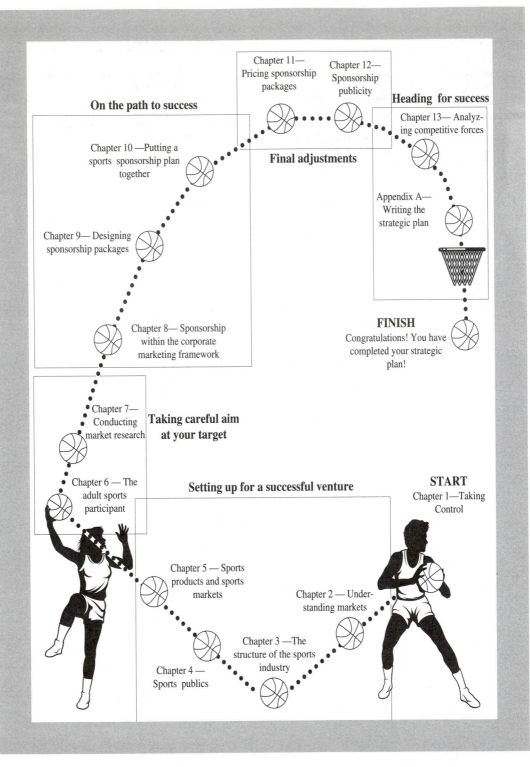

CHAPTER THIRTEEN

Analyzing Competitive Forces

• •

> I am a citizen, not of Athens or Greece, but of the world.
> —*Socrates (469? - 399 B.C.)*

What happens outside your organizational structure is just as important as what happens inside. There was a time when external competitive business forces did not concern sports managers. Listen in on discussions among sports managers today, and you will quickly see that their external environment deeply concerns them. One key question they want to answer is, What forces within the environment affect our financial survival?

THE INDUSTRY ANALYSIS MODEL

A useful method for analyzing forces affecting the sports industry is a process introduced to the corporate world by Michael Porter in 1980.[1] Porter isolated five forces, the structure of which shapes the way individual companies, in our case sports organizations, can compete successfully. Figure 13.1 illustrates the five forces. By analyzing and understanding these five forces sports managers can develop a profile of the specific aspect of the industry in which they want to operate. This makes it possible to identify competitive opportunities.

Take, for example, the intense competition among sports organizations for sponsors. If you do not have a profile of the forces that shape the sponsorship industry, you will not be able to formulate a strategy that will allow you to work at a competitive advantage over other sports. A sponsorship industry analysis

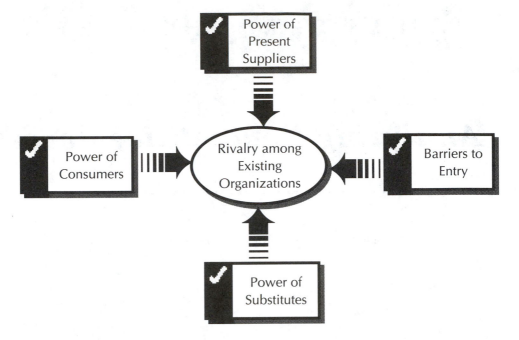

Figure 13.1 The Five Competitive Forces Affecting Sports Organization
(Reprinted with permission of The Free Press, a division of Macmillan, Inc., from Michael E. Porter, *Competitive Strategy: Techniques for Analyzing Industries and Competitors.* Copyright © 1980 by The Free Press.)

helps define benefits valued by sponsors and allows you to position yourself as better than, or different from, your competitors.

In this chapter we discuss Porter's industry analysis model as it applies to the sports industry. You can use this model whenever you need to analyze a specific situation. To show you how you conduct such an analysis, we will discuss an actual case study of how one Olympic sport used the model to identify distribution opportunities for its sport.

The Five Forces

Rivalry among existing sports organizations

Whenever there are several sports vying for limited resources such as sponsorship money, you will find yourself enmeshed in competition with your friendly—and not so friendly —rivals. An example many of you may be familiar with is college athletics departments. Powerful sports like football and basketball will strive to keep the majority of the resources for themselves and away from the non-revenue-producing sports. In turn, these smaller sports struggle among themselves for their share of the remaining resources.

Competition can be beneficial when it increases the overall demand for the industry's products. For example, two tennis clubs in a town can both win if in the process of competing they expand the overall market for tennis. Similarly, two or more recreational golf courses in a confined area can fight for market share while simultaneously stimulating the market for recreational golf. The NFL and the NBA fight merchandising battles, and in doing so they increase the demand for sports-branded apparel.

However, intense competitive rivalry can also have an adverse effect on profitability. College football teams, for example, have competed fiercely for television time. The result is such a proliferation of college football on any fall Saturday that the rights fees derived from individual games have dropped dramatically. Sports managers must learn to compete with their smaller and less powerful colleagues in nondestructive ways. You see this principle at work among professional sports leagues where there is an effort to reduce the direct competition among league members.

Barriers to Entry

Every time another business entity enters your market, your consumer base is at risk. If it is easy to set up a shop in your specific sport's business area, you may find yourself with many competitors. The sports agency industry, for example, presents almost no barriers to entry. Anyone can hang up a shingle, print up business cards, and declare the title of sports agent. On the other hand, the barriers to entry into a sport may be formidable. For instance, starting a new professional football league may be extremely difficult because of capital requirements, difficulty in obtaining facilities, and difficulty in persuading quality players to join the new league.

Barriers to entry are not always obvious.
Consider these:

- Access to distribution channels—in the United States, high schools and colleges have been important distribution channels for the USOC. When high school or college athletics departments struggle financially, the smaller Olympic sports such as synchronized swimming are often cut from the varsity program. With removal of the distribution system, participation in that sport will decline. The NGB must then seek alternative distribution channels.
- Capital requirements—starting a recreational tennis or golf tournament, annual marathon races, or triathlon competitions requires access to the necessary sponsor backing, facilities, promotional materials, and staff.
- Consumer loyalty to existing sports or leisure-time activities makes it more difficult for new sporting events to attract a market. The American love affair with football, for instance, makes is difficult for soccer to attract a spectator market.
- New entrants may find that favorable geographic locations are already taken, making it difficult for them to find a suitable market.
- Sanctioning bodies or governmental agencies often have regulations that prevent entry into the industry. For example, only the International Olympic Committee

(IOC) can give a sport Olympic status. That sport's participants can enter the Olympic Games only if they have the blessing of the IOC.

- Experience requirements—organizing a triathlon competition requires more experience with the event that organizing a 5K walk. Producing a major football bowl requires a great deal of experience.

A strategy that often discourages new entrants is aggressive expansion. NFL expansion into Europe, for example, will probably discourage the formation of other leagues. The more barriers a new entrant must face, the better it is for current competitors.

Power of Substitutes

The third force we must consider acknowledges the potential impact of substitutes. Consider football for a moment. What competition does football have from potential substitutes? If you said none, you may want to reconsider your response. There is no sports organization in existence that does not face direct competition from substitutes. Even football must contend with other leisure and entertainment options people have. We call such options substitutes.

It is often difficult to distinguish between a competitor and a substitute, however, and many times we use the terms interchangeably. The key is simply that you account for all potential choices consumers have available to them. The professional sports industry, for example, must consider all forms of entertainment as either competitors or substitutes. A sports manager who is analyzing the sponsorship industry must also look at arts and concerts as potential substitutes. Sports are not the only communication platform available to the corporate sector. To understand how substitutes can affect a specific sport we need to

- understand how and why sports fulfill the needs of consumers
- know what substitutes are available that can fill these same needs
- identify and evaluate how serious the threat from these substitutes are to sports
- find ways to reduce their threat

Power of Suppliers

In sports any individual or company providing key products or services is a supplier. Universities produce professional football players. Sports marketing agencies produce a sporting event, represent the best athletes, and sell sponsorship and television broadcast rights. Corporate sponsors provide cash, equipment or services. These are all various types of suppliers. Strong suppliers can have a negative affect on the profitability of a sports organization. Agents such as ProServ, for example, are the chief source of top-ten-ranked male tennis players. Thus, ProServ can have a major impact on whether or not a tennis tournament can field "household name" players.

Powerful suppliers will often determine how much of the profits a sports organization can keep. Suppliers with significant power—whether it is in the form of cash, equipment, or athletes—may raise event costs by demanding certain benefits. This, in turn, reduces profits for the sports organization. Sports agent suppliers may also reduce the quality of the competition by threatening to withhold their athlete clients from participating in the competition. Without top-caliber athletes the event will not attract television. You will find that a supplier group is powerful under the following four conditions:

1. A few large companies with vast resources dominate it. For example, ProServ and IMG dominate the sports marketing agency industry. Both companies represent athletes, own and produce events, own and produce television broadcasts, sell sponsorship rights, sell television advertising time, and even act as event television announcers.
2. The supplier's product or service is instrumental to the sport's product or service. For example, ProServ has client players that are highly desired by tennis tournaments.
3. The sport does not represent a large share of the supplier's market. For example, minor sports attract such a small portion of the television audience that they are not important to television programmers.
4. The supplier has the potential to forward integrate into the sports industry. For example, sports marketing agencies can produce their own sports events to compete directly with sanctioned tournaments.

In analyzing the power of suppliers in the sports industry, you must identify the key supplier groups, which ones are the most powerful, and how that power will affect you. Only then is it possible to identify steps to circumvent that power.

Power of Consumers

This force recognizes the power that buyers exert upon suppliers. The more alternatives buyers have, the more power they have. For individual sports, identifying and understanding buyers is important to extracting higher profits. For example, all sports could agree to seek different groups of buyers and this would reduce the power buyers have by minimizing the options at their disposal. Realistically, this hardly ever occurs, since certain kinds of buyers are usually more attractive to a wide variety of sports organizations. If yours is a small organization, you will need to search for less desirable market segments where there are fewer competitors and find creative strategies to profit from them.

APPLICATION

Once you have diagnosed the forces affecting your sport, you move to the next step—understanding the causes of each force and isolating ways to maneuver against them. Such maneuvering could encompass a combination of offensive and defensive strategies. You might, for example, find a different market position for your sport; alter the balance of forces through strategic moves; anticipate shifts in the factors underlying the forces and respond to them in such a way that the competitive balance changes in your favor. This sounds complicated, but if you think critically and creatively you will be surprised at how many opportunities become evident. This is easily illustrated with a research project done for U.S. Synchronized Swimming. In the following case study you will learn how to use the industry analysis model to investigate competitive forces. The case focuses on an investigation of the Parks and Recreation system as a distribution channel for synchronized swimming.

....

CASE STUDY | Synchronized Swimming

Two important factors inhibit participant expansion in synchronized swimming: familiarity and distribution. Let's examine familiarity first. If this is a problem with your sport, what can you do? One of the first things you might decide to do is study other products to see how managers deal with the problem. The product does not necessarily have to relate to sport, for we can learn from almost any situation. So let's take cosmetics.

Cosmetic companies in the 1970s wanted women to be familiar with their eye products. Eye cosmetics required women to adopt an unusual behavior—decorating their eyes. To create a mass market for eye shadows and eye liners cosmetic firms established demonstration counters in stores throughout the country to teach women how to use their products. Along this line of reasoning, the first phase of introducing an unfamiliar sport to an area of the country is to set about creating awareness and familiarity with the sport. Do you have demonstration centers where people can learn about your sport? An example of a demonstration center for synchronized swimming is the water show. Focus interview data have indicated that many girls develop an interest in synchronized swimming while watching one of these shows.

Distribution also inhibits participant expansion opportunities. In the case of synchronized swimming there is an inadequate distribution network for the sport. A club generally exists because an interested individual has taken the initiative to start it. Consequently, there are pockets of clubs throughout the country, but the sport is not widely diffused. Some sports already have distribution channels through the school system (track and field, swimming) or through a private club system (gymnastics). Sports like synchronized swimming, however, lack built-in distribution channels and must find ways of developing them.

Forcing a potential distribution channel to cooperate will not work. Universities, for example, resist considering synchronized swimming for varsity sports—unless, of course, the sport has the potential to contribute financially to the athletic program. The sport does happen to have this capability, but at this point in time it has not developed a marketing plan to promote itself successfully. So for the time being it may be better for the sport to spend its time and limited resources searching out more "willing" partners.

A Potential Strategy

As synchronized swimming managers searched for distribution possibilities, they wondered if Parks and Recreation programs could be viable distribution channels. For synchronized swimming to penetrate the Parks and Recreation system, the managers needed to know what key forces drove this complex organization. In light of these forces, what should synchronized swimming do to succeed in this environment? They used Porter's model to guide their research project. The five competitive forces underlying the structure of the Parks and Recreation system are illustrated in Figure 13.2. To determine the impact of each of these forces, synchronized swimming managers conducted in-depth interviews with key personnel within thirty different programs. They asked twenty-one questions designed to assess the feasibility of using

Figure 13.2   The Five Competitive Forces Underlying the Structure of the Parks and Recreation System

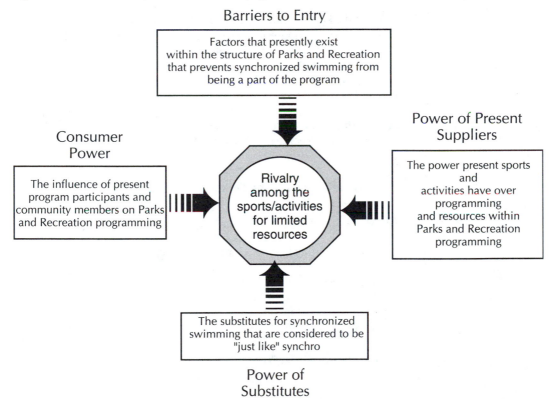

the Parks and Recreation network as a distribution channel for synchronized swimming. The interviews lasted between thirty and forty-five minutes.

Two of the 30 parks and recreation programs interviewed had small synchronized swimming club programs that were struggling to survive. One of these programs was a year-round club with twelve girls; it was now without a coach and subsequently cancelled for the summer. The second, though it had been in operation for 20 years, was only a summer program. This year the group was smaller than usual and the instructor had difficulty getting sufficient girls to perform the end-of-summer show. In a few cases an interested community member had suggested a class and offered to teach it. However, no one signed up for the classes. There were also two instances where synchronized swimming had existed several years before but died because of waning interest. Except for these situations, none of the other Parks and Recreations programs in the sample offered synchronized swimming to its consumers. Read through the following summary of the interviews, and as you read each question, try to identify the key issues. After each section you should complete the Competitive Force Analysis Worksheet. To give you some guidance the Barriers to Entry Worksheet (Figure 13.3) has been completed for you (see page 292). There are four steps to the process:

1. Identify the key issues from the research for each force.
2. Evaluate the importance of each force to the entry of synchronized swimming into Parks and Recreation pools.
3. Briefly describe why the force is significant.
4. List the significant problems and the steps synchronized swimming can take to counteract them.

Assessing Barriers. The goal here is to determine barriers within the Parks and Recreation structure preventing entry of synchronized swimming.

Q. Is There a Reason You Don't Have a Synchronized Swimming Program?

The responses to this question fell into three categories:

- No one in the community had requested a synchronized swimming program.
- There was a lack of interest in the sport in their community.
- A qualified instructor was not available.

A busy pool schedule was mentioned only a couple of times.

(Analysis: Busy pool schedule is not a factor.)

The most common reason for not having a synchronized swimming program was perceived lack of interest in the community. However, Parks and Recreation is a reaction-oriented organization. If no one specifically asks for a particular program, aquatics directors assume there is no interest. If one of two conditions exists—either someone asks for synchronized swimming or someone offers to instruct—Parks and Recreation would make an effort to provide a program.

(Analysis: There is a perceived lack of community interest.)

Q. What Do You Know About Synchronized Swimming?

The common response to this question was "not much." Some had seen it on TV or had been to water shows. A few giggled at the question and said:

- "Oh, I know they put gelatin in their hair"
- "That's where they kind of dance in water."
- "I'm sorry I'm not much help. It's a team sport right? Do they compete or is it just done for the joy of it?"
- "I know you need a pool and water!"

(Analysis: Gatekeepers do not know much about the sport.)

Q. Who Makes the Decisions About Pool Programming?

In some of the Parks and Recreation departments the aquatics director or pool manager had complete autonomy over pool programming. In others, a board of control made the decision. Sometimes the board based its decisions on the recommendations of the aquatics director; other times the board simply made decisions that were based on past experiences. Where the aquatics directors and pool managers had autonomy, they were highly involved, enthusiastic, and knowledgeable. It was "their" pool and "their" program. They boasted about "their" pool being the nicest facility around and "their" aquatics programs being recognized as a good one. These individuals also tended to have been on the pool staff for a reasonably long period of time.

Those who had little decision-making power, on the other hand, seemed to be recently hired. Staff turnover at the pool appeared high, perhaps explaining the "newness" of the aquatics staff. Individuals with little autonomy were more detached from the pool than autonomous individuals. Nor did they express as much pride in their pool or their aquatics programs. It appears that it may be easier to gain access to a specific Parks and Recreation pool if the aquatics director or pool manager has some autonomy, that is, if there is less bureaucracy.

(Analysis: Gatekeepers without autonomy lack desire to add new programs.)

Q. What Kind of Information Do You Need to Implement a Synchronized Swimming Program?

The response to this question would aid the NGB in putting a package of material together for distribution to the Parks and Recreation system. The requests included the following:

- lesson plans
- a description of the necessary equipment
- a brochure describing synchronized swimming
- past history of the sport
- skill levels the girls require
- resource pamphlet—where to obtain more information
- promotional strategies—how to raise the awareness about synchronized swimming
- the cost of running a program
- how much time it takes
- suggestions on how to fit it into a pool schedule
- how to get a coach
- where a coach can go for training

(Analysis: This is a potential gatekeeper material package.)

Q. If We Asked You to Start Synchronized Swimming Classes What Would You Want to Know?

- What type of person should we hire/what qualifications?
- How much would it cost?
- What staff/equipment would we need?
- What kind of guidance are you going to give us?
- Should they do a water show—how do you do a show?
- What does the staff training involve?
- What does the program entail?
- What are the benefits of the program?

- Where do I get more information?
- How do you publicize it?
- What about the insurance?
- Is this a long-term program, or is it a fly-by-night outfit?
- Are there competition opportunities in the sport?
- Where does a girl to go to pursue synchro further?
- What problems are other Parks and Recreation programs experiencing with their synchronized swimming programs?
- How many people can you accommodate in a pool?
- Is there a nationally recognized program we could use?
- Where can we get instructors trained?
- Is this a growing sport in any other parts of the country?
- What age groups are involved?
- How will this draw more people to our pool?
- How do I go about getting a coach?
- How long should the classes be?
- How many do you put in a class?
- Where do I start—what do I do?
- Why would you want us to do it?
- How do you expect us to recruit people for the program?
- What kinds of people do you want in the program?
- Are the girls training for something, or is it just for fun?
- Will there be someone to back us up when we run into problems?

(Analysis: This is a potential gatekeeper implementation package.)

Q. How Do You Feel About Adding a New Sport or Activity?

Parks and Recreation systems are quite positive about trying new programs. The philosophy is that their role is to serve the community. However, finances have played a role in recent years and will continue to play a more dominant role in the future. Most departments have budget limitations. Almost every respondent asked how much a synchronized swimming program would cost and whether other Parks and Recreation departments had break-even programs.

(Analysis: Need to find successful Parks and Recreation programs.)

Now you should study the Barriers to Entry Analysis Worksheet (Figure 13.3), which has been filled out for you. Note the key research findings regarding the barriers, how signiicant these barriers were believed to be, a brief comment on what makes each significant, and the summary of the significant barriers along with actions that can be taken to overcome them.

BARRIERS TO ENTRY

STEPS

1. Identify the key barriers to entry from the research interviews.

2. Evaluate how significant this barrier is.

3. What makes it significant?

4. List the significant barriers and an action that can be taken to counteract each.

Summary of Research Findings

Perceived lack of community interest	Gatekeepers don't know much about the sport	Gatekeepers with lack of autonomy lack desire to add new programs	Gatekeeper material package	Gatekeeper implementation package	Budget issues
Very (circled) Mod Slight Not	Very (circled) Mod Slight Not	Very Mod Slight Not (circled)	Very (circled) Mod Slight Not	Very (circled) Mod Slight Not	Very Mod Slight (circled) Not
If this is true, an awareness campaign will be needed.	If they don't know about the sport they are likely to assume it is similar to lap swimming.	Can't do much about this - stay with autonomous pools.	Need this information if they are expected to add the sport.	Will not know how to implement unless they are told how to.	Can be a factor but not likely to stop implementation.

SIGNIFICANT BARRIERS

SIGNIFICANT BARRIERS	ACTIONS THAT CAN BE TAKEN
Perceived lack of community interest	Do survey to find out attitudes of community. Then develop campaigns. Need to set up demonstration centers (i.e., watershows).
Gatekeepers don't know about the sport	Develop videotape to tell gatekeepers about the sport. Video can also be used by them to promote the sport in their pool.
Gatekeeper material package	Put packet together based on list asked for in survey. Distribute free to all pools.
Gatekeeper implementation package	Put packet together based on list asked for in survey. Distribute free to aquatics directors wanting to start a program.
Budget issues	Need to provide information on cost of synchronized swimming to Parks and Recreation and suggest ways to reduce cost.

Figure 13.3   Barriers-to-Entry Analysis Worksheet

Assessing Substitutes.   The objective of this information is to determine if gatekeepers perceive other activities as being similar to synchronized swimming. During the preliminary phases of the research, one Parks and Recreation superintendent asked how synchronized swimming was different from other swimming. He could see no additional benefits from synchronized swimming that could not already be obtained from lap swimming. To him, swimming was swimming and that was that. Then he hesitated, apparently realizing he had simply closed his mind off to synchronized swimming, and said, "You tell me. What are the benefits of synchronized swimming?" After been told about the intrinsic value participants obtained—the creativeness, the interaction, and the beauty of the sport that were not inherently a part of lap swimming, the superintendent's eyes sparkled. "Now," he said pointing a pencil in mid-air. "I hadn't thought of that. If there is a group of people out there who want to express themselves through a sport in this way and we are not providing them that opportunity, then that would concern me."

Although the respondents we interviewed might privately have believed that the benefits from the two sports are similar, none openly expressed that opinion during the interviews. Generally, it seemed that the majority were open to offering synchronized swimming.

(Analysis: There may be the belief that synchronized swimming satisfies the same needs as lap swimming.)

Now complete the Substitute Analysis Worksheet (Figure 13.4) before proceeding to the next section.

Assessing the Power of Present Suppliers.   The goal of these questions is to determine how present programs may affect the entry of synchronized swimming.

*Q. What Are the Financial Goals
for the Programs?*

Knowledge about this area usually related to the amount of autonomy the respondent had. Those with the most autonomy projected the most knowledge. In these cases the response was usually "to break even." Most, however, stated that they didn't know, but they thought the goal would be to break even. Some Parks and Recreation departments have a nonreverting fund, which consists of money from registration fees that is set aside for special events. Apparently these departments get a budget that will cover their running costs, and any fee they charge for their programs is extra money.

Swimming pools are an essential part of most cities in this country, but they are expensive to operate and require subsidization. To try to

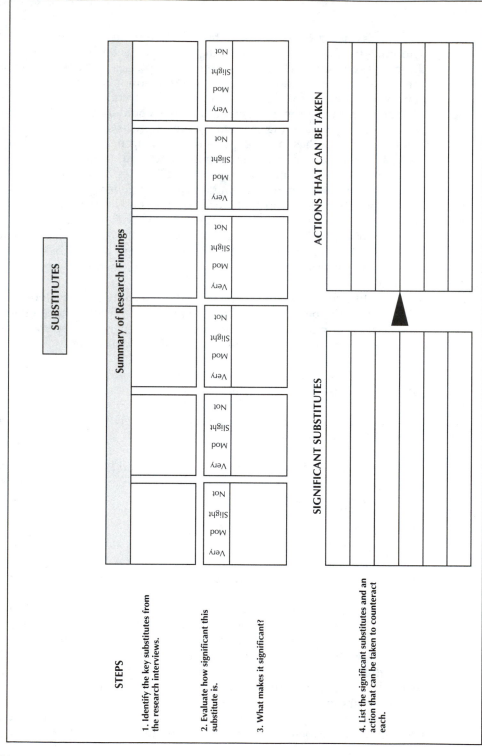

Figure 13.4 Substitute Analysis Worksheet

recoup all the costs is not considered in the best interest of the community. However, there are renewed efforts to increase pool attendance to reduce this subsidization. Water slides have been added to some facilities. Some pools have been renovated, and a few departments have built completely new facilities.

(Analysis: Other swimming programs do not recoup all their costs.)

Q. How Do You Evaluate Programs?

Most Parks and Recreation programs do not have a formal program evaluation process. Programs looked at in the study were predominantly evaluated through signups, class attendance, and whether or not people kept coming back. Usually the only financial concern was to try to break even.

(Analysis: Signups and class attendance are important.)

Several departments collected user survey data. However, these were more the exception than the rule. One evaluation program involved a four-step process. First the parents were surveyed about the class, whether their children improved, whether they had fun, and so on. Next the instructors themselves were surveyed regarding their evaluation the success of the summer program. The supervisors also filled out a questionnaire about how they thought the class was going. Finally the class was evaluated financially: How much was it subsidized? How much did it cost?

(Analysis: Overall, program evaluation is based upon easily observable factors. Soft or intangible variables such as improved mental well-being and improved self-confidence are not used.)

Q. How Would You Evaluate Synchronized Swimming?

There was considerable hesitancy with this question. Some simply said they didn't know; they were not familiar enough with synchronized swimming to answer the question. Others thought that they would probably evaluate the sport with the same subjective procedures used to evaluate swim lessons, namely, class signups, class attendance, and repeats.

Now complete the Supplier Power Analysis Worksheet (Figure 13.5) before proceeding to the next section.

Assessing the Power of Consumers.   The objective of this information is to determine how much influence consumers have over Parks and Recreation programming.

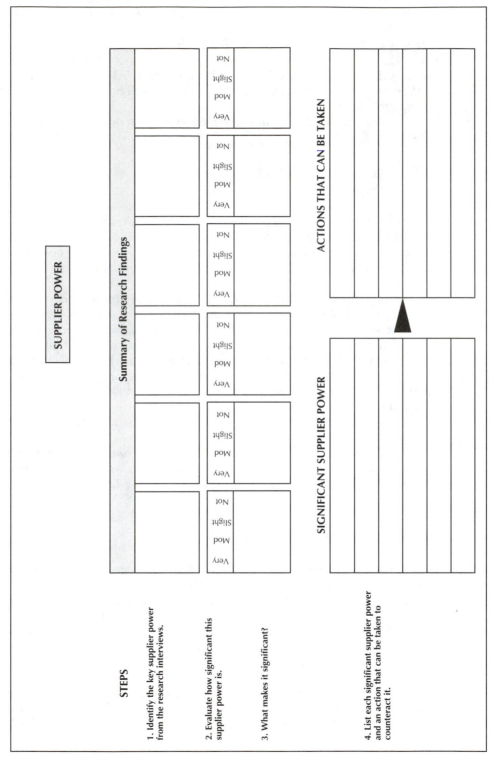

Figure 13.5   Supplier Power Analysis Worksheet

Q. Why Do You Feel There Is Little Interest in Synchronized Swimming?

It was generally felt that lack of interest was due to unfamiliarity with the sport. Some thought that the majority of adults could probably tell you something about synchronized swimming, but most young girls could not.
(Analysis: Consumers lack familiarity.)

At this point in the discussion respondents were asked what image members of the community had of synchronized swimming. Most believed there was probably no image at all, at least none to speak of. That is, there were no feelings about the sport one way or the other. People just didn't know enough about synchronized swimming to really have an opinion.
(Analysis: Synchronized swimming has no image.)

Q. How Would People Go About Getting Synchronized Swimming Classes in Your Pool?

The community members would have to show interest first by going to the Parks and Recreation personnel and specifically requesting the program. Preferably, they should also have a qualified instructor available . The class would then be placed in the brochure and there would be a trial period to "see how it goes over." As one recreation director put it, "You can't beat an old dog to death—we usually let a program run a year or two and see how it goes. But when the time comes, you have to say enough is enough, the people are just not interested."
(Analysis: Community must show an interest. Need qualified instructors.)

Q. How Do You Publicize Your Aquatics Programs?

Most Parks and Recreation departments make a program brochure available to the community. These are distributed in one of three ways: They are sent home with the children through the school system, distributed with the local newspaper, or made available at various strategic locations throughout the city. A few also use radio and advertise in the newspaper—but this is not common. Of the departments canvassed, most generally felt that advertising took too much money and was not very successful. Some did a direct mailing to participants of previous classes.
(Analysis: Publicity is passive; that is, consumer will probably sign up for familiar programs.)

Q. What Is Your Most Successful Promotional Strategy?

The responses here varied. There is no scientific measure of promotional effectiveness. For some the newspaper was ineffective; for others it was effective. Some felt that brochures were the bible for parents—something they held onto for several months. Others felt brochures were not effective. Many believed that the best method was simply to place posters about the programs at the swimming pool. The notion here was that people who came to the pool already had a basic interest in swimming, would see the posters, and would sign up for the classes. At one pool, the addition of the water slide contributed to learn-to-swim enrollments. More people were coming to the pool because of the slide and were seeing the posters. Word of mouth was also frequently mentioned as the best publicity.

(Analysis: Parks and Recreation do not know how to successfully promote their programs.)

Q. Do the Parents or Their Children Take the Initiative to Sign Up For Your Programs?

This question usually elicited a clarification question from the respondents: "Do you mean any of the recreation programs or just the aquatics programs?" As it turned out, there are apparently differences. When it comes to the swimming programs, most felt that the parents—usually the mother—took the initiative because she wanted her child to learn how to swim. However, for other recreation programs, it was believed, the children themselves were the instigators of the idea to sign up.

(Analysis: Since synchronized swimming is not a learn-to-swim class, it will likely fit into the recreation program category. Therefore, girls may be the target for synchronized swimming—not the parents.)

Q. Do You Do Any Research on Your Consumer?

Most departments have never done much in the way of consumer research. One or two of those in our study had done a basic user survey. Others felt that they heard enough voices from the community every day to have a reasonable enough feel for what the needs were. Yet others didn't know; if there had been any research, they had not seen the data. A few recognized the need for consumer research but didn't have the computers necessary to undertake a study. In one instance there was an interest in knowing who the pool consumers were so that the program brochure could be better targeted.

(Analysis: Parks and Recreation probably do not know their consumers very well.)

Q. Do You Try to Target Any Particular Groups?

Government departments are philosophically against targeting specific segments of the population to the exclusion of others because doing so would lead to perceived favoritism of certain social groups over others. It is not surprising, then, that the Parks and Recreation departments studied for this report did not target their programs to any specific groups. The communities themselves selected what they wanted. Tennis, for example, attracted a certain socioeconomic groups, and swimming was more general in its appeal. Children under twelve years of age were the predominant market segment for the swim classes. Participation dropped off after this age even though there were swim clubs they could join—a trend attributed to the high school swim programs.

Now complete the Consumer Power Analysis Worksheet (Figure 13.6) before proceeding to the next section.

Assessing Competitive Rivalry.   The goal of these questions is to determine whether some activities have priority over pool time.

Q. What Is Your Pool Usage Like?

It appears that all pools were having a good year. Both pool usage and class enrollments were up over previous years, and many pool managers attributed this to the hot summer. One pool had almost tripled its learn-to-swim enrollments over the past three years. However, very few felt that they were at full capacity. Money to hire more staff was a problem.

(Analysis: There does not appear to be much competitive rivalry for the pool.)

Q. What Other Facilities Are Available In Your Area?

During the preliminary research done prior to this project, one individual suggested that we find out about other facilities in the area, since this might be a factor in the willingness of Parks and Recreation departments to experiment with new programs. The rationale was that areas in which Parks and Recreation had competition for the consumer would appear to be more progressive in their programming.

As it turned out, potentially competing facilities such as YMCAs and health clubs did not appear to be a factor in whether or not a Parks and Recreation system was willing to explore aquatics alternatives. Most

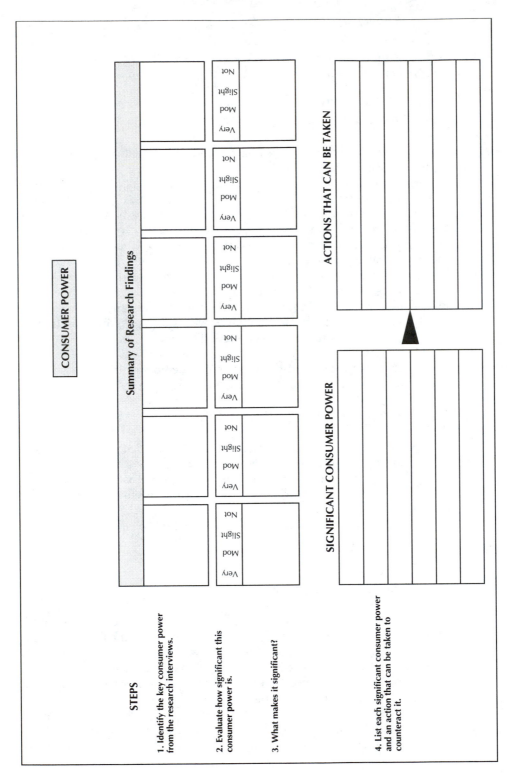

Figure 13.6 Consumer Power Analysis Worksheet

operated as if they were the "only game in town," but one or two pools would not offer a class if the YMCA was offering it. However, in most cases other facilities were not a factor in pool operation.

(Analysis: Parks and Recreation does not appear to be affected by other competitive forces.)

Q. How Do You Differ From These Other Organizations?

No one really had much of a response to this question. There is apparently little research on consumer usage of different types of facilities.

(Analysis: Parks and Recreation does not appear to know where it fits in the recreational marketplace.)

Q. If Synchronized Swimming Were to Be Offered, Do You See It Taking the Place of Something Else?

Most departments answered no to this question, although some said they would try to slot it in during the learn-to-swim programs, when the pool was not being fully used. Others felt there was still some available pool time during which synchronized swimming classes could be offered. However, there were a few situations where lack of pool space would present a problem. Under no circumstances would the learn-to-swim classes ever be touched. These were sacrosanct—the assigned mission, so to speak, of Parks and Recreation swimming pools. "I firmly believe that everyone should know how to swim, and I want to make sure that happens," one aquatics director stated passionately. "But," she continued, "synchronized swimming is a great idea, and if I knew more about it I might be able to add it. I know enough about swimming to go about starting a program—but for synchronized swimming, I know nothing."

(Analysis: Learn-to-swim programs will not be sacrificed.)

Lap swimming was generally considered a weak use of the pool but something that could not be touched. Parks and Recreation departments are community oriented. Lap swim was an open time for anyone in the community to swim for exercise and even though most people did not take advantage of this time taking it away from those who did would create too much controversy. Open swim is a very popular use of the pool. Aquatics directors and pool managers mentioned that they would be very reluctant to cut back on either of these two programs.

(Analysis: Lap swimming is a political "hot potato.")

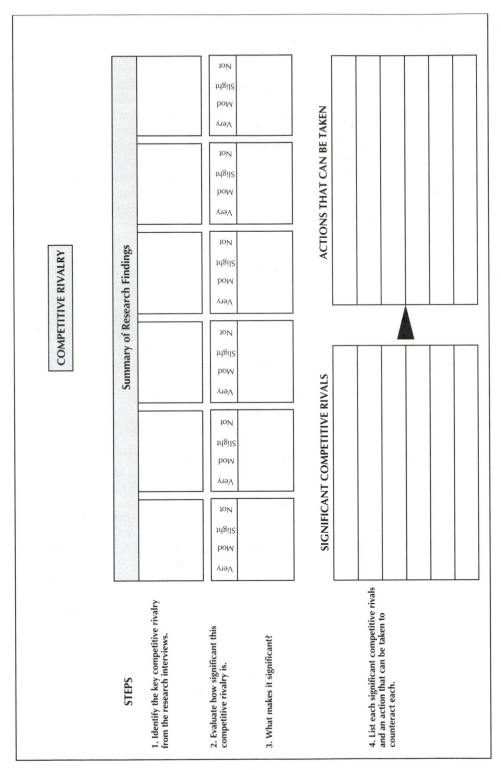

Figure 13.7 Competitive Rivalry Analysis Worksheet

SUMMARY ....

This chapter discussed a strategy you can use to analyze the competitive forces within your environment. We adapted a model developed by Michael Porter to help guide us in the procedure. The model tells us that we should consider five forces: barriers to entry, power of suppliers, power of consumers, substitutes, and rivalry among the existing competitors. We analyzed an actual research project designed by the managers of synchronized swimming that would help them assess these forces that might prevent Parks and Recreation programs from acting as distribution channel for this sport. Now comes the hard part—developing a plan of action. On the basis of the data collected from the Parks and Recreation programs, discuss what U.S. Synchronized Swimming must consider before Parks and Recreation can act as a distribution channel for synchronized swimming. Develop a plan for the introduction of synchronized swimming into the Parks and Recreation system. Send it to the executive director for U.S. Synchronized Swimming—you never know, you may develop the plan that will help this sport grow.

STRATEGIC PLAN WORKSHEET–CHAPTER 13

What you should know about your competitive forces

Your Goal ....

To assess the five competitive forces that may affect your event

Things to do

- Assess barriers to entry (Worksheet 13.1)
- Assess substitutes (Worksheet 13.2)
- Assess supplier power (Worksheet 13.3)
- Assess consumer power (Worksheet 13.4)
- Assess competitive rivalry (Worksheet 13.5)
- List your marketing strategy options (Worksheet 13.6)

WORKSHEET 13.1

Assessing Barriers

	A great deal	Moderately	A little to none
Are competitors different from each other?			
Are consumers attracted to another sport?			
Are consumers knowledgeable about your sport?			
Are there regulations that make it difficult to enter the market?			
Are the capital requirements for entry into the market high?			

List the main sources of barriers limiting entry into a specific market area.

_____

_____

_____

_____

_____

_____

How can barriers be erected? _____

_____

_____

_____

_____

How can barriers be reduced? _____

_____

_____

_____

_____

WORKSHEET 13.2

Assessing Substitutes

What needs do the products you offer serve for your consumers?	What other products also serve these needs?		
	A	B	C
1.			
2.			
3.			
4.			
5.			

List the substitutes that have the greatest threat.

_____

_____

_____

_____

_____

List your consumer groups that might be attracted to these substitutes.

_____

_____

_____

_____

_____

How can you reduce the attractiveness of the substitutes that are affecting your market?

_____

_____

_____

_____

_____

WORKSHEET 13.3

Assessing Supplier Power

Who are the most important suppliers?	Is this supplier group dominated by a few?	Are there substitutes to their products?	Does your sport represent a large portion of supplier's revenues?	Is this supplier's product important to you?	Does this supplier have a lot of power in your market?	Can you switch to another supplier?

Which of these suppliers are having the most impact on your sport? _____

_____

_____

List actions you can take to reduce supplier power. _____

_____

WORKSHEET 13.4

Assessing Consumer Power

Who are the most important consumers?	Is this consumer group dominated by a few?	Do these consumers represent a large portion of your revenues?	Is the purchase decision a major one for consumers?	Is this consumer group important to you?	Is this consumer group pursued by competitors?	Can you find an alternative consumer group?

Which of these consumer groups are having the most impact on your sport?

_____

_____

_____

List actions you can take to reduce consumer power.

_____

Which consumer group should you concentrate on?

_____

What are some important stategies you should consider in attracting this consumer group?

_____

WORKSHEET 13.5

Assessing Competitive Rivalry

Who are the most important competitors?	Is this competitor helping to expand the market for your sport?	Does this competitor represent a large portion of your market?	Can you convert this competitor into a friend?	Is this competitor important to you?	Is this competitor pursued by consumers?	Can you differentiate yourself from this competitor?

Which of these competitors are having the most impact on your sport?

_____

_____

List actions you can take to reduce the rivalry.

_____

Which competitor should you concentrate on?

_____

What are some important strategies you should consider to counteract the impact of this competitor?

_____

WORKSHEET 13.6

Identifying Marketing Strategy Options

Based on your assessment of the five forces, how should you proceed in your marketing strategy?

Barriers to entry

_____
_____
_____
_____
_____

Consumers

_____
_____
_____
_____
_____

Substitutes

_____
_____
_____
_____
_____

Competitors

_____
_____
_____
_____

Suppliers

_____
_____
_____
_____
_____

REFERENCES ....

1. Michael E. Porter, Competitive Strategy: Techniques for Analyzing Industries and Competitors (New York: The Free Press, 1980).
2. See Christine M. Brooks, A Marketing Plan for Introducing Synchronized Swimming into the Parks and Recreation Structure. Project Funded by the United States Olympic Federation for U.S. Synchronized Swimming, Inc., 1988.

APPENDIX A

Writing Your Strategic Plan

. . . .

SOME GENERAL COMMENTS ABOUT STRATEGIC PLANS

Style.   When you write your strategic plan, express yourself in the first person. Avoid flowery language and superlatives. Phrases like "fantastic profits" and "tremendous consumer appeal" mean absolutely nothing and will trigger bells and alarms in readers. Use clear layman's language. Most of the people who will read your plan will know nothing about the sports industry.

A strategic plan must be comprehensive but concise. A sketchy plan will be perceived as a sure sign of incompetence. On the other hand, nobody reads a long-winded plan. The goal is to give readers a clear, concise insight into your idea and to give them confidence in your ability to accomplish your plan.

Suggested Outline.

- Executive Summary
- Table of Contents
- The Market
- The Industry
- The Product
- Research and Development

- Sponsorship
- Publicity and Hospitality
- Competitive Analysis
- Image Assessment
- Market Strategies

The Executive Summary. The Executive Summary is the doorway to the rest of your plan. You must interest key readers in your idea. It is here where readers decide to read on. The purpose of the Executive Summary is to highlight key points of your plan not to merely list the topics.

The Remaining Topics. Follow the guidelines you are given on the next few pages. The guide presented here closely resembles the process you will have to follow in a sports business venture.

1. Go through the entire guide to familiarize yourself with the task you have ahead of you.
2. Decide where to begin. Start with the section you can most easily handle with the information you have already available.
3. Make sure you understand the objective of each section.
4. Read through each section carefully, noting areas where you will have to do some additional research before you are able to answer the questions.
5. Go to work immediately. You should not expect to complete each section on the first attempt. Do as much as you can the first time through, then do the research necessary to complete it.
6. Answer each question in rough draft as fully as it needs.
7. Decide on the subheadings you want to include in each section.
8. Write each section of the business plan in your own style.
9. Critique your work for each section by consulting the list of common errors, which is provided at the end of each module.
10. Have your plan proofread by a person well versed in English grammar. Finally, put it in an attractive binder and hand it in to your professor for evaluation.

MODULE 1—THE MARKET

(Use the data you gathered on the worksheets in Chapters 2 and 6 to write this section.)

Your Objective. To demonstrate that you understand your markets, that your idea has the opportunity to penetrate those markets, and that you understand factors within the environment with the potential to impact the success or failure of your idea.

What You Should Accomplish. Use facts from actual research and your personal experience to show why your idea can succeed. Demonstrate that there is a market for your idea and that you have the product to attract a share of that market.

Subheadings to Include.

- Target Market and Its Characteristics
- Market Trends and Growth Potential
- Research Summaries

- **Target Market and Its Characteristics**
  Describe your target market. Discuss how your idea meets the needs of your target market. Describe the physical activity behavior of your market and its demographics. Include any research you have done yourself, or research you hired an outside agency to do for you.

- **Market Trends and Growth Potential**
  Discuss the trends for your sport and how the market might change over the next two to five years. Describe the growth potential of your market and how it might affect your market share. What are the risks associated with each target market?

- **Research Summaries**
  Summarize significant published facts and trends about your markets. Make sure you document the source of your information. Based on the data, pinpoint opportunities that exist. You should clarify for your reader exactly how you will take advantage of those opportunities by meeting the needs of the target market better than existing methods that are available to them.

Common Errors

- Not knowing the size of your market base
- Not understanding the consumer need you are filling
- Failing to fully assess the market potential for your idea and how it is affected by social and economic trends
- Thinking of your consumer as one mass market; that is, failing to segment your market and developing a profile for each segment separately
- Failing to back up your assumptions with data

MODULE 2—THE INDUSTRY ....

(Use the data you gathered on the worksheets from Chapters 3 and 4 to write this section.)

Your Objective. To give your reader a brief overview of your industry

What You Should Accomplish. Demonstrate that you understand the economic structure and scope of your segment of the sports industry.

Subheadings to Include

- Industry Characteristics
- The Publics
- Industry Trends

  - **Industry Characteristics**
    Briefly describe your segment of the sports industry. Discuss its profile in terms of structure, size, geographic spread, history, and profits.

  - **The Publics**
    Briefly describe the sports publics as they affect your idea. Summarize each in terms of an important-unimportant scale. Discuss any competitors you have for your idea in terms of their product and their market niche. Present more detailed information about a competitor that is likely to have a direct impact on your idea.

  - **Industry Trends**
    Summarize where your segment of the sports industry is headed. Focus on whether or not it is declining, improving, or stable. Discuss what changes are occurring that will have an impact on your idea.

Common Errors

- Basing industry information on your own opinion
- Giving too much detail
- Failing to have a good grasp of your publics and their relative importance
- Demonstrating inadequate knowledge of the sports industry and how your idea fits within it

MODULE 3—THE PRODUCT

(Use the data you gathered on the worksheets from Chapter 5 to write this section.)

Your Objective. To describe your product in terms of its special features and consumer benefits

What You Should Accomplish: In very simple language explain your idea and who it serves. Also discuss your plans for maximizing your market opportunities.

Subheadings to Include

- The Idea
- The Primary and Secondary Components
- Adaptation for Market Expansion
- Liability Issues

- **The Idea**
  Describe your idea and for whom it was designed. Discuss how it fits the needs of your consumer, its special features and what sets it apart from other ideas. How does your idea differ from those offered by competitors?

- **The Primary and Secondary Components**
  Discuss the product as it meets the needs of your primary and secondary consumers.

- **Adaptation for Market Expansion**
  Summarize how you can adapt the idea to meet the needs of different market segments.

- **Liability Issues**
  Discuss the liability and insurance issues related to the idea. How do you plan to limit liability?

Common Errors

- Describing the idea too technically, too ambiguously, or too broadly
- Failing to identify variations of the idea to meet the needs of different market segments
- Failing to understand liability issues
- Having weak developmental plans for the future or not recognizing possible future market need shifts
- Failing to indicate the consumer need that the product is serving

MODULE 4—RESEARCH AND DEVELOPMENT

(Use the data you gathered in your research from Chapter 7 to write this section.)

Your Objective: To outline the research you have done and the significant findings

What You Should Accomplish: In very simple language discuss how you developed the product from the idea stage to a viable business opportunity. Tell your reader what you learned from your research and what you still need to do to make your idea a marketable product.

Subheadings to Include

- Idea Concept Development
- Research and Idea Evaluation
- Major Findings
- Current Research Status

- **Idea Concept Development**
  Discuss the initial product concept and how it has changed and improved as a result of your research. What new markets or variations of your idea did you discover?

- **Research and Idea Evaluation**
  Describe all related research and idea evaluation activity. This includes discussing published surveys, articles, or studies that you have found. Use these as evidence to back up your belief in the potential success of your idea.

- **Major Findings**
  Summarize significant findings. Describe the impact they have on your idea.

- **Current Research Status**
  Discuss where your research stands now. How much of the idea has been tested? What still needs to be done to ensure that your idea will meet your target market needs? When will your research be completed?

Common Errors

- Developing your idea based on superficial information
- Doing inadequate research
- Trying to justify your idea with insufficient data
- Failing to discuss research reliability
- Failing to plan for future trends

MODULE 5—FINANCIAL DATA —SPONSORSHIP PROJECTIONS ....

(Use the data gathered on the worksheets from Chapters 8–11 to write this section.)

Your Objective: To illustrate your sponsorship or other financial opportunities for funding your idea.

What You Should Accomplish: Provide your reader with an analysis of your sponsorship packages and targeted companies. Document the funds you will need and show that your sponsorship plan will take care of these needed funds. Show that your sponsorship projections are realistic and based on reasonable assumptions.

Subheadings to Include

- Overview of Idea Cost
- Sponsorship Packages
- Targeted Companies
- Sponsorship Pricing Strategies

- **Overview of Idea Cost**
  State the amount and type of funding that will be required for your idea. Give a breakdown of how you will use the money —facility rental, umpires, equipment purchase, T-shirts. State when you will need the money. Draw a graph showing the amount and timing of the funds.

- **Sponsorship Packages**
  Describe your sponsorship packages. Discuss what your packages offer companies and how they will fit within their marketing mix. Describe why the sponsorship packages are attractive to companies and how they compare with other sponsorship opportunities within the industry. Describe payment schedules for sponsors.

- **Targeted Companies**
  Provide a list of all companies you are targeting and why you feel they are prime prospects. Back up your comments with research.

- **Sponsorship Pricing Strategies**
  Show that your sponsorship fees cover your costs. Your pricing should be based on realistic expectations. Provide a break-even analysis for each sponsorship package.

Common Errors

- Failing to fully identify all costs of bringing your idea to market
- Inadequate research on targeted sponsoring companies
- No logic in sponsorship pricing structure
- Unreasonable sponsorship projections based on unreasonable assumptions

MODULE 6 —SPONSORSHIP PUBLICITY ....

(Use the data you gathered on the worksheets from Chapter 12 to write this section.)

Your Objective: To describe your sponsorship publicity services, their special features and benefits.

What You Should Accomplish: Explain your publicity services, what they do for a sponsor that is special or different from present opportunities available, and whom they serve.

Subheadings to Include:

- Description of Publicity Services
- Special Features
- Liability

- **Description of Publicity Services**
  Describe your sponsorship media publicity plans (include a copy of your media plan outline). What are your evaluation strategies?

- **Special Features**
  Describe features distinguishing your publicity services from other similar ideas. Describe any special arrangement regarding publicity evaluation assessment. Do you have the necessary labor to provide publicity services?

- **Liability**
  Discuss the liability and insurance considerations that are inherent in the publicity program. There may be none, but if there are describe how you plan to limit your liability.

Common Errors

- Describing the publicity services too technically, too broadly, or too ambiguously
- Failing to cover liability issues
- Failing to discuss your labor requirements and how you will obtain them
- Failing to show that you are fully prepared to provide these services

MODULE 7—COMPETITIVE ANALYSIS ....

(Use the data you gathered on the worksheets from Chapter 13 to write this section.)

Your Objective: To show you are fully aware of the competitive forces at work in your marketplace.

What You Should Accomplish: Give a brief overview of other industry participants. Explain why you feel you have a competitive edge.

Subheadings to Include

- Competitor Profile
- Barriers to Entry
- Substitute Products
- Supplier Power
- Consumer Power
- Competitive Edge

- **Competitor Profile**
  Briefly summarize your notes from Worksheet 14.5.

- **Barriers to Entry**
  Briefly summarize your notes from Worksheet 14.1.

- **Substitute Products**
  Briefly summarize your notes from Worksheet 14.2.

- **Supplier Power**
  Briefly summarize your notes from Worksheet 14.3.

- **Consumer Power**
  Briefly summarize your notes from worksheet 14.4.

- **Competitive Edge**
  Discuss your strengths and weaknesses in relation to your major competitors. List the key variables down the left hand side of the page. On the top of the page place your competitors and your idea. Now compare your idea with your competitors for each variable. You should summarize product superiority, price advantages, market advantages, labor, participants, facilities, and management strengths and weaknesses.

Common Errors

- Not identifying known major competitors
- Underestimating the power of suppliers, consumers, and substitutes
- Failing to demonstrate your competitive edge
- Assuming that you have no competitors
- Failing to be aware of competitors' plans in the market

Glossary

. . . .

Advertising. Any paid form of nonpersonal presentation of ideas, goods, and services by an identified business.

Affect. The feeling or emotional component of psychological reactions towards products. It can be positive or negative. Needs, wants, and desires are basically affective in content.

Affinity consumption. Allows the sports follower close association with a sport. Products include sports clothing, game and video highlights, books, and magazines.

Affinity market. Products come in three groups: popularity, prestige, and metamorphosis products.

Amateur Sports Act. Passed in 1978 and was designed to end the incessant squabbling among amateur sports organizations over the control of amateur sports. The Amateur Sports Act gave the U. S. Olympic Committee the final authority over amateur sports.

Athlete coalition. A formal group of athletes who compete as individuals to form a salable product such as a circuit or tour.

Athlete unions. Their purpose is to counteract the power of the club or team owners. Presently only seen in professional sports.

Athletes. The physical assets of the sports product, they consist of recreational participants, amateur athletes, and professional athletes.

Athletic platform analysis. An investigation into which component or combination of components the athletic platform — the athlete, the team, the event, or the sport — lends itself best to accomplishing corporate objectives.

Athletic platform. Consists of four components: athlete, event or competition, sport, and team.

Attitudes. A predisposition to respond toward an object, act, or situation in an evaluative way. An attitude is persistent over time, carrying cognitive (knowledge), affective (emotion), and conative (intention) elements. It also indicates intensity.

Audience. The person or party receiving a communication.

Barriers to entry. The level of difficulty for another entity to enter a specific business area.

Channel of distribution. The existing institutions and functions that facilitate the exchange between marketer and customer. In the case of sports a distribution channel is any institution that permits the sport to reach an interested participant.

Coalition clusters. A formal collection of independent sport units—clubs in a league, tournaments in a tour, national governing bodies in the U.S. Olympic Committee, or universities in the National Collegiate Athletic Association.

Communication. The sending and receiving of information; affect and influence from one party to another.

Competitive market pricing. Based on what managers think the market will bear given the competitive environment. Competitive pricing is usually determined by what the sport organization has to offer and what is offered by other sports organizations.

Competitive strategy. How a sports organization chooses to meet or stimulate consumer needs for its product. It entails setting goals, defining consumer needs, analyzing competitors, analyzing markets, selecting targets, and developing products.

Corporate sponsorship market. A group of corporate sponsors who maintain an integrated relationship with the event. They purchase the right to target and communicate with ready-made clusters of consumers and the right to use positive images affiliated with the sport for their commercial benefit.

Cost-plus pricing. A pricing tactic whereby a price is set as a percentage increase over costs.

Custodian coalitions. Prime purpose is to ensure the survival of a specific form of amateur competition, for example, Olympic sport in the case of the U.S. Olympic Committee, or collegiate sport in the case of the NCAA. Athletes are analogous to children who require financial, coaching, and moral support during their competitive developmental years.

Deductive research approach. A research approach that begins with a set of loosely gathered, relatively unstructured data with the idea of exploring or discovering potential hypotheses.

Distribution channel. The system of institu-

tions used to deliver goods to the final consumer.

Economic impact studies. A strategy for assessing the value of a sports event to the local economy.

Entrepreneurial manager. Develops new products from sports, expands the markets for sports, encourages innovation, and makes a major contribution to its overall size and scope.

Environments. The physical, economic, technological, and other social conditions that effect the success of a sports organization.

Exclusive sponsorship. The only sponsor associated with an athletic platform component.

Expectations. Anticipation or judgment that some event or state of affairs will occur.

Experiences. One category of events characterizing an exchange. Experiences are the thoughts, feelings, expectations, rules, ideologies, and so on, felt by the parties to an exchange.

Experimental research. The manipulation of one or more independent variables and the observation of their effect on one or more dependent variables.

Exploratory research. An unstructured or loosely structured data collection method whose purpose is to collect information for evaluation rather than hypothesis testing. This is done typically through focus groups, in-depth interviews, projective techniques, or participant observation.

External publics. A group of independent organizations largely outside the immediate control of sports managers that can influence the economy of the sports organization. They include organizations or groups advancing their own interest through sports (city, country, university, or corporation); sanctioning bodies (U.S. Olympic Committee, U.S. government, NCAAs); intermediaries (sports agents, sports marketing firms and sports promoters); and competitors (all forms of leisure, entertainment, and other products that compete with the sports organization for the time and money of its consumer group).

Hospitality sales. The marketing function consisting of efforts to persuade a company to try a hospitality program or to continue using one.

Independent sport units (ISUs). Produce the

primary sports product—the sports activity. They may come in the form of amateur, recreational, or professional clubs or individual athletes.

Inductive research approach. This research approach begins with some theory or hypothesis and then designs a project that proves the hypothesis true or false.

Industry life cycle. The stages through which an industry progresses. These stages are sometimes referred to as embryonic, growth, maturity, and decline.

Industry. A group of organizations producing products that are close substitutes for each other.

Internal publics. Consist of those groups associated with the primary product—the sport itself. They include those groups involved in the manufacturing process (support publics, employees, and supplier publics); groups involved in the distribution process (television, stadiums, high schools); and groups involved in the consuming process (participant and nonparticipant consumers).

League coalitions. A contractual relationship between several clubs or teams in one single sport.

Licensing. An arrangement whereby a firm produces a product that uses an athletic platform tie-in. An athletic platform may give the licensee various kinds of rights—trademark rights, logo rights, symbol rights.

Magnet companies. The type of company that tends to attract other companies as cosponsors of an athletic platform.

Market analysis. Evaluation of what is happening in the marketplace. It helps a sports organization determine consumer needs and demands and competitive threats. It is also concerned with what the overall aggregate market of consumers looks like and what changes and trends can be forecasted.

Market data. Facts about the characteristics of the marketplace. These help a manager make sound marketing decisions.

Market diversification. A growth strategy encompassing the introduction of new products in new markets.

Market expansion. The growth strategy characterized by the marketing of existing products in new markets.

Market growth strategies. Methods for increasing the market for a sport. There are four types of strategies.

Market penetration. The growth strategy aimed at obtaining a larger share of an existing market.

Market research. The formal gathering of data by the sports organization and used by managers as part of their decision-making activities.

Marketing concept. The ideal standard or philosophy perspective wherein a sports organization attempts to meet its own goals, satisfy consumers, and fulfill social responsibilities.

Marketing mix. Generic tactics marketers can use to adapt to and influence responses in the marketplace. Also known as the 4 P's (product, place, promotion, and price).

Marketing. The set of activities concerned with the initiation, resolution, and/or avoidance of exchange relationships.

Medium. Any device, symbol system, or means used to convey communication. The most common advertising media include television, radio, magazines, newspapers, billboards, posters, sky writing, mail, telephone, and the Yellow Pages.

Medium. The communication channel through which a message is conveyed. Sponsorship is a unique medium.

Message. The information or data conveyed in a communication and consisting of factual, affective, and influential symbols.

Metamorphosis product. A product that is enhanced if the public transposes the reputation of the sport, event, or athlete to the product. Attaching Michael Jordon's name to an athletic shoe, for example, transposes it to a very special shoe that people may believe can make them jump higher, dunk better, or run faster.

Module strategies. A number of very specific decisions on what target market strategies to implement via each module of the sponsorship package.

Module tactics. A listing of specific activities required for sponsorship target market strategy implementation.

National Governing Body. Responsible for the governance of a specific sport. Reports to the U.S. Olympic Committee.

New products. Consist of six types: new-to-the-world, new product lines, additions to existing product lines, improvements and revisions to existing products, repositioning, and cost reduction.

Official supplier. A special case of subsidiary sponsorship. Provides products that often have little obvious connection with the athletic platform.

Participatory events. Activities within a hospitality setting that require guest participation, for example, Pro-Am tournaments.

Perceived risk. The judged costs, losses, or possible negative consequences associated with consumption.

Point-of-purchase displays. A promotional device consisting of posters, tablelike displays, or other material placed next to merchandise or used to highlight merchandise.

Popularity product. A sport, athlete, event, or team that receives high levels of media exposure.

Prestige product. An ordinary product that takes on a prestigious image by associating with a specific sport, event, athlete, or team.

Price. The cost of a sponsorship package to the consumer. Price is usually expressed in monetary terms but can also encompass time, psychic costs, and service costs. Price is viewed as something that must be given up to acquire the sponsorship. Occasionally, price is a signal of quality, prestige, or other unique value.

Primary sponsorship. A sponsorship category that tries to ensure that these sponsors have the opportunity to maximize their exposure with minimal effort.

Primary sports infrastructure. This is where the production process occurs. It consists of five components: two related to management (coalition clusters and independent sports units) and three related to labor (athlete unions, individual athletes, and sports agents).

Primary sports markets. Consist of the immediate consumer of sports—participants, spectators, and volunteers.

Product differentiation. A strategy used to achieve an advantage over competitors. This is accomplished through product design, advertising, and in certain instances distribution and sales practices.

Product. Any offering actually or potentially desired by a target market of consumers. A product may include a physical object (equipment, team); service (personal trainer); idea (fitness, good health, excitement); or place (exercise facility). Products satisfy physiological, psychological, or social needs.

Promotional spend. The money a company allocates to promote the event or its sponsorship.

Publicity objectives. Goals that a sponsorship media planner believes to be the most important in helping attain a sponsor's communication objectives.

Publicity. Any form of nonpaid commercially significant news or editorial comment about ideas, products, or institutions.

Qualitative research. The use of unstructured methodologies—for example, in-depth interviews, participant observation, focus groups, and projective techniques—to interpret data.

Reach. The number of people exposed to the vehicle.

Receiver. The person or party receiving a communication. Also termed audience or target.

Relative-value pricing. Based on the market value of the benefits offered by the sponsorship if other communication mediums were used.

Sampling. A type of consumer promotion whereby a brand is given to a consumer free of charge. The sample may be the normal size of the product as it is presented for sale, or it might be a reduced portion.

Sanctioning body. Acts to protect the interest of athletes and fans.

Secondary infrastructure. All those business activities associated with the distribution and service of the output produced by the primary infrastructure. These include facility owners, museum curators, book and magazine publishers, camp managers, equipment manufacturers, event producers, television broadcasters, and media personnel.

Secondary sports markets. Consist of people and organizations that consume sport tangentially. They include the advertising, corporate sponsorship, and affinity markets. There is another motive behind their consumption beside the sport itself.

Simmons Market Research Bureau. A national survey of media and markets in the United States. This survey also obtains data about American sports spectatorship and participation behavior.

Sociocultural environment. The social and cultural factors that interact with our personal attitudes and needs to influence our behavior.

Sponsorship budget. The amount of money spent by a company on a sponsorship program. The amount is set on the basis of executive subjective judgments or rules-of-thumb to meet or break the competition, or objectively according to specific goals and the tasks needed to accomplish those goals.

Sponsorship hospitality. A means of entertaining guests at a sporting event.

Sponsorship modules. Broadly conceived methods of using the athletic platform. These modules are organized into a unified sponsorship package specifically aimed at attaining the goals of the targeting unit.

Sponsorship objectives. Goals for sales, market growth, market share, profitability, product line performance, brand image, and so on that a corporation has set for its sponsorship program. These are usually derived from broader organizational objectives or serve as intermediate steps.

Sponsorship publicity. Any form of nonpaid commercially significant news or editorial comment related to the athletic platform that includes the name of the sponsor.

Sports advertising. Effective way of reaching sports consumers by way of banner space in the stadium, and announcements during the event and in the event program.

Sports agents. A breed of commercial sales representatives who market the talents of the most highly skilled athletes. They have recently expanded into event production, television, and event ownership.

Sports markets. Clusters of people who actually or potentially desire a sports product.

Sports product market wheel. Strategy for stimulating ideas for new products and new markets.

Statistical analysis. Procedures based on probability and used to summarize data, test hypotheses, and make predictions.

Strategic plan. A detailed outline of your analyses; evaluation and selection of market opportunities so that you can reach your market objectives. It tells people what you want to do, the support your venture will need, the markets for your product, and how you will ensure profitability.

Subsidiary sponsorship. This is a second level of sponsorship involving several companies that are divided into product categories.

Substitutes. Any products or services that satisfy the same needs and act as competitors for each other.

Supplier. Any individual or company providing key products or services.

Survey research. The collection of responses from people through a questionnaire administered face to face by a researcher, over the phone, by mail, or by computer.

U.S. Bureau of the Census. Provides you with past and future population figures. It is available in most libraries.

Vehicle. A particular carrier within a medium such as the *New York Times*, CBS, or *Sports Illustrated*.

Villain products. Commercial products, such as cigarettes and alcohol, that are perceived to cause social problems.

Index

. . . .